To Jeremy

LAY THE FAVOURITE

BETH RAYMER has an MFA from Columbia University. In 2007 she was awarded a Fulbright scholarship. She lives in New York City.

LAY THE FAVOURITE

A TRUE STORY ABOUT PLAYING TO WIN IN THE GAMBLING
UNDERWORLD

Beth Raymer

Yellow Jersey Press
LONDON

Published by Yellow Jersey Press 2010

2 4 6 8 10 9 7 5 3 1

Copyright © Beth Raymer 2010

Beth Raymer has asserted her right under the Copyright, Designs
and Patents Act 1988 to be identified as the author of this work

First published in Great Britain in 2010 by
Yellow Jersey Press
Random House, 20 Vauxhall Bridge Road,
London SW1V 2SA

www.rbooks.co.uk

Addresses for companies within The Random House Group Limited can be found at:
www.randomhouse.co.uk/offices.htm

The Random House Group Limited Reg. No. 954009

A CIP catalogue record for this book
is available from the British Library

ISBN 9780224083324

The Random House Group Limited makes every effort to ensure that the
papers used in its books are made from trees that have been legally
sourced from well-managed and credibly certified forests.
Our paper procurement policy can be found at:
www.rbooks.co.uk/environment

Mixed Sources
Product group from well-managed
forests and other controlled sources
www.fsc.org Cert no. TT-COC-2139
© 1996 Forest Stewardship Council
FSC

Printed and bound in Great Britain by
Clays Ltd, St Ives Plc

LAY THE FAVOURITE

CHAPTER ONE

The Crew

The thing I liked best about working at Komol was Jowtee, the invisible spirit who controlled the restaurant's destiny. I had never actually seen Jowtee but the kitchen staff swore he existed. They said he was a seven-foot-tall Native American Chief, a ghost from the Indian burial ground beneath the strip mall. If I didn't feed him, pray to him, and bring him presents, something disastrous would befall the restaurant. As the only non-Thai, I had to believe them. So in between seating, waiting, and busing tables I found time to keep Jowtee happy. At the booth that was reserved for him, I'd serve Jowtee imported bottled beer in a frosty mug, whole fish fried in hot sauce, and coconut ice cream for dessert. I'd bring him daily horoscopes and decks of cards from neighboring casinos. After lighting his candle, I'd close my eyes and telepathically beg him to help turn my life around and get me that cocktail waitress job at the Bellagio.

Jowtee heard my plea. At least part of it.

During a particularly slow dinner shift, one of the regulars offered to help get me a better job. Her name was Amy and she was a massage therapist. Every Saturday evening she came in by herself and ordered vegetable green curry, extra spicy, and took her time eating it, her oversized black sunglasses never leaving her face. One night, on her way out, she slid into the front booth next to me and watched as I filled out my Stardust and Four Queens cocktail waitress applications.

"These jobs are shit," she said, flipping through the papers. "I have this one client I give massages to. A professional gambler. Want me to see if he'll hire you?"

I was twenty-four and had moved to Las Vegas to be with a guy I had been dating for a few months. We broke up soon after I arrived. I didn't know a single person in town. But no one else seemed to, either. It was 2001 and Vegas was the fastest-growing metropolitan area in America. Fifteen hundred people were moving into the city each week. Everyone I met was very much like me and had just ended up there.

After the breakup, I rented a room in a motel just north of the Strip in a neighborhood known as Naked City. In the fifties, it had been home to strippers who sunbathed in the nude to avoid tan lines. Now, bail bondsmen, hookers, Vietnam vets, and irritable motel clerks added color to the place. My motel was three blocks from the Little White Wedding Chapel and Johnny Tocco's Boxing Gym and four blocks from the downtown casinos: Binion's Horseshoe, the El Cortez, and the Aztec—home of the fifty-nine-cent strawberry shortcake. The cigarette burns in the motel's bedspreads were big enough to fit a leg through and the staccato of stilettos across the floor upstairs made it hard to get a good night's sleep. But at seventeen dollars a night, it was affordable, and it allowed dogs. So Otis, my sixty-pound Chow Chow, and I moved in. The wooden nightstand showcased the room's only décor: a Rand McNally road atlas and a Magic 8 Ball.

Before moving to Vegas, I was living in Tallahassee, Florida, and working at a residential home for troubled teenage girls. During one Sunday morning shift, the girls kept asking me if I would let them run away. I could get their shoes out of the locked closet, open the back door, wait fifteen minutes to give them a head start, and then call the cops. I could tell the psychologists that they threatened me. That one of them held a knife to my back—no; my face—then stole the keys from my pocket. Come on, they begged, we just want to see our boyfriends and smoke. *Please?*

All three of them were seventeen-year-old white girls who got into a lot of fistfights, dealt pot, and dated gangbangers. Usually when they asked me to let them run away I'd change the subject. But on that morning, as the girls over-plucked their eyebrows and pleaded with me to set them free, I felt sad for them. The only thing they looked forward to was filling paper cups with mouthwash, shooting it back as though it were bourbon, then pretending they were drunk. They were never allowed outside, and their lunches and dinners consisted of microwavable pasta dishes high in fat. As a result, they had acne and their clothes were too tight. I didn't get their shoes from the closet, which seemed too calculated. But I did let them run away. Standing by the door, I watched them laugh and scream in disbelief, grasping for one another's hands, their bare feet skipping across the parking lot's blacktop. Fifteen minutes later I called the cops. Two days later I was fired.

A cocktail waitress job seemed like a better fit. But with no connections or casino experience my application went straight to the bottom of the heap. After applying to the fancy casinos on the Strip, I moved to the downtown casinos near my motel. Sure, I was welcome to apply for a position at the El Cortez, but I'd have to wait for sixty-five-year-old Rosie from Cheyenne, in her surgical stockings and CULINARY WORKERS LOCAL 226 pin, to die before I could even get an interview. The only reason I had a job at the Thai restaurant was because my ex-boyfriend's parents, who were nice enough to offer me a job upon arrival, owned it. They weren't expecting me to break up with their son, however, and working there had become tense.

I gave Amy twenty percent off her curry and the following day she left a message. Interview at noon with Dink, 1459 North Rainbow.

*   *   *

The office park sat in a patch of desert eight miles off the Strip. Every few steps, Otis stopped to sniff and pee on the benches. Dragging him past the professionally dressed men and women enjoying their smoke break, I pulled the address out of my pocket. I hadn't imagined gamblers doing business alongside divorce lawyers and accountants. In my denim miniskirt and Converse sneakers, and with Otis scruffy and panting at my side, I felt more like a teenage runaway than an interviewee. I pulled my hair out of its ponytail so that it fell over my shoulders and hid my bra straps.

In a row of offices with signs like Nevada Insurance and Coldwell Banker, stood a suite with no sign and white plastic blinds covering its windows. Next to the door was a square address plaque and scrawled in its center, in Wite-Out correction pen, was "Dink Inc." From inside, a television blared. The sound of a bugle summoned horses to the starting gate at a racetrack. I knocked.

The door opened, revealing a guy about six-foot-four, two hundred and eighty pounds. His hair was a heap of shiny, springy brown curls, the kind you see in ads for home perms. Tucked into his armpit was a *Daily Racing Form,* and in his hand was a puffy white bagel overstuffed with lox. He introduced himself as Dink, then took a bite of his sandwich. With mouth full, he asked if my dog had an opinion on the Yankees game.

Dink was in his late forties, but his bashful smile and distracting habit of twisting his curls around his pointer finger made him appear much younger. He dressed like the mentally retarded adults I had met while volunteering at a group home. His Chicago Cubs T-shirt was two sizes too small for his expansive frame. Royal blue elasticized cotton shorts were pulled high above his belly button. White tube socks were stretched to the middle of his pale, hairless shins.

Inside the suite, a long banquet table was cluttered: hockey digests; baseball encyclopedias; a baseball prospectus; sports pages from *USA Today,* the *New York Post,* the *Las Vegas Review-Journal;* dozens of calculators; telephones; mechanical pencils; computer monitors; and several copies of *Fuzzy Creatures Quarterly,* a magazine that offered tips on how to better love and care for one's hamster. At the front of the office, a tower of six forty-inch televisions balanced on a flimsy metal stand, each tuned to a different sport. Dink took his seat at the head of the table. In front of him, stacks of cash were piled as high as his bottle of Yoo-Hoo. I stared at the money, mesmerized.

He nodded to one of the TVs and in a heavy Queens accent he said, "We need Minnesoter and undah, for a decent amount."

Having no idea what he was talking about, I said, "Okay," and took a seat.

In the long silence that followed, Dink twirled and twirled his curls, engrossed in the basketball games and horse races. The action on TV reflected off his eyeglasses, which were as thick as hockey pucks and cloudy with thumbprints. Rising from the floor were stacks of books, all of which appeared to be on the subjects of hockey and New York punk bands except for one on the very bottom: *Hide Your A$$et$ and Disappear: A Step-by-Step Guide to Vanishing Without a Trace.*

On the TV, a player for Minnesota made two free throws. Unsure of whether or not this was a good thing for Dink, I stayed quiet and massaged Otis's back with the bottom of my sneaker. Dink clicked the eraser of his mechanical pencil, then scribbled something down in his raggedy five-subject notebook. He asked me how well I knew Amy.

"Very well," I lied. I smiled.

He took a swig of his Yoo-Hoo and asked me what I knew about gambling.

The day the Fort Lauderdale airport started offering casino junkets that flew nonstop to the Bahamas was the day my family started taking vacations. My dad, a car salesman, found out about the offer from the guys at the dealership. Basically, he guaranteed that he would spend a certain amount of time at the Paradise Island Casino blackjack tables, and in return, we got free airfare. The next thing I knew there were four airline tickets on the kitchen counter and Dad was coming home from work carrying *books*. Dad never came home from work carrying anything but Miller Lite tallboys. The only book in our entire house was the Lee Iacocca autobiography Dad won for selling the most cars at the Fourth of July tent sale.

The books were small and glossy and bore titles like *A Winner's Guide to Blackjack* and *Beat the Casino*. They had lots of pictures and were only about sixty pages long. Perfect for an eleven-year-old like me. The week before the trip, after my mom and fourteen-year-old sister went to bed, I sat at the kitchen table and practiced dealing hands of 21 to my dad and my three Cabbage Patch Kids.

On the afternoon my family arrived at Paradise Island, Dad handed my mom, my sister, and me each a crisp one-hundred-dollar bill. He recited our family vacation motto—Money is no object!—then bolted for the casino the moment the airport shuttle's door slid open. Mom caught the trolley to the outdoor market, my sister went off to buy pot, and I went in search of my dad, eager to sit beside him at the tables and watch him play.

It was my first time in a casino but certainly not my father's. In the early years of my parents' marriage, he and Mom flew out to Vegas a couple of times a year and stayed at the Tropicana. In 1976, a nun from the orphanage called my parents and told them there was a two-week-old baby girl available. My parents had married young and had been trying to have kids for twelve years. They had adopted my sister three years earlier. Now there was a new baby, from a different family. Were they interested? Mom cried "Yes!" but as soon as she hung up, Dad reminded her of the tickets they had, to see Elvis in Vegas that weekend. The next morning they picked me up from Catholic Social Services, named me after the Kiss song "Beth," which was playing on the radio, left me with Aunt Bonnie, and took off to Vegas. On the evening of the show, Dad found himself at the blackjack table, in the middle of a "hot streak." Despite my mother's pleading, Dad refused to quit playing, and they missed Elvis. Twenty-two years later, during their divorce,

Mom repeated this story in front of the judge as proof that my father was a problem gambler.

I finally spotted Dad (hard to miss in his red, white, and blue Ford trucker hat) at the blackjack table and took a seat beside him. It didn't take much to realize that the gambling laws in the Bahamas were very, very loose. As long as I sat next to my dad, the dealers let me play. They taught me to motion for another card by skimming the bottom of my cards against the felt, and how to gesture "stay" by gliding my hand, palm down, across the cards in front of me. When I was dealt blackjack, Dad would yell "Bethannana! Big-banana!" and give me a high five. I'd take a sip of his beer and wiggle my toes inside my pink glitter jellies in excitement. When I lost all of my chips, Dad peeled another hundred-dollar bill from his money clip and slipped it to me, adding, "Don't mention a word of this to your mother."

The same words were muttered when we went to the dog track in Florida. On the Sundays Dad didn't have to work, we took the T-tops off the white '77 Stingray Corvette, and went to the matinee races at the Palm Beach Kennel Club. A thick humid air rushing through the car, George Jones blaring from the stereo, and the backs of my knees sticking to the red leather seats, I read the racing form I'd cut from *The Palm Beach Post*. My dad first took me to the track when I was seven, and there he taught me the basics of a racing form. Even though I knew how to tell the difference in seconds between the dog's time and the average winning time on the track and knew enough to check up on how long it had been since the dog had last practiced or competed, these facts mattered little. My seven-year-old sensibility ruled. I was a girl; I liked girl dogs. I was skinny; I liked skinny dogs. In the time it took me to circle the names of the lightest girl dogs of all twelve races, we had arrived.

Before each race, in exchange for the twenty dollars in betting money he gave me, Dad had me run down to the paddock where the dogs could be viewed, and report back whether any of them had taken a shit. This was part of his handicapping strategy. Dad believed that the dogs that went to the bathroom right before they ran were lighter and would therefore run faster. On the rare occasions that a dog would make too wide a turn and crash snout first into a concrete wall, or get electrocuted by faulty machinery, I brought the race form home with me. Alone in my room, I tore the dog's name out of the form, tucked it under my Virgin Mary nightlight, and recited ten Hail Marys.

Though gambling caused many fights between my mom and dad, I associated it with some of the happiest moments of my childhood. I rarely saw my father in higher spirits than when he handed the dealer a stack of hundreds, and watched the money spread into a perfectly shaped fan across the grass-green felt. It gave me a jolt too. I clapped as the dealer did this. I knew that when we returned to the hotel room there'd be a fight. But for the moment, at the tables, I was at peace. Dad wasn't irritated or storming off to work. He was here, beside me, giving high fives to strangers. Together we were going to win enough to buy a new Corvette, a new house. These casino resort vacations top my list of good memories, right up there with running out of my room Christmas morning to find my stocking stuffed with shiny, hot pink scratch-off lottery tickets.

Those were some of the things I knew about gambling, and I told Dink all of them during the interview. After spending so much time with no one to talk to but Otis and Jowtee it felt good to talk to someone, so I went on for an hour, describing the motel I lived in and my morning routine of walking to the El Cortez for the ninety-nine-cent breakfast. I told him about my first weeks in Las Vegas and how I became obsessed with Flip It, the game where spinners flip dollar tokens up onto a shelf and a metal bar pushes an already existing stack of coins toward the edge. The coins that fall over the edge, you win. After work, I would drive to the Stratosphere, one of the handful of casinos that had Flip It, and circle each machine, peering into it at all angles. After determining which machine's tokens would be the first to fall, I'd begin to play. One evening, the casino manager took me aside. I thought he was going to yell at me for knocking my hip against the machine, which I sometimes did to help push tokens over the edge. Instead, the manager told me that he'd seen me the last few evenings and advised me to stop playing. Flip It was a gimmick. It was for "retards."

"You were addicted to Flip It?" Dink asked.

"I wasn't *addicted*," I answered, rolling my eyes.

"How am I supposed to trust you with my money? You're gonna rob me to go play Flip It."

"No, I'm not," I said. I hadn't realized he planned to entrust me with his money. I too began twirling my curls.

"Good. Hours are eight 'til five with a four-hour lunch break between ten and two, Monday through Saturday. Sundays we work eight to four straight. Pay is twenty dollars an hour, off the books, but you get bonuses, vacations, free meals."

Despite the experience gleaned from my dad's small-time gambling, I was not qualified to work for Dink Inc. Dink was a professional sports gambler. He bet on the NBA, NFL, PGA, NCAA basketball, NCAA football, tennis, WNBA, the Little League World Series, Miss America Pageants, the National Spelling Bee, and the Coney Island hot dog eating contest. He specialized in horses, hockey, baseball, and also dabbled in poker. When he spoke of money lines, run lines, ten-cent lines, spreads, odds, and propositions, it all went over my head.

"It's okay," he said. "You come highly recommended by someone I have a lot of faith in."

Suddenly, a guy a little older than me walked into the office without knocking. His Y-back tank top flaunted his self-tanned, salon-waxed, well-built upper body. He tossed a wad of money onto the table. It was rubber-banded in the middle and folded in half. Dink introduced him as Robbie J, one of "the crew." He greeted me with a wink and patted Otis on his head. I smiled hello.

"You think I'm good lookin'?" he said.

"You're okay," I said.

"Oh sweetie, I'm more than okay." He flexed his biceps.

Dink's cell phone rang. An office phone rang. The computers began to ding.

"New York's moving, what do you want me to do?" Robbie J asked.

"Call Jazz," Dink said.

Robbie J picked up two receivers and feverishly dialed two separate phones, simultaneously. Dink grabbed for his phone and dialed a number.

"Responsibility to come on time to this job is number one," Dink continued. His palm cupped the receiver pushed to his ear. "You have to have the mind for numbers and be able to pick up things that have to do with numbers, number two. And *don't steal*, number three. Most people fail at one of those." He uncupped his hand. "Nine-nine-two Dinky, lookin' for a line on the New York Liberty, WNBA. Over for a dime, please."

Still seated in his office chair, Dink wheeled toward the window. "There's more crew members, two very important ones. But one's in a cage and one's on a yacht in Europe." He unpeeled two glossy photographs from the wall and handed them to me. One photo was a close-up of a fat brown hamster with watery black eyes. The other was of a petite blonde in her fifties with lips painted coral. She cradled dozens of banded stacks of hundred-dollar bills and proudly presented these bundles to the photographer, as though they were a newborn baby. "That's Jyrki, my hamster"—named after Jyrki Lumme, a former NHL defenseman. "And Tulip, my wife."

Dink noticed that another race was about to start on one of the televisions. "I'm gonna bet the two here. First-time starter. Could be a total zero.

"One-six-four Ivy," he said into the receiver. "Hollywood Park, race four. The two to win for a nickel."

The horses shot out of the starting gate and Dink bounced up and down in his chair as though he were the jockey. Robbie J continued talking hurriedly on the phones. The two horses won and Dink shouted, "I'm a genius! I'm a genius!" He hovered over his racing form like a schoolboy trying to keep other kids from cheating, jotted something down, and quickly turned the page. "So?" he said. "You want the job?"

I had no idea what my job would entail, but it was the best interview I had ever had.

"Yes," I said. "I want the job."

The next morning, I drove to the casino where Dink and I were scheduled to meet. The pitiless sun scalded the floor of the High Desert. Along the shoulder, brittle branched shrubs caught the litter tossed from passing cars and nearby construction sites. In the distance, rising out of rippled sand dunes, appeared the Rampart casino, a Mediterranean mansion surrounded by fifty acres of lush landscape. It was the first time since moving to Vegas that I had seen grass. Along the entranceway, jackrabbits found shade beneath the palm trees' sprawling canopies.

The casino's sports book had the feel of a Fortune 500 retiree's office. Watercolors of horses and boxers hung on the mahogany walls. In the back was a small bar with lit-up shelves showcasing highball glasses and bottles of top-shelf liquor. When I walked in, a group of old men turned and looked at me.

"Ya lost, doll?" asked a man in his seventies. His steel-gray hair went nicely with his wire-framed glasses.

"I don't think so," I said, shyly. "I'm meeting someone here."

"Who?" they wanted to know.

"Dink," I said.

They smiled. "Dinky! Whadda ya meetin' Dinky for?"

"I work for him. I just got hired."

"You work in this business before?" asked a man whose eyeglasses were even thicker than Dink's. "Bobby, by the way. Bobby the Owl."

"No," I said.

"You're lucky," said the Owl, "Dinky's a good guy to work for. He buys his crew breakfast and lunch. If you can, try and bring us in some bagels, will ya?"

"Excellent hockey bettor, Dinky. Guy's made a fortune off that godforsaken sport," said a young man at the ticket counter. Behind him, numbers flashed on an electronic board as massive and complicated as the giant train schedule in New York's Penn Station. But instead of train schedules it listed every upcoming sporting event in the world.

"Lemme give ya your first piece of advice," the old man said. "After you leave here, go and get yourself a pair of galoshes. Your new boss is a crybaby. He thinks there's a black cloud followin' him all the time. His team's up. Score's one hundred to seventy-two. He has minus six. Guy's a nervous wreck. Fidgetin' round his chair like he's got hemorrhoids. Nice wife though. Pretty. You should meet my wife. Beauty-ful woman. If you wanna see her, she'll be on display today at three o'clock in the high-limit slot room."

"Dinky!"

Dink walked into the sports book, setting the room abuzz. The old men gravitated to him like reporters at a postgame interview. They wanted to know who he liked in hoops and what he thought about last night's winner at the buzzer. And what about today's games, was there any value in the Bruins line? Dink crossed his arms over his chest. He answered some of the questions with questions of his own, dismissed others, and tugged self-consciously on the bottom of his too-tight Caesars Palace T-shirt. A cocktail waitress passed by with a tray of coffees. She was young and blond and half naked and not one of the men turned to look at her.

"Hey, I know you!" came a voice behind me.

I turned around to see Chunky, a regular from the Thai restaurant. He used to come in and leave me hundred-dollar tips on his forty-dollar bill. Not wanting to walk the ten steps to the betting window, Chunky asked if I could make a bet for him. "Belmont, race two, fifty-dollar quinella for the five and the seven." He handed me the money for the bet, then slipped me a hundred-dollar tip.

"No, I'll do it for free," I said. "I need to learn."

"Take the money," the men sang in unison.

"Take it," Dink said. "Chunky's on a roll. You're struggling in life. If he wants to give you money, let him give you money."

"I'm not struggling in life," I said.

"You live in the worst neighborhood in Vegas," Dink said. "Trust me, you're struggling."

"I live there so I won't struggle," I said.

"That means you're struggling."

I took the money and wrote Chunky's bet onto the back of my hand so I wouldn't make a mistake at the window.

Above us, horses raced on each of the fourteen television screens. Each time Dink began to teach me something about placing a bet, loud cheers and moans interrupted us. After a while, we stopped talking gambling and sipped our Coca-Colas.

"Do you like music?" Dink asked. "There's a Dink Inc. office field trip tomorrow. No one else can go. Adult responsibilities."

The field trip included flying to San Diego, catching a Mighty Ducks game in Anaheim, and seeing Dink's favorite band, the Old 97's. All expenses paid by Dink Inc.

"Really?!" I shrieked. Then, in a calmer, less eager voice, I said I'd love to.

"Here," he said. Using both hands he pulled his wallet from his back pocket. It was as thick as a Big Mac. Money oozed from its corners. He handed me three hundred dollars. "To cover field-trip-related expenses."

The next morning I took Otis to the Courtyard animal hospital and spa and paid extra so he could have storybook hour and a suite to himself. Inside McCarran Airport, beside the Megabucks slot machines, I found Dink waiting for me. A New York Knickerbockers duffel bag hung from his shoulder; a white terry-cloth headband pushed his curls away from his face. He held his sports ticker, a beeper-sized gadget which displayed live scores, an inch from his eye. In an effort to bring the text into focus, he cocked his glasses, squinted his left eye shut, and scrunched up his nose. He peered into it with the intensity of a seventh grader looking at his first "tip and strip" nudie-girl pen. From the side of his mouth, his tongue curled upward.

Only when the captain prepared for takeoff did Dink turn away from his ticker and lower his glasses.

"Terrible. Dreadful. Horrendous," he said, heavy-eyed. "Today was not a profitable day."

It was my first time flying first class. Not quite believing in my luck, I ordered champagne.

CHAPTER TWO

Dinky

When Dink Heimowitz was eleven years old his mother, Freda, took him and his friend Howie on a subway ride to the 1964 World's Fair in Flushing, Queens. Alongside the General Motors Futurama exhibit and the stained-glass windows of the Vatican pavilion was a more modest display that captured Dink and Howie's attention.

It was the Minnesota state exhibit. As the two friends admired a large stuffed moose, something caught their eye. Hanging on the wall, above the moose's antlers, numbers scrolled across a small black screen: the updated scores for the Minnesota Twins game. Twins 4, White Sox 3, bottom of the sixth.

A sports ticker. Dink was awestruck.

"Can you believe it?" Dink whispered to Howie. "In the future, no matter where we are in the world, we'll be able to see baseball scores!"

Scores. Even as a kid that was what interested Dink most. Not which team was winning or losing, but by how much.

One morning, on his way to Hebrew school, Dink came upon a group of older kids crouched in a circle. They looked over their shoulders, making sure the rabbi was nowhere in sight, and then flipped their baseball cards toward a wall. The kid whose card landed closest to the wall won. "Flipping" was a game of skill. But these kids weren't just playing to see who could win the most cards; they were gambling. And Dink, with his thick eyeglasses, lanky frame, and high IQ—the highest in Hebrew school—joined them.

From flipping cards, the kids moved on to pitching pennies, which led to nickels. But by that time, Dink had gone. His seventh-grade math scores were so high that he skipped the eighth grade. The next year he was accepted to Stuyvesant High School in Manhattan, the most selective public school in the city and one of the most mathematically rigorous schools in the country. As a fourteen-year-old sophomore, Dink ran the Stuyvesant baseball pool. Thirty-five cents to bet on which major league team would score the most runs in a week. You picked your teams from a hat.

But Dink's gambling education wasn't limited to flipping cards and running baseball pools. At home in his tiny Rochdale Village apartment in Queens, he learned horse-betting techniques from his father, Solomon, a mailman who moonlighted as a two-dollar horse bettor.

There were only a few things in life that Solly enjoyed: the *New York Daily Mirror*, the TV show *Car 54, Where Are You?*, and agonizing over his weekly horse bet. Each Monday, Solly began studying the newspapers and keeping charts of horse workouts at the Aqueduct and Belmont raceways. Solly bet two dollars on one horse per week, and fretted over where to put those dollars. Every day, he walked over to the OTB and thought about which horse he should bet on. He came home, pulled a cigarette from his hard pack of Camels, ran his palm over his slicked-back blond hair, and reread the papers. Finally, after twenty-six hours of studying the workouts, Solly placed a bet.

On the following morning, Solly fetched the paper, carried it over to the kitchen table, and stood, stoically. His immaculately pressed gray flannel suit enhanced his tall, slim physique. He lit a cigarette.

Across from him, Freda sat, dishtowel over her shoulder, separating the dairy from the nondairy silverware. In the living room, Dink, their only child, entertained himself by playing an indoor variation of stoopball. He raucously bounced a ball off the wall and yelled *Foul!* when the ball hit furniture.

Solly unfolded the paper directly to the sports section and quickly covered the horse-race results with his thumb.

Inhale.

With the hesitancy of a man reading a love letter that his wife has written to someone else, Solly slowly dragged his thumb over the print, revealing the words one letter at a time.

Exhale.

"I *knew* I shouldn't have bet that horse! I liked all these other horses and they all won! Why'd I pick this bum?"

He'd grab his hat and extinguish his cigarette. Mutter something about his wife being a jinx. Then catch the train for his hour-and-a-half commute to the James A. Farley Post Office in Manhattan.

On the rare occasions Solly won, he sang "Oyfn Pripetshik," his favorite Yiddish song.

Whatever the outcome, the moment the front door slammed, Dink gathered his father's charts, picked a horse, usually based on its name, and made a bet in his mind to see if he would win.

Frosty Lady, driven by Carmine Abbatiello, paid $2.80 to show. Dink was a junior in high school and it was the first bet he ever made at a racetrack. Roosevelt Raceway in 1968 was the nation's largest, most prestigious institution for the advancement of budding mathematicians and degenerate gamblers. On any given night, fifteen to twenty thousand people trotted around the grandstands, chewing on their miniature pencils. They put their money on long shot Shirley MacLaine or big favorite Nevele Pride, and twisted their *Daily News* into a bludgeon while rooting at the top of the stretch. That's exactly where fifteen-year-old Dink was when Frosty Lady's nose thrust first across the finish line. He made eighty cents on his two dollars and thought that betting horses had to be the best way, ever, to make money. Dink stood six-foot-two and had a deep sense of purpose and belonging; the mutuel clerks never once asked to see his ID. He went to the track nearly every day thereafter. With his winnings, he bought a busted-up '59 Chevy Bel Air. Sparks shot from the steering wheel each time he drove over a pothole.

Eventually the track became the axis around which all of Dink's life revolved. It was where he made friends and money, took dates. Where he watched Hank Aaron break the home-run record. Where he was the day his father died, where he met his wife. And it was where he was introduced to many of the people who helped him throughout his career.

Lenny Goldfarb was a chubby gay bookmaker from Brooklyn who often hung out with Dink and his friends on the steps outside of Yonkers Raceway. He was always interested in seeing if there was any sexual potential with any of the young guys in the group, but even more interested in recruiting customers.

"Dinky!" Lenny hollered one night, as he approached Dink on the steps. Dink was only sixteen, but already a freshman at Queens College. "Dinky. Look. Why don't ya get your friends together, and tell 'em to bet with me. I'll give ya twenty-five percent of their losses. All you gotta do is make sure they pay when they lose, then give the money to me."

A quarter sheet. Free money! Dink's friends always lost when they bet on sports. Dink always lost too. Now all Dink had to do was simply exist and let his friends lose and he'd get twenty-five cents for each dollar they owed Lenny.

By being a part of Lenny's business, Dink pocketed twenty, thirty extra dollars a week. More important, though, he learned how a bookmaker made money. In taking bets from gamblers the bookie is only concerned with making sure that, no matter what a game's outcome, the amount he owes the winning gamblers is matched by the amount of money losing gamblers owe him. He could always gamble, and take a position on games to try and make more money, but as long as he balanced his book, he would profit from the ten-percent commission he charged for taking a bet. This fee is called the vigorish, or the vig, the juice, the take. It's a bookmaker's livelihood. It's also what makes his business illegal. In the United States, the layman is not allowed to charge a fee for taking a bet. That privilege belongs solely to the government-operated or -licensed racetracks, jai-alai frontons, casinos, off-track betting parlors, and state-sanctioned lottery systems.

Dink saw no harm in getting in on the government's monopoly. After a few months, he caught on to the business and realized that if he booked his friends himself, he could make even more free money. That was the end of Lenny Goldfarb.

Dink gave his eight friends hundred-dollar limits and installed a phone line in his bedroom. In between poker games at the Queens College cafeteria and episodes of *The Gong Show,* he attended his accounting classes. In the evenings, he booked his friends. At night, he went to the track. "You need a secretary!" his mother scolded when he returned home from his long day. "Your phone hasn't stopped. Louie Saphron called. Said he doesn't want anything to do with the Jet bet."

To avoid his mother's suspicious stares and the probing that followed, Dink retreated to his bedroom. He fed his hamster and graded his friends' bets to see how much they lost, then fell asleep watching the Knicks game.

Dinky brought home beautiful marks, wore his hair short, and stayed away from drugs. He loved his pleasures, though, and the way he put sports and friends before all else worried Freda. She thought Dinky needed structure so she had Solly set him up with a job at the post office. *Greetings from Amarillo, Texas! Utah, let this be heaven.* Dink figured he was faster at sorting mail than most and, therefore, entitled to read the backs of postcards. After four weeks he got fired for being nosy. After college, Dink worked as a sales-tax auditor. He incessantly sided with the store owners, doing everything in his power so that they wouldn't get screwed. He got called to task for showing up in jeans and sneakers and five months later he got fired. A relative got Dink a job at the New York State Housing Finance Agency. Eight months later, he quit.

Other than having to explain to his mother why another job hadn't worked out, Dink couldn't have cared less about getting fired. With each tax form he reviewed, he found it increasingly difficult to continue his I-better-do-something-with-my-life-just-in-case attitude toward a career in accounting. It wasn't like Dink to consider his future. The only time he did so was when he thought about tomorrow's eighth race. Yet, here he was, twenty years old, at Yonkers and Roosevelt Raceway, consulting friends on whether or not he should try to become a full-time bookmaker.

The general advice from people in the business was this: Do it! Just don't ever deal with bad people. Deal with normal people and gamblers. Don't deal with the mob.

People who weren't in the business said: It's illegal! Try to see the big picture, will ya, Dinky? You don't want to be surrounded with pathetic people your whole life. Stay with accounting. In the long term, you'll work at a firm and be a partner one day.

Below the New York Rangers pennants taped to his bedroom walls, Dink lay in his twin bed and watched *The Tonight Show*. From the crack beneath his locked door, he saw the outline of his mother's shoes. He could smell her lit cigarette. She was eavesdropping, as usual. Johnny Carson swung his phantom golf club stage left and Dink started thinking: *There were pathetic sewer workers, there were thriving sewer workers. Pathetic lawyers chasing ambulances and charismatic lawyers not chasing ambulances. It wasn't what you did; it was how you did it. Bookmaking was illegal, but there weren't any victims. The fine was three hundred bucks and a night in the pokey.*

The risk-reward profile seemed reasonable.

Dink thought about his dad at the post office. The long commute. The nine hours of standing. All for $6,100 a year. Where was the value? The older gamblers at the track were so much cooler than the accountants and the mailmen. They did what they wanted. They enjoyed life.

Dink didn't want to be a miserable accountant. He wanted to feel important. He wanted to use his math skills, get an informational edge, and match his wits against someone else's. He wanted to make book.

Dink moved out of his parents' house, into an apartment in Forest Hills, Queens, and slowly expanded his list of clients. Friends of friends, acquaintances, people from the track; with each customer Dink acquired, his size-fourteen sneaker slipped a tad deeper into New York City's gambling rabbit hole. Five mornings a week, at the 108th Street drugstore in Queens, Jeff the pharmacist held a card game in the basement. Down the block, at the Poseidon seafood restaurant, Jimmy Fish housed poker games starting at noon. Lum's, the Chinese restaurant near Main Street, was the place to go for thirteen-card pai gow. Gam Wau, on Northern Boulevard, offered a high-stakes rummy game after the lunch rush. The Bohack Supermarket two blocks down from Dink's apartment wasn't a supermarket, after all. It was a Vegas-style casino run by a rabbi.

Dink heard about the casino from a friend at the track. The NYPD wanted to raid the operation, the friend explained, but they couldn't, on a technicality: Rabbi Schwartz rented the supermarket under the agreement that he was going to turn the Bohack into a synagogue and offer the community some religion. And Rabbi Schwartz stood by his word. Bohack *was* a legitimate shul. In the first aisle, propped atop a wooden pulpit, was an open Torah. You could touch the Torah and daven. Or you could make a right and shoot craps.

In the vacant supermarket-cum-temple crammed with gambling paraphernalia, Dink and one hundred or so others gathered nightly. Rabbi Schwartz, in navy blue suit and maroon tie, strutted up and down the cereal aisle overlooking the action at the roulette table. In the dairy section, men leaned over craps tables and looked on as the shooter diddled with the dice. In the storage area, aisles away from the noise and commotion, poker players sat around a wooden table, their faces barely distinguishable under the halo of the room's fluorescent lights.

In less than a year, the police shut the doors of Bohack after they discovered Rabbi Schwartz had a prior arrest for impersonating a priest. Dink and the rest of the congregation regrouped at a Mafia-run gambling parlor near Austin Street.

Dink came out ahead as a bookmaker because his customers were all *schmendericks*: good-natured suckers, they bet on the Knicks, the Jets, and the Mets every time they played.

Trouble started with the wiseguys.

In the bookmaking business, the term "wiseguy" isn't used to describe someone involved in the Mafia. It's used to describe a shrewd, successful sports gambler. And, seemingly overnight, Dink's office was crawling with them.

They got in through an agent. Just as Dink was offered a kickback if he encouraged his friends to place bets with the gay bookie, professional gamblers offered agents a return if they found bookmakers who were willing to take their action. In terms of marketing strategy, gamblers resemble Mary Kay saleswomen.

"Dinky, want some more customers?" an agent asked.

"Sure," Dink said. "Give 'em my number."

Dink continued with his usual routine. He opened his office at five p.m., called a fellow bookmaker, and asked what point spread, or what *line*, he was using. If his colleague dealt the Pistons minus seven, Dink dealt the Pistons minus seven. If he dealt the Packers minus three, Dink dealt the Packers minus three. Each Monday, Dink settled his accounts with his customers. He met them at the track or inside the Queens College cafeteria, and either paid them what they had won, or, more commonly, they paid Dink what they had lost. The only thing that changed in Dink's workday was the amount of time he spent alone at the kitchen table, hunched over a calculator and yellow legal pad, trying to figure out how the hell his old customers, his friends, never won, and the new guys, who were so friendly on the phone and bet obscure teams like Western Michigan and Troy State, never lost.

What Dink didn't know was that at eight a.m., while he was sound asleep, his new customers had already started their workday. Their pencils were sharpened and they were looking over their charts, considering the matchups. At JFK Airport, their associates lingered at the arrival gates of major cities that had sports teams, waiting for planes to empty so they could collect the discarded hometown newspapers and bring them to their boss.

At noon, while Dink ate a bowl of cereal and prepared to watch *Ryan's Hope,* another set of associates was out gathering information. At the Union Plaza Hotel in downtown Las Vegas, the sports book manager held his stogie while scribbling the day's odds on a chalkboard. The messengers, known as beards or runners, copied the odds onto their clipboards and sprinted to the nearest pay phone and reported to the boss. The boss compared the Las Vegas line, *the* line, to the lines of all the other bookmakers with whom he did business, searching for the odds that were the weakest.

At four p.m., while Dink moseyed home after the afternoon races at Aquaduct, his wiseguy customers were still working. They had thoroughly read the sports and weather pages of the *Chicago Tribune,* the *Milwaukee Journal,* and the *Pittsburgh Post-Gazette,* among others. Laboring over their own calculators and legal pads, they jotted down the facts they found most useful: injuries, suspensions, precipitation levels, wind directions, team morale, referee schedules, and distinctive home-field advantages. They analyzed the information and determined the games where the point spread gave them a thorough advantage.

And at five p.m., they dialed the number of the new fish. That kid in Queens, Dinky. The one who never adjusted his lines. Who never knew of pitching changes or thunderstorms or injuries.

"What you got on the Cowboys?" one of Dink's wiseguys asked him one morning. It was early, not even ten o'clock. Dink had yet to call his colleague. He didn't know what he had on the Cowboys.

"I'm not open yet," Dink said.

"I gotta get down before I go to my kid's Bar Mitzvah. Just tell me what you got on the Cowboys."

"I'm not prepared yet," Dink said.

"Well, what'd ya have 'em at last night? Just gimme that line."

Dink turned the pages of his notebook, searching for the odds he'd given out the night before.

"Thirteen," Dink said.

"All right. Gimme the Cowboys minus thirteen for two dimes."

Dink hesitated. Dealing a line before checking with fellow bookmakers to see what line they were using was like selling an antique before you had researched the item. He didn't want to be taken for an amateur, but he also didn't want to seem rude, didn't want to lose a customer.

"Okay," Dink said. "Cowboys minus thirteen for two dimes."

There was no Bar Mitzvah. The customer had learned that the quarterback for the opposing team was injured. The Cowboys were going to win by a landslide. Bookmakers were no longer taking bets on the game.

. . . except for that one kid in Queens.

"I don't feel good," Dink said.

He sat beside a friend, Ernie, on the steps outside the track. Dink had on his signature outfit of jeans, sneakers, and a red satin Montreal Canadiens jacket two sizes too small. The snaps strained to stay closed. Like Dinky, they looked as though they were in pain.

"I owe out a lot of money," Dink continued. "And everything I do every day indicates that I'm gonna owe a lot more money."

Dink's "a lot of money" was $120,000.

"You know, Dinky," Ernie said, "you can *not* pay people and they'll let you live. Just tell 'em you're broke. If you ever get money you'll give it to 'em. But for now, say you're broke. Say you quit."

"If I quit, what do I do? I'll owe out money and have no income. I have to pay. I don't wanna go broke."

To most gamblers, going broke is a rite of passage. It's the only real way to foster a disregard for money. Only after a gambler goes broke, and recovers, does he build the fortitude needed to take bigger risks. This is the knowledge the old-timers had passed down to Dink and his friends, most of whom were already broke. But Dink didn't buy it. Going broke was his greatest fear. If he went broke it would shatter the one belief that sustained all of his self-esteem: that he was a good bookmaker.

"You need a lender?" Ernie asked.

"You know one?"

"I know one. But you gotta make sure you pay him, Dinky. The guy's not such a good guy. I don't really want you to borrow from him unless you have to."

"I have to."

The transaction took place at a social club in the Bronx. Beneath the low ceilings, in a poorly lit back booth, a Florsheim shoebox slid, slowly, across the vinyl tablecloth. It stopped at the tip of Dink's fingertips, gripping the table's edge. His face half shadowed, the loan shark spoke his only words: two percent interest a week.

Dink settled his accounts with the wiseguys—including one customer to whom he owed one hundred grand—and people took notice. At twenty-eight, Dink may have been too young to fully grasp the gambling market, but he wasn't some schmoe who disappeared when he lost. He was an honest, reliable bookmaker, and with his reputation in mint condition, Dink found it easy to acquire customers. Wiseguy gamblers passed Dink's phone number to unwiseguy gamblers who passed the number on to their college buddies who passed the number on to their dentists who passed the number on to their accountants who passed the number on to their colleagues who were serving time for embezzlement. Soon, Dink was no longer susceptible to the risk that came with taking bets from dozens of seasoned professionals and only a handful of rubes. He now had the most valuable asset in the bookmaker's arsenal: volume.

So much so that he rented the second floor of a row house in

neighboring Whitestone and hired his friends Bobby Nebbish and
Fat George to man the seven phones that never stopped ringing.
His friend Lobster came on board as a partner and the two invested in a wire service that gave them updates on injuries, scores,
and line changes from the Las Vegas casinos. They attached tape
recorders to each of the phones so that if a customer claimed that
he had not made a particular bet or that he bet more or less than
what Dink's clerk had written down, Dink was able to replay the
tapes and quickly settle the dispute. As a New York Rangers and
New Jersey Devils season ticket holder, Dink began watching the
games less like a fan and more like a gambler. A customer of Dink's
noticed that his hockey line was sharper compared to other bookies and the two began to exchange opinions and share handicap secrets. By trial and error, Dinky developed his own systems and was
soon betting four, five thousand dollars on hockey games. One of
the drawbacks of being a hockey handicapper, however, was that
information was harder to obtain. The western Canadian newspapers arrived at newsstands three days late. One of Dink's employees
suggested that they call someone who had a job-needed posting
in the want ads of the *Calgary Sun* and the *Edmonton Journal,* and
offer them five hundred dollars a week to call the office every
morning and read the sports section over the phone. Dink called
"light typing needed," who turned out to be an eighty-seven-year-
old widow. She told him he was insane, and said no. "Good with
children" also told him he was insane, but said yes, and became
Dink's first official hockey reader.

Within ten months, Dink returned to the Bronx social club
where he paid his final installment on the loan shark payment
plan.

Over the next five years, the money came in faster than Dink
could spend it. He was officially a millionaire. Not yet a multimil-
lionaire. But, still, a millionaire. Some of the money he kept inside
a lockbox in his apartment. He hid twenty-five grand inside his
Strat-O-Matic baseball board game and another ten thousand inside empty Ajax containers. More of his money was stacked inside
several different safe-deposit boxes around town. His closest

friends held on to a few grand. He invested in punk bands, race-horses, and the *schmata* industry. He paid sixteen hundred dollars a month for a two-bedroom inside the Bay Club, a high-rise complex in Bayside, Queens, complete with basketball and tennis courts, steam rooms and saunas, a swimming pool, valet parking, and its own underground mall. And in the center of the lush thirteen-acre estate, beneath a quaint wooden bridge, the Bay Club ducks paddled gracefully around a reflecting pond as sparkling green as the Emerald City.

On the afternoon Freda came to visit, her black orthopedic shoes sank into the cream-colored shag carpet. Her tiny brown eyes scanned the room: the leather couch, the marble table, the view of the Manhattan skyline. She brought her hand to her heart.

Freda grew up in the Madison House settlement on the Lower East Side. Her two brothers were Orthodox rabbis. Most of her friends were widows whom she met at the local Jewish center. No one Freda knew lived in such an opulent home.

She had never realized her son desired such riches. God knows he never bought new clothes or paid to have his hair cut. She spoke with Dink on the phone every day, yet she still didn't understand how he made money. Despite how impressed Freda was with her son's apartment, she couldn't bring herself to tell him so.

"I don't want to know how you can afford this building," she said.

"The building's not mine," Dink said. "Just the apartment."

"Whatever it is you're doing, you need to stop. I can tell you're not living a clean life."

"Mom, I told you. I'm gambling. I'm doing good."

"If you're doing so good, why don't we go to the Big and Tall store and buy you some clothes that fit? It annoys me to death the way you dress. "

Dink flipped through the channels until he came upon *The White Shadow.*

"Your father would disapprove of your position in life. He would want his child to do the right thing in every respect. I think it's disgraceful, anyone who gambles. You need to apply to medical school."

"Mom! I'm thirty-three years old."

"Fine, study law."

"Not gonna happen."

"Go into teaching. There are plenty of children out there who need to learn math."

"You go teach math."

"Accounting."

"Not a chance."

After the last race, Dink drove his brand-new '86 Cadillac Seville along the Bronx River Parkway, alone, at twilight, listening to the scores on the radio. This was the part of the day he looked forward to most.

Ten ten WINS. You give us twenty-two minutes, we'll give you the world.

He rolled down the windows and the wind splashed his brown curls across the front of his glasses.

Here we go to the National League . . .

After the commentator announced each score, Dink snapped his fingers.

Mets lost to the Cubs in extra innings, 3–2.

Snap.

Pirates topped the Phillies, 7–5.

Snap.

Dink was making money on nearly every game. Sports pages, candy-bar wrappers, and loose ten- and twenty-dollar bills flew around the backseat. If Dink had let go of the steering wheel and reached out, a small fortune could have flown right into his hand.

Inside Dink's 150th Street office, five telephones rang. The 1987 regular football season had come to an end and Super Bowl XXII was just two days away. The moment the clerks hung a phone on the receiver, it rang again. The handles were hot to the touch.

"Sports," Fat George answered. "What can I get for ya?"

He handed the phone to Dink, who sat at the head of the table. "Hello."

"Dinky, A.J. Listen. There was a bust at Lou's office in Brooklyn, 'bout twenty minutes ago."

With the Super Bowl came heat. This, Dink knew. His first arrest happened the day before Super Bowl XV, Oakland versus Philadelphia. He was booking with his friend Doug. Together, they were busted and brought to the holding cell on Northern Boulevard. Dink asked the cop if he and Doug could have connecting cells. "This isn't the Hilton," the cop replied, then granted them the connecting cells. The following afternoon, they paid the four-hundred-dollar fine and made it home late in the fourth quarter. They opened shop the following evening.

Dink also knew that the police organized hits simultaneously. If you didn't get busted within five minutes of a neighboring bookmaker being busted, chances were you were safe.

Dink stood up from his chair and looked out the office window to the garbage cans and leafless shrubs lining the driveway.

"I think I'm good," Dink said. "Thanks for calling."

Ten minutes passed. The telephones rang. So did the doorbell.

Armed with only a number two pencil, Dink descended the narrow staircase. In the doorway stood seven FBI agents dressed in SWAT uniforms.

The FBI interviewed Dink and his crew separately. Everyone but Fat George told the truth. "I didn't give up on anybody," George whispered, returning to the office after being questioned. "I don't know anything. I didn't roll on anybody." His loyalty, though sweet, was unnecessary. There was no disputing that the office had one purpose: bookmaking. While the agents sifted through the trash, collecting notebooks and sports schedules and scraps of paper, the phones rang incessantly. Every fifteen minutes, the sports wire divulged the newest line, the latest injury, and the updated scores, with its usual *ttt-ttt-ttt*.

The head agent handed Dink his business card. "I'll get back to you," he said. "We know who you're working for."

At the Bayside Diner, Dink, Lobster, Bobby Nebbish, and Fat George sat at a round table.

"It has not been a wonderful day," Dink said. He considered the menu, then set it aside. He always ordered the tuna on rye. Today wouldn't be any different.

"I didn't roll on anybody," Fat George said.

"George!" Lobster said, losing patience. "We were there! We were bookin'! It was obvious."

"I didn't say that," Fat George said. "I told 'em, 'I don't know a thing.' "

"At least we're not sleeping in jail tonight," Nebbish said.

"I don't know," Dink said. "I think it's worse that they let us go home. I might have a real situation here. The FBI is kind of scary."

Lobster leaned closer to Dink and whispered over his menu, "Dinky, relax. You're not in the Mafia. You're just a Jewish bookmaker from Queens. That's kinda clear."

Dink was just a Jewish bookmaker from Queens. Everybody knew that. Growing up in Rochdale and Forest Hills and being in the gambling business, Dink had spent plenty of time around Italian mobsters. But they respected that Dink didn't want to get involved in their businesses and have sit-downs. The Italian mobsters let the Jewish bookmakers be Jewish bookmakers and the Jewish bookmakers knew they could always go to Italian mobsters for help, but then they owed them.

"He said he knows who I work for," Dink said. "How much trouble can you get in if the FBI thinks you just work for somebody?"

Long after his crew finished their sandwiches and left, Dink stayed at the diner. He couldn't make sense out of the raid. Why hadn't he gotten arrested? Lou, the bookmaker who got busted in Brooklyn, was mob related, and the FBI didn't take him to jail, either. Same with Joey Useless, in Manhattan, whom the FBI raided after they left Dinky's. Three busts, three different types of bookmakers, and no jail.

"You want some more tea?" the waitress asked.

"Whatever," Dink mumbled.

"It's not whatever. A new tea bag you get charged for. Hot water you don't."

He was going to have to shut down. With the FBI privy to his every move, he knew that betting and booking and being seen with bettors and bookmakers wouldn't be of help to anyone. But his business! For seventeen years he had worked at building his clientele and his reputation, not to mention his ego. He had persevered through the years when he was a terrible bookmaker to become a great bookmaker. His business had been prospering. It was worth something. For a moment, he considered selling it. His customers alone were worth probably four hundred thousand. If he sold it to someone competent, they could put four other clerks in those four seats and make five, six hundred thousand dollars a year without putting in a lot of work.

But now was not the time to be orchestrating deals. As he finished his tea, he realized that it was over. Tomorrow he would go to the office and collect his belongings. From a pay phone on Queens Boulevard, he would call a close friend and give him the business, for a small consideration. In the evening, he would drive to the track, sit on the steps, and get advice from the old guys. But he would never again be a bookmaker.

CHAPTER THREE

The Best of It

Holding a screwdriver in my right hand and the doorknob in my left, I leaned against the frame of the office door. The change-a-lock instructions lay at my feet. "I swear to God, I didn't know her," I said. "She recommended me because I gave her twenty percent off her curry!"

"You said you knew her well," Dink said, turning the page of *Fuzzy Creatures*. He seemed too calm for a guy who'd just been robbed by his masseuse.

I shouldn't have lied during the interview. I hadn't known Amy at all. Perhaps that's why I was more shocked than Dink to discover upon returning from San Diego that she had let herself into the office and stolen cash and winning wagering tickets. Dink wouldn't tell me how much, but even with Dink in the room, swiping ten grand in casino chips off his desk was as easy as sweeping bread-crumbs into the palm of your hand.

In San Diego, we stayed at a five-star hotel in rooms with private balconies. For breakfast, we ate ham-and-cheese omelets at a restaurant overlooking the Pacific Ocean. Dink paid for every-thing. When I mentioned I wanted to go to film school one day, he insisted we stop by the University of California at San Diego and tour the campus. He really was a sweet, generous man.

"I only said I knew her because I wanted the job," I said, taking a seat next to him.

Dink finished the article about the potential hazards of organic hamster treats and closed the magazine. "I'm just giving you a hard time. I think she had a cocaine habit."

"Really?" And then I remembered her black, oversized sunglasses.

"A terrible one. Sometimes she came to work nine hours late. On 9/11 she told me the government was looking for her and she didn't come to work for two weeks."

"Then why'd you tell me you had faith in her?"

"She was nice," he said. Then, like a father taking an awkward situation and turning it into a learning opportunity, he shook his finger and added, "There are a higher percentage of thieves out there than you think."

"Do you think she'll show up for work tomorrow and pretend like nothing ever happened?" I said, thinking that's exactly what I would do if I were Amy.

"No. I think she'll run off to Reno. That's where everyone goes after they steal from me. I think they all have a meeting there, at the Royal Moose, like in *Rocky and Bullwinkle*. They all belong to Local 12, the Villains, Thieves, and Scoundrels Union."

I returned clearheaded to the job at hand: changing the locks on the office door so that my reference could never again break and enter.

Over the next three days, Dink sat with me in the office and gave me gambling tutorials. By the evening of our last session, my five-subject notebook was nearly full. Not with statistics and notes regarding important sports betting information, but intricate doodles: balloons and flowers and jungles with monkeys half hidden by palm trees. I hadn't understood a thing Dink taught me. To look busy, I drew.

"We shop for the best value," Dink said. "If we don't get the best of it, I'll be broke and you'll be out of a job. When I die, I want my tombstone to say 'Dinky. He died with the best of it.' "

It would be months on the job before I would understand the lessons Dink tried to teach me in those sessions. The first lesson I learned was that while it may be illegal to be a bookmaker, it is not illegal to gamble for a living. The second lesson was that despite the tens of thousands of dollars in bets he made each day, the money Dink bet was always his own. He did not take other people's bets and was therefore not a bookie. Professional gambler was the occupation he listed when he filed his taxes. The bets he lost he used as tax write-offs. The fact that he had an office and employees, though it gave him an aura of officialdom, simply reflected the complexity of his betting. He couldn't do it alone.

As a sports gambler, Dink's job wasn't simply to figure out which team would win. As I learned, if all you had to do to win money betting baseball was predict the winner, you, me, and everyone else in the world would bet on the first-place team every time they played and by the end of the regular season, we'd all be rich. But gamblers can't make money by just betting on a team that wins more often than it loses. That's because bookmakers create odds—otherwise known as lines—that, in essence, penalize people who bet on the favorite. The line is an attempt by bookmakers to make both teams in any given matchup appear equally attractive. They want their books balanced; they want as many people to bet on the underdog as on the favorite.

The key to winning money is knowing a good line when you see one. Value, not just who you think is going to win or lose, is the overriding consideration.

To understand value, Dink first determined for himself what he thought the line should be. He had become just like the wiseguy gamblers who had beaten him for hundreds of thousands of dollars when he was a novice bookmaker. Dink researched as much as possible about teams and specific matchups, weighing the relevant factors in order to arrive at his best educated guess as to each game's likely outcome. I had assumed that as a professional gambler Dink researched teams, weather, and statistics and made bets for himself based on that information, but it took me a while to understand what "shopping for the best value" entailed. Whether or not we thought a certain team was going to win didn't matter. If the price was right, we bought it. When Dink said that we must always get the best of it, he meant that we must find a line that gave him an edge—a line that offered the most reward with the least risk. That, to me, didn't seem like gambling. It seemed like we were bargain hunting for luck.

First, Dink had determined for himself what the line had to be to make it worth betting on. Then he had to find a line that came closest to that magical number. Like a company's stock price, lines for each game were in constant flux, changing according to the demands of the market. To know how the market valued a particular game, Dink, like all professional gamblers, turned to the Internet.

Gone were the days of waiting in airports for out-of-town newspapers or searching for a bookmaker in the backstreets or bars. Starting in the mid-'90s, gamblers could suddenly go online and read reviews of offshore gambling businesses. They could open their *Daily Racing Form*s and see advertisements for gambling parlors based in the Dominican Republic. The first time Dink saw such an ad, he couldn't believe it. Bookmakers? Advertising? At worst it was a police scam, he thought, and at best it was a swindle. Dink spoke to a lawyer. "Internet gambling is untested waters," the lawyer explained. "But for now, it's legal." He told Dink to go for it.

Dink tested the waters and the waters were great. He didn't have to wait for bookies to open. He could bet any time of day. Oddly, it seemed to make gambling so much more socially acceptable. Everyone, young and old, was talking sports-betting shop. It was just as normal as day-trading.

To keep track of the lines offered by sports books around the world, professional gamblers used Don Best Live Odds, an online service that for six hundred dollars a month gave a running tally of the lines each sports book offered for any day's games. In fact, Don Best Live Odds did for gamblers and bookmakers what Bloomberg terminals did for hedge-fund managers and stockbrokers. Where Bloomberg streamed stock quotes and the latest financial data, Don Best displayed the latest injury reports and lineup changes. It broadcasted line adjustments from a dozen offshore offices and a handful of licensed sports books in Las Vegas in real time.

As a Dink Inc. employee, I needed to learn how to read the lines on Don Best as they flashed across the office's five monitors. Taking a closer look at the computer screen, I saw not just numbers and plus and minus signs; I saw fractions. I hadn't passed a math class since junior high. A rush of incompetence washed over me. Feeling my face blush, I pulled my notebook close and added stripes to a toucan's beak, completing my jungle scene.

At a quarter to eight I arrived at Dink Inc. for my first shift, convinced I would make a fatal mistake with Dink's money.

Across from me, Robbie J worked on his rundown sheets—long pieces of paper with tiny blank boxes designed for listing the day's matchups and the lines on each game. October brought preseason NBA, hockey, NFL, college football, and baseball playoffs. Fearing that it would take me too long to complete these sheets and that I would miss something, I wrote mine out the night before. With the televisions turned off, the office was quiet. The only sound came from underneath the table where Otis lay, licking his paws.

Tony, the casino runner, ogled an amateur porn site, stroking his thick beard and shifting his posture, as we all waited for Dink to arrive with his bankroll. Tony's job was to visit several different casinos and call Dink with the lines each sports book had posted. This is what was referred to as "shopping for numbers." Runners were necessary for two reasons. One, Don Best broadcasted the lines from just a handful of Las Vegas's 110 licensed sports books. If Tony hustled, he was sure to find a bargain at one of the sports books elsewhere in Clark County for Dink to bet. The other reason was that betting limits were higher in person than they were over the phone. If Dink found a cheap price on a team, why bet five hundred dollars over the phone when he could wager five thousand in person? What good was getting the best of it if you couldn't bet the most on it?

In addition to Tony, Dink also had a casino runner based in Reno. Her name was Louise and she was eighty-five years old. Until Dink hired her, she was having a hard time making it on her Social Security alone.

As bet-out clerks, Robbie J and I also shopped for numbers, but instead of driving around Vegas we did our shopping by calling bookmakers or visiting their Web sites. This included the legal bookmakers, based offshore, and illegal bookmakers, based in big cities and small towns across America.

I took out a stack of index cards that I had made to memorize this new foreign language. The part of the business that caused me the most confusion was that the method of betting varied with each sport. You didn't bet on baseball the same way you bet on basketball, and in hockey you could bet any number of ways. There was the Canadian line, a puck line, an East Coast line, and even a line called the Grand Salami.

I flipped an index card.

Grand Salami: The grand total of goals scored in all the hockey games of the day. It can be wagered to go Over/Under.

Robbie J looked at me and raised his perfectly waxed eyebrows. Wrinkles bulged across his shaved head.

"Flash cards?" he said, giggling.

"I'm nervous," I said.

" 'Cause I'm so good-lookin'?"

Even Money:

Flip.

A bet in which no vigorish is laid.

"No. Because I keep thinking I'm gonna bet thousands of dollars on the wrong team."

Tony and Robbie J offered different advice, but their sentiments were the same. Dink came up with the plan, we followed it.

"Dinky's the architect, we're the construction workers," Robbie J said. "Just copy what I do and try not to get too distracted by my beautiful muscles."

Dink held the *Las Vegas Review-Journal* sports section close to his face and underlined the box scores with his thumb. While driving. Dink drove an aqua four-door Nissan Altima. It was an ugly car, and Dink could definitely afford something nicer, but he bought it as a "self-punishment vehicle" for doing so poorly last baseball season.

There was barely enough room in the car for both Dink and his bouffant. His belly nudged the steering wheel. He was too big to wear a seat belt comfortably, so to drown the *ding ding ding* of the seat-belt reminder system he blasted his Donovan CD. His car jumped the curb as it pulled into the office parking lot.

He entered the office with a bounce in his step. Baseball, with its grueling five-month-long, 4,080-game regular season and its five-inning lines, alternate run lines, and strikeout propositions, had finally wound down and Dink could now focus on football, horse racing, and his beloved hockey. He carried stacks of hockey schedules and a brand-new spiral-bound *Jim Feist Football Workbook,* a compilation of ten years' worth of results for both college and pro teams with team logs, spread breakdowns, matchup reports, and reminders of the type of surface on which each game would be played. Dink purchased these materials from the Gambler's Book Shop, downtown. The Book Shop was stocked with information on how to beat any casino or gambling system ever devised. It also carried novels like *Sex, Lies, and Video Poker,* and do-it-yourself divorce kits.

Plopped on top of Dink's workbook was a brown paper lunch sack from which he pulled out ninety thousand dollars in one-hundred-dollar bills. He tossed the rubber-banded brick to Tony, who stuffed it into his pockets. A quick discussion of a few games that piqued Dink's interest and Tony was off.

Between my two phones, I had sixty bookmakers programmed to

speed dial. Beneath the speed dial cover plate was a list of book-makers' offices, each with a different code name and password. I had spent plenty of hours becoming acquainted with the tele-phones. It was important to be quick on them and to know which bookmaker booked which sport, what time they opened, closed, and what their maximum limits were. One of the bookmakers on my list was Texas Toast, a farmer in south Texas who was also a poker player. A notoriously slow speaker, he took twenty minutes to give a rundown of his day's odds. Dink always assigned him to his new clerks.

Robbie J picked up his receiver and punched a speed dial button with the eraser of his pencil. I picked up mine.

"Yep," Texas Toast answered.

"Hi. Uh, nine seven six popcorn. Can I get a rundown?"

There was a long silence. In the background, I thought I heard a cow moo.

"My Gawd, popcorn, you sound like a child. Here we go. . . . N . . . B . . . A. Golden State . . . four . . . and . . . a hook. Eighty . . . eight. Bucks . . . six . . . and . . . a hook. Ninety . . . two."

I wondered what a hook was. Too shy to ask, I pretended to fill in the blank boxes of my rundown sheet and then called the next bookmaker on my list.

An 800 number and a man with a Caribbean accent answered: "Sports. Dis is Bush."

"GJ nine seven two Dinky," I said. "Can I get a rundown?"

"Of course, Ms. Dinky. Starting with College Football. *Jee-or-jee-uh, Boo-dog,* ten and a half . . ."

Robbie J held a receiver to each ear.

He spoke into one phone: "Gimme the Bulls first half, over oh one minus the oh nine for two dimes."

Then the other: "I'll take the Heat over the eighty-nine flat for a dime."

In between confirming one bet and making another, he slid a three-ply ticket from the pile in front of him and jotted down the name of the office with whom he bet, the bet itself, and the amount he bet to win. With the motion of someone throwing a Frisbee, he tossed his tickets one by one to Dink. Over the table the tickets flew, their top and bottom pages fluttering like moth wings. Two thousand, five thousand, twelve thousand dollars' worth of bets soared toward Dink. In one quick motion, Dink snatched the tickets out of midair as though they were pesky bugs.

I lost track of where I was on the rundown and hung up on Bush in midsentence.

"What'd he have on Morehead?" Dink asked me.

"Who?" I said.

"Morehead," Dink repeated.

"I didn't call Morehead," I said.

"No, moron," said Robbie J. "Morehead's a football team."

"Morehead's a college," Dink corrected.

"The office you just called, what did they have on Morehead?" Robbie J asked.

I looked down at the tiny boxes on my sheet. They were all blank.

"Forget it, we missed it." Dink yelled. "Call Fort Knox. Fuck, we're on the wrong side. Go! Go! Go!"

I didn't have Fort Knox programmed to my speed dial so I picked up the phone and pretended to call a bookmaker just to make it appear as though I was doing something.

"Beth, you gotta say who you're calling so no one else wastes their time calling the same office. Okay?" Dink said.

"Okay," I said.

The computers beeped, along with the fax machine. One of the fourteen phones rang. I had no idea which one.

"So?" Robbie J snapped and I nearly jumped out of my seat. His hand gripped the receiver so hard his knuckles turned white. He was waiting on me to make a call. "Who are you on the phone with?"

"Uhm," I said, and hung up.

I found the ringing phone. It was Tony, prepared with his rundown, calling from a men's bathroom inside the Stardust casino. The Stardust was the preeminent Las Vegas sports book because it was the first sports book to post the day's lines. For professionals like Dinky, these lines—calculated by handicappers but untested by the market—were pure potential. Any mistake, any miscalculation or oversight—maybe the line didn't take into account the college quarterback who stayed up till two in the morning downing tequila shots—was begging for a smart bettor to take advantage of it.

Gamblers called these virginal lines the early lines and there wasn't a wiseguy in the country who didn't want to get down on them. To protect itself from getting hammered by the smart bettors, however, the Stardust managers limited the number of bets they took before they had a chance to adjust their lines. It was a first come, first served setup to bet the early lines and competition became so fierce that some gambling bosses paid homeless people to sleep in the Stardust sports book. The homeless player wasn't making a bet, he was just staking claim to a position in line until ten to eight, when the regular runner moved in, slipped the bum twenty bucks, and took his place in the line. Eventually, in preparation for the next day's odds, the homeless players began camping out on the sports book's purple-and-green-flowered carpet at seven at night. The managers put an end to the situation by incorporating a lottery. Get here at a quarter to eight, guys, they told the runners, and draw a number from a hat.

"Gimme Dinky," Tony said, and I handed Dink the phone.

The televisions cut to a breaking news story. With September 11 just a month behind us, news flashes and terror alerts had become commonplace. Still, we held our breath and looked to the TVs with apprehension. The anchorman reported that letters laced with anthrax had been discovered in Reno.

"Reno?" I said. "We better warn Louise."

"I think Louise is safe at the sports book," Dink said.

Close-up images of Osama bin Laden in his white turban appeared on the television. Another clip showed him walking along a mountainous brown-gray desert with an AK-47 hanging across his chest.

"Guy's livin' in a cave. That must be a real riot," Robbie J said.

He punched a skinny red straw into the foil of his protein-drink box.

"How much is the reward for capturing him?" I asked.

"Twenty-five million," Robbie J said.

"Think of what we could do with that kind of money!" I said.

"I'd invest in the Yankees to win the World Series," Dink said.

Bin Laden vanished from the TV screen and in his place appeared Las Vegans who claimed to have served some of the 9/11 hijackers during a trip they made to Vegas earlier that summer. A teenage employee at Hungry Howie's said the hijackers ordered a pizza from him "with the works, minus the ham." An Alamo Rent A Car employee explained that he had rented one of the hijackers a brand-new Chevy Malibu, complete with a Triple A discount. At the Olympic Garden, reporters interviewed strippers who had lap-danced for one of the hijackers. "Some big-man terrorist," said a sarcastic brunette in a push-up bra. "He spent about twenty bucks for a quick dance and didn't even tip." When asked what the hijackers looked like, the girls quickly exclaimed, "Cheap!"

How does Sin City appear through the eyes of Islamists? Tonight at seven.

Louise called from a pay phone outside the Peppermill casino. Her voice shook, not with fear of anthrax, but with elderliness, and she began her rundown. "They have the Seattle Seahawks minus three . . ."

By lunchtime we were up thirty-three grand.

After a frenzied four-hour shift, we drove to the Red Rock country club to watch the afternoon games at a friend of Dink's who was also a professional gambler. Along a brick driveway lined with Corvettes, Jaguars, and luxury SUVs, Dink parked his Altima. We walked beneath an outdoor chandelier, through a marble-floored foyer, up a wrought-iron spiral staircase, and onto the second floor, which overlooked the eighteen-hole Arnold Palmer–designed golf course. Opened French doors led to the friend's office, commonly known as the Den of Equity.

Ten middle-aged men of all moods, sizes, and smells fraternized around the den, fiddling with their sports tickers and talking shop.

"You guys are gonna think I'm full of shit," said a man with hair plugs, who seemed to be at the center of conversation. "But I met this girl. Redhead. Big tits, no kids . . ."

With just a few exceptions, these men had known each other since they were in their twenties. In New York, they had played in the same card rooms and were regulars at the track. They remembered each other's first cars and first wives. They had watched each other go to prison for tax evasion, bookmaking, and race fixing. They'd seen each other flush at the final table at the World Series of Poker and so broke that they couldn't pay their electric bill. Through the years, they had bet each other thousands of dollars on things as meaningless as whether or not the winner of the spelling bee would be wearing glasses and as consequential as the results of their prostate exams. When they felt that one gambler was in over his head with a girl who was spending fourteen thousand dollars a pop on pocketbooks, they held a gold-digger intervention.

Michael, the Den of Equity's host, was a short, grumpy old man who looked like he'd just downed a glass of curdled milk. He was reputed to be a ruthless bettor, but he couldn't manage to turn on any of his state-of-the-art appliances. He hired assistants to teach him how to use the mouse on his computer. When he couldn't find the TV's volume button, he asked friends to come over and help. His office, however, was so spectacular—the gambling books in the mahogany bookshelves, the valuable Brooklyn Dodgers paraphernalia, the four flat-screen televisions built into the wall cabinet—that the friends and assistants never left. Thus, the Den of Equity became the game-day hangout and Dink saw it as a great place to introduce me to his friends.

"Everyone!" Dink said, hoisting up his shorts. "Meet Beth, the newest Dink Inc. employee and Flip It aficionado."

Falafel, an Israeli backgammon player, was the only one to say hello.

Noticing that the host was looking at me, I smiled.

"*What*?" he snapped.

Dink and I sat on a couch in the corner. "Your friends don't like me," I whispered over the noisy televisions.

"They like you," Dink said, loudly. I shushed him.

"They like you," he whispered. "But they barely tolerate women. I guess I kind of forgot that."

Beautiful day in Wisconsin, the defending Super Bowl champion Baltimore Ravens against the Green Bay Packers. Hello everyone, what a great matchup we have for you today.

With no interest in the games, and feeling unwelcome, I stayed at Dink's side and opened my mouth only to eat chocolate-covered strawberries when they came my way. When it came to sports, I enjoyed baseball the most and I had my favorite players—Pedro Martinez and Vladimir Guerrero. Before I met Dink, I had never watched a hockey game; now that I was beginning to understand the rules and becoming familiar with the players, I found the sport exciting. But I loathed football, an animosity that brewed at Florida State, where I had had classes with some of the players. During lectures, they'd blast their Walkmans and rap to themselves while popping zits on their shoulders. When I was a little girl, I always watched football on the couch with my dad. I'd had a crush on Jim McMahon and when he ran onto the field I'd hold up a homemade sign that read "I ♥ you Jim! Do the Super Bowl shuffle!" But Florida State and the obnoxious tomahawk chop, which stayed in my head for years, ruined the sport for me.

The host's young Mexican wife, an ex–cocktail waitress from Binion's, breezed through the room in a low-cut silk dress, looking as posh and polished as a movie star. A diamond-encrusted Star of David, a present from her husband when she converted to Judaism, fell into her cleavage. She offered the guests fresh-squeezed orange juice, toasted bagels and lox, and more chocolate hors d'oeuvres. She delivered a prepared plate to her husband, who sat behind his glazed desk. As lissomely as she entered, she departed. And once again, I was the only female in the room if you didn't count sideline reporter Bonnie Bernstein.

And, let's go down to Bonnie Bernstein. Bonnie?

The camera cut to Bonnie, standing on the sidelines, composed. A silver clip kept the wind from blowing her hair into her face. A quilted magenta coat protected her from the Green Bay chill. She brought the CBS microphone close to her mouth and began to speak.

Our host muted her commentary. "Cunt," he spat.

Dink came to her rescue. "Hey, don't be rude to Bonnie. She's one of the tribe."

"Cock! Sucker! I have too much on San Fran under. Anybody wanna piece of it?"

"I'll take two dimes."

"I'll take three."

"How do you have two dimes to bet on the game but you can't pay me back the money I loaned you at Saratoga?"

"I got a joke for you guys. Two Muslims and a Jew are sittin' next to each other on an airplane . . ."

On the TV below, players piled on top of each other.

He fumbles the ball and here comes the Ravens and . . . they . . . got it!

On the top TV, the Redskins prepared for kickoff.

"FUCK you, Schottenheimer, you inept FUCK," Hair Plugs shouted. The camera cut to the coach pacing the sidelines and Hair Plugs lunged at him, the way high school bullies do when they want to make someone flinch. I thought he was going to spit at the screen. I had to look away.

"Baltimore's shootin' their load a little too early."

"Niners' defense is horrendous. This may be a very profitable day."

"Can somebody mute Dierdorf? *'An inopportune time to fumble.'* Is there ever an opportune time to fumble, jerk-off?"

"Fuck. I forgot my Xanax."

On the divan sat a man so entranced by the game's unfolding drama that he absentmindedly peeled psoriasis scabs from the back of his hand and popped them like movie candy into his mouth.

"Eating it's not gonna make it go away," Dink said, and then turned to me and asked, "Are you having a nice time?"

I nodded my head yes.

"You're allowed to talk, you know."

I shook my head no.

"You wanna piece?"

In addition to my salary, Dink gave me "pieces" of games we watched together outside of the office. It was an all-reward, no-risk situation. If he won, he'd give me two, three hundred dollars. To make it more fun for me, he said. He gave me my first piece of a game while we were in San Diego. Now, one week later, I was up eight hundred dollars for the week, in pieces.

I nodded yes.

"We need Falcons and under. Our root is for no one to score. But if someone must score, we want it to be the Falcons. We need the Redskin total to go over thirty-four in the first half, that's a big one. We need Tennessee to get destroyed . . ."

Falafel was reprimanded for rooting too loudly for his three-hundred-dollar bet while his friend, the host, had five grand riding on the opposing team. This, Dink said, was one of the reasons he liked having me work for him. I didn't gamble on sports, so if Dink needed one team, he could rest assured that I didn't have a bet on the other side and was secretly rooting against him. That situation happened quite often with the guys in the office. It was one thing to like a certain team; it was another to root against your boss, who's paying your salary.

"WHY IS THERE A RECEIVER ALONE IN THE END ZONE?"

Eyeballs bulged and faces reddened. Palms smacked the top of the coffee table. Teeth bit deep into knuckles. Hair Plugs took a knee. I smelled the first wave of body odor.

Touchdown! Washington.

I was confused. Was that good for Dink?

Dink read my mind. "That's good for us," he whispered.

*   *   *

We returned to Dink Inc. to bet on the later games. Field goals, foul shots, flip shots, and snaps pushed the afternoon into night-time. Trying to remember who and what we needed on each event was exhausting. In the first half we rooted for a team to score a lot of points, and in the second half we rooted for them not to score. We rooted for a team to make a field goal and twenty minutes later we rooted for them to fumble. It was important for one team to win by 3 or 5, but definitely not 4.

"See these tickets," Dink said. There were enough of them now to fill a shoebox. "This is what I've been talking about. These bets could be sold for something. Hopefully the gambling gods will be on my side, but I can go to sleep tonight knowing I have the best of it."

My brain was mush. I didn't have the energy to even feign inter-est. Dink noticed the sullen look on my face and assumed my spir-its were low because I had yet to make a bet. To boost my morale, he allowed me the honor of making the day's last wager.

"Okay, here. You're gonna do this right now," he said. "Call Top of the World and ask for game two twenty-four, Minnesota money line for one dime."

"Come on, baby, you can do it," Robbie J said.

I lifted my cheek off the table and reached sluggishly for the phone.

"Sports."

"Hi, six four six Double D."

"Go 'head, Double D."

"Game two twenty-four, Milwaukee money line?"

"Game two twenty-four, I got Bucks minus the fifty-five, total at one twenty-one."

"Okay," I said. I slid a three-ply ticket from my own little pile. "I'll take the fifty-five . . ."

"No, no, no, not *take*," Dink said.

Oh, God. Enough already. My instinct was to hang up.

"Stay on the phone," Dink instructed, in a hushed tone. "Mil-waukee's favored. You don't take the favorite. You *lay* the favorite. You take the dog."

"You there, Double D?"

"Yeah, hi. Actually, can I *lay* the fifty-five to win a dime?"

On the Don Best screen in front of me, the basketball game changed from minus 155 to minus 159. I realized Dinky's opinion was so respected that when he or his crew bet money on a game, the office we bet with changed their odds. I thought that was cool as hell.

"You got it. Bucks money line risking fifteen-fifty to win a dime. Name and password for confirmation."

"Six four six Double D."

Robbie J blew me a kiss. My heart swelled with pride. In girly cursive, I wrote the bet neatly onto a ticket and tossed it to Dink. For the remainder of the evening, the three of us unwound. We pushed the boxes of leftover pizza to the side and stretched our legs over the banquet table. Otis slept at my feet, surrounded by empty two-liter bottles of Coca-Cola. It was like a Norman Rockwell portrait of a family, but instead of bowed heads and palms in prayer, we rooted for the Bucks to hit a three.

CHAPTER FOUR

Going, Going, *Gonif*

It wasn't that I had misrepresented myself to Dink on the afternoon of our interview. I *had* worked as a social worker. As the weeks passed, though, and Dink showed interest in the details of my past, I considered, for the first time in my adult life, whether it might be best just to tell someone the simple truth about what I had been up to for the past two years. Watching Dink try to make sense out of the disparate anecdotes I shared with him made me feel guilty. Whenever I met someone new, my tendency was to ask a lot of questions, many of them squeamishly personal. Dink was so candid. Whenever I asked him about the frustrations of gambling life or regrets he might have, or the particulars of his financial situation (How much were you making when you were my age? What was the most you ever lost in one year? One day?), he always answered with honesty and careful consideration. He was becoming a friend and deserved better.

I waited for an evening when we were alone in the office. Dink was seated at the head of the table, contemplating a racing form. Sitting in my chair, I tucked my legs under me and leaned my body over the table, toward him. I held myself up with my elbows.

"Yes, Ms. Raymer?" he said, eyes on page.

"Remember how I told you I was a social worker?" I started, trying to be nonchalant. But casualness was never my forte and over the next sixty seconds I hit every point on the emotional spectrum. Ambivalence to worry and back again. My face blushed, I laughed, went serious, broke a sweat, and then took a deep breath to regain my composure. I gauged Dink's reaction, though I hadn't told him a thing.

"I remember," Dink said.

"Well, remember how I got fired for letting the girls run away?"

He folded the form and put it aside. "I remember." His attention was now all mine.

Well, here's the thing. After I got fired from the residential home, I had to find another job. I was living in Tallahassee, and it was summertime. My rental had no air conditioner. It did have a large front porch that looked out onto a red dirt road, so that's where I spent the mornings of my work-life hiatus, dropping ice cubes into my coffee, listening to the cicadas hum their courtship songs, and browsing the *Democrat* classifieds. The ad that caught my attention was the size of a postage stamp. *Nude Dancers Desired, Real Money, Real Fast*. It was strange to read such an ad in the newspaper of a city that prohibited strip clubs. Nude or even seminude entertainment was definitely outlawed in Tallahassee, something my male friends often griped about. I adorned the ad with a doodle.

The coffee kicked in and I couldn't resist checking myself out in the bathroom's full-length mirror and assessing my chances as a dancer. I had no idea what the sex part of the job would entail, but the promise of "real money" made my blood sing. I had the feeling I'd be free. Nude dancing brought to mind a glorious universe free of time sheets, dress codes, schedules, or rules. I'd be in charge of me. I took a pair of heels from my roommate's closet and situated myself into positions that accentuated my curves.

Nightmoves was listed in the phone book under Live Entertainment and the six (seven, counting me) girls who worked there went by the title "in-home stripper." For $150 an hour, we performed at a client's home, office, or occasional parked car. Our services included a striptease, a body rub, and what would soon become my personal favorite, adult conversation—a phrase characterized less by the sharing of hushed dirty desires and more by intimate stories of erectile dysfunction, the humility that accompanies balding, and general discussions on how to protect finances during a divorce. At twenty-two, I found these topics incredibly "adult."

The Nightmoves girls, including Madam S., were all under twenty-five years old. Madam S. started the business when she was sixteen, after both of her parents went to jail for embezzlement. To support herself, she quit school and began walking around her neighborhood with a boom box, asking men if they'd like to see her dance. Tiny jean shorts and a gingham bikini top exposed her long, lean legs and perky breasts. Men ogled her body and asked her age. Madam S. twisted the small silver hoop in her nose and talked price. Seven years later she was piercing different body parts, getting into fistfights, and dating temperamental drug dealers. But she was also a very ambitious businesswoman with an expertise in networking and as a result her black book of clients was as thick as the GED workbook that lay beside it.

At the interview, Madam S. had been happy to see someone with a "sweet smile" and for that reason she gave me the job and the stage name Angel. "Nobody understands Nightmoves until they *do* Nightmoves," said Madam S. on the afternoon of my first shift. Her boyfriend sat on the floor, between her legs, rolling a blunt. She chain-smoked and braided his hair. I lay across from them on the living room couch. My nerves jumped with the beat of a Public Enemy song pulsing from the stereo.

In the sparsely furnished duplex that doubled as Nightmoves' headquarters, my new co-workers watched *Days of Our Lives* while waiting for calls. They passed joints and celebrity magazines, their covers limned with coke. They spoke of the best dealers in the area and the most affordable day care and answered the ever-ringing telephone with a sweet, breathy "Nightmoves Entertainment, where the night never ends."

"Can we go over the negotiation process again?" I said.

"Charge the customer for *eve-ry-thing*. Even hugs." Madam S. yanked her boyfriend's head back for a better angle.

"How much for hugs?"

She shrugged. "Twenty-five?"

"But, do I say, right then, 'That'll be twenty-five dollars'?"

"Fuck, yeah. Get the money upfront, always."

The customers, she said, would be just as nervous as me. They didn't know who the hell the strange woman was stepping inside their home. How did they know that I wouldn't hold them at gunpoint and steal all their shit? We, the women of Nightmoves, knew more about the customers than they would ever know about us. We knew their names and addresses, we saw pictures of their wives and kids, we knew the layout of their homes. We could blackmail them if we wanted to. Some girls had.

Madam S. blew her bangs from out of her eyes and shared her last piece of advice. "In the middle of a call, if the customer needs to order a pizza, he's an undercover cop. They all use the same excuse to update their buddies in the motel room next door."

The telephone rang. She jotted the customer's address onto an index card and handed it to me. "Go get 'em, Angel."

In time, I understood that this was a line of business based solely on trust. There was no playbook or legal system to fall back on. Instincts had to be listened to and trusted. Without them, we, *the women of Nightmoves,* were nothing but birds with clipped wings, stranded on a lofty perch. The job required me to be confident, direct, cunning, and comfortable with uncertainty. I can't imagine any better preparation for a career in gambling.

Once I gained the skill most crucial to my new line of work— assertiveness—I enjoyed the job tremendously. I too developed a sultry phone voice and hung on every possible plot point on *Days.* I had business cards printed, the pink intense, the lettering engraved, and handed them out to ex-professors, bartenders, and lawyers and lobbyists I had worked with during my internship at the Department of Children and Families. In miniskirt and crocheted halter top, I put plenty of miles on my Ford F150, driving to customers' homes in the suburbs, cities, and farming towns along the Florida Panhandle. Having already forgotten the financial constraints that bogged me down just weeks before, I'd toss off my flip-flops, slip on my stilettos, and give Otis, my bodyguard puppy in the passenger seat, a kiss on the snout. Strutting up the driveway to my client's door, I'd double-check the contents of my tote bag: R&B CDs, fishnets, leopard-print bikini, baby wipes, Mace, portable credit-card swiper. Check. One-fifty an hour began the moment my finger felt the heat from the doorbell.

And this was the best part: waiting for the door to open. It's where the adrenaline kicked in. It mattered little whether it was an attractive pilot with a cool, confident swagger or a greasy-haired security guard with dirty fingernails. What I loved was being in strangers' homes and listening to their secrets. Inside the maze of suburban split-levels, hunting cabins, summer homes, and double-wides, intricate, vulnerable human urges were revealed. There was no ordinary structure. Every encounter was unique. Life was in the here and now and I loved the feeling of being wildly alive to it all. Never turning down a call, I took every opportunity to dress up and playact. Some customers took me to shoot pool, some asked me to watch them masturbate. Many asked me to remove my shoes so I wouldn't wake the kids.

There was only one customer with whom I felt uncomfortable. He was an English professor who preferred the lights on low as he instructed me to get naked but for my heels, straddle a bar stool, and read to him from *In Cold Blood*. Out of all the fantasies I was asked to fulfill, this one made me feel the most exposed. That it was a murder story never even crossed my mind. I just didn't have the confidence to read aloud. I was so afraid I would mispronounce a word that I barely managed to enunciate anything. My posture caved. Red blotches the shape of crescent moons appeared on my neck and chest. Sweat trickled from the backs of my knees into the heels of my stilettos, making their plastic arches even more slippery. I scanned each page for words that might trip me up. The first one appeared on page ten: *abstemious*. There was a long pause as I searched for an excuse as to why I couldn't say the word. My damp palms turned the page's edge transparent.

"I don't like this word," I said. "It makes me think of bad things."

The professor seemed genuinely interested. "Bad things? Like what?"

Like it made me feel stupid, for one.

"Can't we do something else?" I said. "Can't I just dance for you?"

Ten months passed. Each afternoon, when I awoke, it became my habit to arrange my savings into piles of one thousand dollars and place them atop my bedspread, side by side. The rows of green stretched before me like a lifetime of summers, each one more promising than the last. There was nowhere I had to be, no outstanding bill I had to pay. I unplugged my alarm clock and forgot about it for a year. The moldy, metallic smell of money lingered in my sheets and before bed I'd pull the covers close to my nose and inhale, deeply, until I fell asleep.

My feelings about the job changed after an evening with Charlie. A friendly fifty-year-old southerner and Nightmoves regular, Charlie told animated stories about his two tours in Vietnam and his life after the war when he began working for the CIA, or so he claimed. It never mattered to me whether or not Charlie's CIA stories were true. The only thing that bothered me about him was that he seemed to have something wrong with his memory. Sometimes I would spend two hours with him in the afternoon, go home, and later in the night he'd call again, forgetting that I had been to his house that very day. Still, I thought his stories were interesting, and I much preferred listening to him than to the downhearted, heavy-drinking cops and accountants I visited.

One evening, I sat on his couch and looked through his photo albums. I saw Charlie as a teenager, his long hair pulled into a ponytail, and Charlie with a buzz cut, grinning in front of a chopper. In one picture, a smiling Vietnamese boy handed Charlie a sharp animal tooth, which Charlie still wore around his neck, attached by a hemp necklace. The albums' last pages displayed more recent photographs: Charlie at fifty, in different exotic locales, his arm draped around girls in their twenties. Assuming the girls worked for places similar to Nightmoves, I asked Charlie why he never invited me to Cambodia or Panama. "Too dangerous," he said. In the photos, the girls were wrapped in Budweiser beach towels and Charlie was sunburned and smoking a cigar. It didn't look so dangerous. I looked up from the album. "Charlie," I said. "Are you *really* in the CIA?"

"Lemme show you something, Angel," he said, in a sarcastic tone I'd never before heard him use. He walked away from me. A closet door slammed, and Charlie returned, carrying a long black semiautomatic shotgun with two barrels. Peering through the scope, he pointed the sight at the bronze bald eagle, wings outstretched, on top of his television set.

From there, Charlie moved the gun swiftly through the air, as though the eagle had taken flight. He followed the bird as it flew from the La-Z-Boy to the ceiling fan to the pile of *TV Guides*, until it landed on the top of my head. Charlie squinted to narrow his aim and his eyeballs shook the way they always did when he had substituted speed for sleep for days on end.

The blood rushed from my limbs. I blinked and saw black. He was going to shoot me or torture me to prove he was no liar, to show this stupid little whore that he *was* in the CIA. I crossed the backs of my hands over my face and turned away from the gun. I found the courage to ask him to put the thing away.

"Miscreant shitheads out to fuck with me," Charlie said in his boisterous Southern drawl. His blinking was outrageous.

I scooted forward to the edge of the couch. The front door was steps away and my bag, with my car keys in it, lay at my feet. Outside, there were neighbors, air, and sky. Otis would be waiting in the passenger seat. My truck was backed into the driveway, the only precaution I took in case I needed to leave quickly. Black dots danced like mosquitoes in front of my eyes. My instincts screamed,

Go. Now. Before you faint. I managed to push myself up from the couch and grab my bag.

It wasn't until I stood that I realized how light-headed I was. Charlie kept his gun focused on the couch as though I were still sitting there. Thinking that maybe I was overreacting, I second-guessed myself and lost momentum. I considered asking him, again, to put the gun away. Then I imagined the barrel of the gun twisting into my temple and I headed for the door. If he raped me, I'd never tell anyone. It was my fault for being there. The front door wasn't as close as I thought. If he was going to shoot me, it was going to be now. Now. I told myself to scream. *Do it. Do it.* I couldn't. I panicked, made a sharp left, ran into the bathroom, and locked myself inside.

"You're scaring me!" I shouted. I felt frantically for the light switch.

"The CIA gives a shit," Charlie shouted back. "The CIA *cares* about insane delusionoids."

Shuffling through my bag, looking for anything that might help me, I imagined my parents at the morgue, collecting my belongings. My sister's drug addiction had caused them years of worry and heartache. I was considered the good kid. Friends, boyfriends, lovers, and family were all under the impression that I worked for a pet-sitting service. One look through my bag—the pager, the panties, the credit-card swiper—and everyone close to me would feel as though they never even knew me. I stashed my business cards inside the fishing magazines stacked beside the toilet.

I heard him walk away from the door. A closet opened, closed. The refrigerator opened, closed. The couch squeaked and Dan Rather's voice filled the room. I heard the sound of Charlie's feet on the carpet, then on the kitchen linoleum. He returned to the door of the bathroom where, on the other side, I waited, back flat against the adjacent wall in case any bullets shot through.

"Listen," he said. He popped open a can of beer loud enough for me to hear. "See? No more guns. Just me and my beer. You can come out whenever you're ready. I'm gonna be here drinkin' a beer."

Certain that if I opened the door he'd point the gun at my head, mock me for being gullible, and steer me wherever he saw fit, I timidly asked if maybe he could call the cops.

"Angel, I'm not gonna bring the cops into this. If I wanted to get you, I would've gotten you already. I know how to pick a lock, for Christ's sake. I *am* in the CIA."

For the next ten minutes, Charlie talked me out of the bathroom the way someone talks a buddy off a ledge.

"Everything's gonna be okay, Angel. I know what it's like to be scared. Hell, I've spent most of my life bein' scared. *Of ghosts!* If you can believe that."

I splashed cold water onto my face and drank from the faucet.

"I'm gonna pay you for your time here. Throw in a lil' extra for freakin' ya out."

From the crack beneath the door, two one-hundred-dollar bills inched their way toward my stilettos.

"I enjoy your company. You're cheerful, I like that. I hope you'll come back. I'm gonna watch TV. Maybe do some Tai Chi."

If he was having an episode, it seemed to be over. Charlie didn't seem like a rapist killer. He was a fan of Oprah and liked nothing more than a playful push-up contest. The imagined horrors left my head and my mind quieted. I cracked the door open to find Charlie just where he said he would be. On the couch, drinking a Coors, watching the news.

The next day was my twenty-third birthday. The weather outside was sunny and bright and I spent the day under a blanket watching a *Godfather* marathon on cable. My bones hurt. Every few hours I'd let out a deep sigh, pull the blanket to my nose, and weep. A young, suspendered Al Pacino offered only lukewarm comfort.

My roommate came home from her job at the health-food store. She opened the front door and the yellow afternoon shot through the dark living room, exposing the dust on the coffee table and the dark circles under my eyes. She eased over to me, bringing with her the stink of a vitamin aisle and a birthday cake. She knew that I was working at Nightmoves and she often worried about my safety. I told her stories about my job, but only the funny ones. I certainly wasn't going to tell her about Charlie.

"This is how you're spending your birthday?" she said. Her latest vinegar cleanse was really working. Her skin was radiant. Peering up at her from beneath the blanket, I felt like a mole.

"Is something wrong?" She looked scared.

"No, no," I said, laughing it off. "It's just sad, you know. All the promises Michael Corleone made Kay."

She prepared my cake and sang me "Happy Birthday."

I continued to arrive at strangers' doors with my belongings—the ones I was so embarrassed about my parents discovering at the morgue—tossed over my shoulder. The only change was my now-elevated sense of fear. Standing inside a customer's home, surrounded by deep woods, I'd psych myself into thinking that there was another person in the house, waiting in the hall closet or behind the shower curtain. Every customer began to resemble Ted Bundy, the serial killer who had bludgeoned Florida State sorority girls to death. Dancing amid the dark walls and the family portraits inside master bedrooms, I couldn't keep my thoughts from turning to the macabre. The wife in the photo wasn't away on business. She was beneath the floorboards. I smiled and made small talk, vacillating as to whether or not I should make up an excuse and leave. A drink was offered and I accepted. Before I took a sip, I switched my glass with the customer's just in case he had laced mine. The air smelled of moist soil as I walked back to my truck. The night mist cooled my face. And though my body shivered with fear, I felt the distinctive, enjoyable rush of having gotten away with something. Life, I guess.

My blossoming death drive came to a halt after I met a customer who worked as a Webmaster. He assumed I was a high school dropout and I never told him any different. From the frame of his front door, he smoked and lectured me on the poor choices I was making in my life. By this time, I had been working at Nightmoves for over a year and all the glamour and thrills that had accompanied the first months had faded. My fear had gradually dissipated and all that was left was genuine boredom. Outcall dancing had become just another job. I no longer wore matching bra and panty sets, nor did I shave my legs or dab my neck with perfume. My dance style grew less seductive and more athletic. A two-minute headstand became the centerpiece of my routine.

"Girl-on-girl Web sites," Webmaster said on the exhale. "That's where the real money is."

I let my legs come down to the floor.

"If you ever want to cash in, just get a friend and bring her on over."

I was open to a new line of work, but I was hoping to go into something that would allow me to travel. I often fantasized about working on a cruise ship or as an international stewardess. I wanted to have a lounge act. I wanted to bake cookies for passengers flying from Miami to Hong Kong. Of course, having a puppy at home made traveling too difficult. A girl-on-girl Web site seemed interesting, but if I was going to go out on a limb and pose naked on the World Wide Web, I certainly didn't want to share the profits with anyone.

Unless . . .

The photo shoot took place on location in the barbeque area of Webmaster's condo development. After spending several hours on the computer, erasing blemishes and the telephone lines in the background, we clipped and snipped pictures of myself until I fit snugly, and convincingly, beside pictures of myself, and *Voilà*! My vision was realized: a pair of twenty-three-year-old incestuous twin sisters. Graduates of Georgetown, I explained in their bio, daughters of a U.S. Supreme Court judge.

I enjoyed doing something artistic, and spent a lot of time developing the twins' characters by writing little vignettes so the subscribers could learn about their individual personalities. The Web site was easy to market, profitable, and I didn't have to share my earnings with anyone but Webmaster, who received 15 percent for his services. I quit my job and introduced the Nightmoves girls to Webmaster and they too launched Web sites. In return, I received a finder's fee and twenty percent of their monthly take. The local library offered a seminar on operating online businesses and, after completing the course, I applied for a business license. On June 30, 1999, Repenterprise Enterprises was born. As president, I promoted all of our Web sites, came up with ideas for future shoots, bought the props and outfits, responded to fan e-mail, kept track of tax-deductible items, and handled the online banking. I recruited more girls and bumped up my cut. Each morning, before my first cup of coffee, I scuttled to my computer to see how many people subscribed overnight. I discovered that there is no bigger thrill than making money while you sleep.

This joint venture with Webmaster lasted seven months and the ending was not amicable. Webmaster's motivation wasn't just to photograph young naked bodies and improve his Webmaster skills. He wanted a girlfriend, and any of us would do. We all started receiving gifts, though he acted as though his affections were exclusive. Pink roses appeared on my doorstep. Dallas received white ones. Jasmine, red. On the afternoon of our photo shoots, black velvet boxes awaited us on the bathroom counter where we did our makeup. Not intending to become Webmaster's girlfriend—ever— we accepted the necklaces and earrings and promised to meet for dates that we canceled the morning of. It seemed easier than to say no and risk hurting his feelings or making him mad, especially since thousands of naked pictures of us, many unflattering, were saved on his hard drive. To make matters worse, nearly every single girl who worked for me had insurmountable problems stemming from drug addiction and poor taste in men. Often I was confronted by their unemployed boyfriends, husbands—fathers, even—who felt that I was taking too much of a cut. The men radiated aggression and most days I felt more like the headmistress of a woman's shelter than the president of a successful business.

Tension peaked just after Webmaster's fortieth birthday, when he purchased a yellow Mercedes Kompressor convertible. Webmaster preferred driving it sans shirt, as if to match his topless ride. The thick, black hair covering his shoulders, chest, and belly rolls gleamed in the sunlight. At red lights, he spritzed himself with ice water and suggested to whoever was in the passenger seat that she too take her shirt off. In no time at all, we ran out of excuses as to why we couldn't accompany him on his afternoon rides. Straws were drawn to decide who would steal his hard drive. We told him one last lie, got what we wanted, and faded from his life.

I was never able to find another Webmaster. Enthusiasm waned. One girl died of a drug overdose. I met a cute film student and over dinner one night he asked me to move out west with him. He was one of the few people to whom I showed my Web site, and he praised me. Not for how good my twin and I looked in sexy French maid outfits, but for the short stories I posted each week about what the girls were up to in their personal lives. He suggested we work at his parents' Thai restaurant for a few months, save some money, and then move to L.A. We would write scripts together, he said, and turn them into movies. We arrived in Vegas, broke up, and when I needed the money, I took the solitaire diamond necklace that had been a present from Webmaster and, severing my last tie to that world, pawned it for ninety-five dollars.

There were two people in my life who knew that about me.

Now three.

I relaxed my shoulders and waited for Dink's reaction.

"You're a *gonif!*" Dink said. His voice boomed like a tribal chieftain announcing the name he had created specifically for its bearer. "You're gonna do great in this business!"

Gonif is Yiddish for a small-time, lovable thief, though at the time I didn't know what it meant. Still, I sensed its complimentary connotation.

His response energized the room. Feeling relieved, I flipped on the lights and grabbed two Cokes from the fridge.

"But you don't think it's something I should be ashamed of?" I asked.

"No. You're a kid. You're gonna do kid things. It was dangerous, I don't particularly like that . . ."

"If my parents ever found out, they would feel like they have no idea who I really am."

"I freebased a few times," Dink said. "I didn't tell my mom."

"If we went to confession, we would be forgiven."

"You were making money without hurting anybody," Dink consoled. "By doing the opposite of hurting anybody! It's not like you were dealing drugs."

"Is that worse?"

"What you did was legal. It's important not to go to jail. Always remember that."

I asked Dink to make me a promise: if, for some reason, the guys in the office came across pictures of me and my twin, he would tell them that I was once a triplet but that my sisters—the incestuous ones in the photo—died. In a car crash.

"Odds are you'll be fine," he said.

"Stranger things have happened."

We sat there, smiling, over Cokes and *Daily Racing Forms*.

"You know what Amy said when she told me about you? She said, 'Hire her, she's one of us.' "

CHAPTER FIVE

The Winner's Circle

I was alone in the office, researching wind direction and humidity levels, when she walked through the door. "You're here early," she said, fiddling through her Neiman Marcus shopping bag. Her black Lycra exercise outfit accentuated her petite, toned physique. The enormous diamond on her ring finger was sunglow yellow and shaped like a cushion. Tulip Heimowitz had returned from yachting on the Rhine.

I set down my can of Coke, stood, and introduced myself. The jeans skirt I'd been wearing to work nearly every day for the last month now seemed excessively short. I tugged at its bottom.

Tulip gave the office the once-over. While she was gone, Dink had given me a four-hundred-dollar redecorating budget. The framed pictures of him posing beside racehorses in the winner's circle were off the floor and hanging on the walls. A little wooden bookshelf held his sports schedules and handicapping books. A potted plant adorned the mini-refrigerator. Tulip's glass-green eyes lingered on a doodle I had drawn and taped to the wall. It featured the little family that had sprouted while she was away: Dink sat at the head of the table eating a bagel and Robbie J, Otis, and I sat around the table, making bets on telephones and watching games on heart-shaped televisions.

Tulip dropped her shopping bag on the floor and plunked her calfskin "hobo" handbag on top of the table. It smelled so strongly of leather it made me nauseous.

"Did you have a nice time?" I asked.

"Mmm hmm. Beautiful. Who have you called so far for rundowns?"

I glanced at the clock on the bottom of the computer screen: 7:55 a.m. Most of the bookmakers we bet with didn't open until a quarter after.

"It's the first thing you do when you get to the office," she said, and turned away.

I gave my skirt one last tug, sat up straight, and picked up the phone.

Upon Tulip's arrival I learned quickly that the best thing to do with my enthusiasm was suppress it. Like a too-cool teenager, Tulip had no patience for the overeager teacher's pet in the front row. When I laughed at Dink's jokes, she cringed. If I volunteered to do something for Dink, she rolled her eyes. Looking at the computer screen one afternoon, I announced, correctly, that the Virginia total was moving and we were on the wrong side. I was finally catching on, and Dink and Robbie J complimented me. If Tulip hadn't been in the room, I would've screamed in excitement, demanding that pizza be ordered in my honor. But with Tulip sitting across from me, and her penchant for mimicking my high-pitched voice, I turned my attention back to the screen and bit the inside of my cheeks to keep myself from smiling.

With the good times seemingly over, I sat, dispirited, in my corner of the table, watching the numbers on the gambling software flash from white to black. Helping Dink update his hockey notebook, I'd divert my eyes from his terrible handwriting and see Tulip filing her glossy nails, the nail dust flying over the cover of her Isabel Allende novel. Sometimes I'd catch her in such a deep daydreaming state I wouldn't bother to look away. Her tanned, narrow shoulders relaxed; her thin lips parted. Her eyes fixated so intently on the item in front of her, a calculator, a pencil, it was as though she were practicing psychokinesis. The full-carat diamonds dropping like tears from her earlobes would send me into my own daydream. Shine, sparkle, haze, until, finally, the cute Cuban clerk from my neighborhood 7-Eleven appeared. In the stockroom, he pushed his body into mine. He kissed me, talked dirty, went up my shirt. A blink, and there I'd be, staring at Tulip, who was now staring at me. Between us, a balled-up piece of paper that Dink had thrown to get our attention. She bugged me, sure, but I couldn't deny she possessed a certain mystique.

There was a time when Tulip found Dink's gambling life exciting. The word she used was "edgy." It was an edgy lifestyle, risky and unpredictable, and Tulip was always attracted to the edge. Growing up in San Diego, she was sent to juvie at the age of twelve for running away to Texas to see the Beatles. During the Summer of Love, Tulip moved to Northern California where she drank too much white wine, dropped too much acid, and forgot to go to college. Despite her morning hangovers, she managed to braid her long blond hair, zip the back of her nurse's outfit, and hitchhike to her job at the convalescent home.

Around this time she met David, a handsome, successful jockey. When David made good on his promise to leave his wife to marry her, twenty-four-year-old Tulip found herself smiling beside her husband in the winner's circle.

Pot brownies, embroidered miniskirts, and cross-country hitchhiking quickly gave way to Stoli martinis, St. John suits, and European holidays. The fourteen-year age gap was of little consequence to Tulip. She reveled in David's adoration; being the wife of a jockey offered her the thrill she craved and the high-society lifestyle, which she took to like mint syrup to bourbon. David's strict regimen impressed her as a sign of self-mastery and maturity. Every morning David trained, and then dehydrated in the sauna. He allowed himself only one meal a day: a T-bone steak, medium rare, no sauce, no sides. The disciplined lifestyle of her older husband left Tulip with all the material comforts of success. The only problem was that there was no one to enjoy them with, no one to help her celebrate her newfound wealth. Not one to gain—or want—acceptance from the other jockeys' wives, whose loyalty remained with David's first wife, Tulip spent more and more time alone.

Loneliness bred boredom and Tulip resumed her partying ways. While David trained and dehydrated, Tulip snorted coke and downed martinis. When David traveled, she invited her brother and sister to come over and the three siblings did drugs and played board games. Though years later she would deny it, I could've sworn I heard her tell a story of one particular evening, when David was away and the three siblings were in need of a fourth person to play Pictionary. After an hour of snorting lines the length of curling irons and thinking of people to call, they decided there wasn't anyone else's company they really desired. Except Chancy. And with that they went into the backyard and retrieved from his stable Chancy, their favorite thoroughbred. For the next few hours the horse stood in the living room and acted as Tulip's Pictionary teammate, chosen to do the guessing, not the drawing. David came home the next morning to find Chancy standing in the living room, dozing, and everyone else passed out on the floor.

But when the siblings weren't around, and Chancy was back in his stable, Tulip was alone, waiting for the cocktail hour that never seemed to come early enough. Drinks at dinnertime seemed arbitrary. And unfair. What about lunch? What about breakfast? Wobbling slightly in her white Chanel pumps, Tulip stood over the kitchen sink piercing the pimiento heart of what must've been her millionth olive with a tiny plastic sword.

Enter Chipper, golf instructor to the lonely housewives of greater San Diego.

Tulip was never in love with Chipper but she did love his game. The way he kept his swing plane lateral, never sliding his hips on the takeaway, but storing up the energy in a tight coil for that moment when his club reached its peak and his hips triggered a perfectly synchronized downturn—hips, shoulders, hands—generating a staggering amount of club head speed. God, he added excitement to her life. Perhaps too much. One day she came home and found Chipper sitting next to David on the living room couch. He had told David of their affair and Tulip was forced to choose between the two.

She chose neither and filed for divorce.

At a friend's house, Tulip stared at the Alcoholics Anonymous workbook splayed across her lap. She was taking inventory of all the people she had harmed through the years, recalling the sadness her addiction had caused to herself and others. One memory came immediately to mind, the one that had weighed on her all these years and sickened her more than all the rest. If she wanted to recover fully, she had to confront it. Her sponsor had warned her that step five was the most difficult. What Tulip would've given for one, just one, super Vicodin. She dragged the phone over to the bed and called her dad.

Between fits and sobs, tears running down her hot cheeks, she apologized. For the time when she was fifteen and she stole all of his quarters. Five hundred dollars' worth. She and a friend. They made it look like a robbery. They did it to get speed and then they shot up.

"Dad," Tulip cried. "I'm so sorry, I need you to forgive me. Please forgive me."

"*Quarters,* sweetie?" He didn't remember any stolen quarters. But of course, of course he forgave her.

Step five. Check.

Tulip graduated from AA and went to work as a clerk, taking bets at Del Mar Racetrack in San Diego. For the first time in twenty-five years she listened to her beloved Beatles albums, sober.

In the grandstands, beneath the tote board, Tulip, with her golden complexion and blond chin-length bob, registered the horseplayers' bets. "The two to win for three dollars, here you go," and she slid the bettor his ticket. She looked forward to a round of golf after her shift. No longer in need of an instructor, she'd play as a single.

The same year that Tulip got sober, Dink, dressed in suit and tie, sat beside his attorney, Burdick—a friend from Dink's fantasy baseball league. The person whom the FBI believed Dink worked for—a Detroit bookmaker named Henry Hilf—was actually just one of Dink's customers. Through his mob ties, however, Hilf had established a nationwide multimillion-dollar bookmaking syndicate that operated in Detroit, Miami, Pittsburgh, Las Vegas, the Ohio Valley, and New York City. The FBI was confident Dink was in the Mafia.

"I booked seventeen policemen who I played softball with. That didn't make me a cop," Dink said to Burdick. "They can't say that because I booked a guy in the mob I'm a mobster!"

This was something that most people, law enforcement included, either had a hard time understanding, or didn't want to understand. Most bookmakers did not know their customers personally. They were, in most cases, just voices over a telephone that placed bets using code names. If an agent or a friend put someone into Dink's office, Dink had no way of knowing if the new customer was a butcher, baker, mayor, or mobster.

"I never met that guy," Dink continued. "I just booked him. I'm in the market where you get a five-hundred-dollar fine and a night in jail. Keep me in that market."

Burdick told him he wouldn't go to jail. He would never be able to make book again without risking prison time, but he would not go to jail.

The Honorable George E. Woods entered the courtroom.

"All rise."

The United States of America versus Douglas Heimowitz. A.k.a. Dinky.

"You may be seated."

"Mr. Burdick. Did your client take bets from Mr. Henry Hilf?" the judge asked.

"Yes, your honor," Burdick replied. "He's a New York City book-maker, that's his job. Nothing more than that."

"Mr. Heimowitz, you're getting a ten-thousand-dollar fine and one year at a corrections center," the judge said. "I don't have any facility. You and your attorney figure that out."

As quick as a coin flip, court was adjourned.

Burdick explained to Dink his two choices: Club Fed or a halfway house. Mortified, Dink ran to a pay phone and called his friend Cathy, at her jewelry store in Chinatown. Most of her family had been in the mob; some were serving time. She was an old hand when it came to listening to people spew their sentencing anxieties.

"Oh, Dinky," she said, calmly. "It's gonna be okay. Pick a halfway house, they're easy. They're like a joke. You go out every day. Everybody's low-level criminals."

"I won't be able to sleep!" Dink said, panic-stricken. "I'm not gonna be able to sleep one night there. What am I gonna tell my mother? Oh, God, the food! I'm gonna get sick."

"You'll learn to sleep," Cathy said. "You'll adjust."

Dink researched his options. One place caught his attention: the Pacific Furlough correctional facility in San Diego. The weather would be nice. Ira, his closest friend from childhood, lived there. Dave the Rave had a condo right on the beach. Roscoe, a longtime acquaintance, owned a deli nearby and if Dink worked there he could fulfill the sentencing requirement that he have a job. The Furlough was only fifteen miles from Tijuana. He could explore the Mexican sports-betting market. And, most important, he'd be close to Del Mar racetrack.

"Nonsense!" Freda said. "How can they do this to you?"

"I'm a bookmaker."

"Do they know you graduated from Stuyvesant?"

Behind them, on the living room wall, hung a four-foot-tall acrylic painting of Dink reading from the Torah on the day of his Bar Mitzvah. A royal blue yarmulke covered his curls.

"Ma, I'm gonna be out every day. I'm gonna work at my friend's deli."

"You're a bookmaker?"

"It's not real jail. It's night jail. I'll be out ten hours a day. I'll watch *Tom and Jerry* every day. You're allowed to bring your own TV."

"Tell me the prosecutor's name. I'll call our state congressman and have him send the judge a letter."

"Not gonna happen. One year in night jail, Ma. That's all."

Before his sentence began, Dink flew to San Diego and rented a room in his friend's condo. On his first visit to the track, he went to the grandstands. Beneath the tote board, taking bets, was a young lady with large breasts. Her name was Diane and she and Dink began dating. When the line at Diane's window was too long, Dink went to the clerk stationed to the right of Diane. The petite blonde, Diane told him, was once married to a jockey. Dink cashed in his winning tickets and tipped Tulip twenty bucks. He was generous like that. And anyway, she was cute.

During the visits Dink made to Tulip's window, the two became friendly enough that they shared their stories. He was about to serve a year at the Furlough. She was in the middle of a divorce, staying with friends.

"You're welcome to stay at my place, 'cause I'm gonna be in night jail," he told her.

She took him up on the offer.

Dink stood on a patch of burnt grass holding his Knicks duffel bag and an eighteen-inch color TV. The Pacific Furlough correctional facility was an old Army barracks painted institutional green and surrounded by a chain-link fence. The guard beside the gate pressed his finger to his nostril and blew. Snot smacked against the cracked sidewalk.

Inside, when Dink's eyes adjusted to the dark, he saw rows of pillowless bunk beds pushed close together. A breeze from the Pacific squeezed its way through the Furlough's barred windows and wisped across the black and brown faces of the men in the TV room as they watched *Under Siege* for the third time that day. The draft blew through the bathroom, which had no doors on the stalls, no lids on the toilets, and into the cafeteria, carrying with it a stench that made a plateful of corned beef hash taste as bad as it looked. Dink held his breath as he unpacked his bag. He would try anything in the square world to get away from this smelly, snorey, shitty place.

Refuge was found at Roscoe's deli. A small-time gambler and petty thief, Roscoe, it was rumored, was in the Witness Protection Program. Paranoid that everyone was stealing from him, Roscoe emptied the till a dozen times a day. He got over on every possible angle, underreporting his earnings, and saving pennies by buying non-brand-name mayo and muffins where he could swing deals. But he let Dink work the cash register six hours, five days a week, and for that Dink was grateful.

To kill an extra hour before returning to the halfway house, Dink attended Gamblers Anonymous meetings. With no intention of quitting gambling—*ever*—Dink relaxed and listened to stories from men and women who didn't lose much, just all they had. The head of the chapter was a teller at Del Mar who stole money from the racetrack, bet it into the machine, lost, and had to reimburse the track. One man claimed that he lost all of his money by betting his savings on a fixed race. The horse that was supposed to win was ahead by ten lengths when, three steps from the wire, he broke his leg. He swore he would never go to the track again (Dink later saw him at the track). Another man produced sports for television. He borrowed money and stole money, bet millions on football and baseball games, and finally lost his job. "I produce sports!" he said during one meeting. "If I can't win, how can anybody else win?"

All these people thought that they were smart. Then they lost all of their money, and decided they were sick. Dink wondered why they didn't decide that they were just stupid.

After GA, Dink would stop by the condo to shower. He enjoyed seeing Tulip. They talked about the track, her AA meetings, movies she had seen. Tulip looked forward to Dink's shower visits. He always made her laugh. It didn't surprise her one bit, the evening she found herself on her tiptoes, giving Dink a kiss.

First Diane, now Tulip. Dink had more women while he was in the halfway house than ever before. What was it about night jail that women found so sexy? The answer was easy: the eight o'clock curfew. Put a time limit on anything and life gets exciting. At a small table in the back of Yogi's Sports Bar, the new couple ate dinner together nearly every night. Once the dishes were cleared, Tulip sat on Dink's lap and rooted for the teams he needed to win.

It was at the Furlough, belly down on his top bunk, transistor radio against his shoulder, that Dink honed his gambling skills. With such an early curfew there was little else to do but listen to games and study sports. His bookmaker lifestyle may have seemed very far away, but Tijuana wasn't. And the sports books there took bets ten minutes after kickoff as long as no one had scored. A team could have the ball on the 10-yard line and you could bet on that team, or the total. It was sports betting's best-kept secret. Dink employed Ira, his oldest, most trustworthy friend, as his runner.

"Avoid customs. Park the car and walk over," Dink instructed, handing Ira twenty grand.

His blue jeans stuffed with cash, Ira walked across the San Ysidro border. Immediately, he was besieged by contagious-looking three-year-olds begging for money. Past the kids and the cabstands and the Chavez fight posters tacked to plywood shacks, the Caliente hotel and casino rose in the distance.

Back at Roscoe's deli, Dink was busy making the square world suit his needs. Directly across from the cash register, the newly installed sports ticker was just as glorious as Dink had imagined. The teenage employees Dink worked with every day stood by and watched as he stared up, slack-jawed, beholding the in-game updates that flashed in red, green, and gold, like sun-dappled stained glass.

"Why do you work here?" one of them asked.

"I'm interested in opening my own deli, one day," Dink said.

He turned his attention back to the ticker: *Welcome to Sub-Marina! Mets 3 Cubs 2, bottom of the eighth.*

During his year of rehabilitation, Dink gambled—and won—more than he had ever won bookmaking in Queens. He beat the Tijuana sports books and because he was in good standing with the bookmakers back east, they gave him high limits and took his bets. It was all on the books and when his sentence was over he collected his winnings. *Arty owes me $80,000, I owe you $60,000. Can you pick it up? You'll owe me $20,000. Louie owes me $90,000, I owe you $100,000, pick it up and I'll give you the other $10,000 next week. You know how it is.*

With his debt to society paid in full, and a four-hundred-thousand-dollar bankroll, Dink and Tulip headed to Vegas and launched Dink Inc. Tulip, enticed by something new and exciting, became Dink's first casino runner, stationed at Caesars Palace. Seven years had passed since their first date when Tulip finally asked, "Honey, are we *ever* gonna get married?"

"You have an open invitation," Dink said.

They flew to New York and bought an engagement ring from Dink's friend Cathy at her jewelry store in Chinatown.

It was during their first year of marriage, while the newlyweds were still negotiating their roles and discovering ways to work together, that I began working at Dink Inc. Tulip had recently cut back her hours, which was a source of tension between them. Dink had been a boss since he was twenty-two years old. Transactions were involved in every single relationship he had in his life and he had a difficult time understanding that Tulip was his wife and that she was not on the payroll. Tulip's lifestyle—the clothes, the jewelry, the cars—made her an expensive proposition. He didn't mind paying for her Pilates and daily rounds of golf, but it angered him when she spent money out of boredom. A job kept her out of the malls and also "helped with her mental sharpness." Dink didn't think she did enough thinking in her life; she didn't challenge herself. Right, Tulip thought. As if having a husband who gambled for a living wasn't challenging enough.

One afternoon Tulip came into the office, just wanting to say hi. Playing on the four televisions were two hockey games and two baseball games. Dink was down fifty grand for the day and it wasn't even two p.m. The moment Tulip turned the brass knob of the office door, two teams he needed to lose simultaneously scored a goal and hit a home run.

"No!" Dink screamed. He squeezed his eyes shut and beat the palm of his hand against his forehead, making his curls jump. He shot his hands to heaven, invoking the Almighty, as if He should be helping. "Tulip!" he shouted. "You're a jinx!"

"I am not," she said, injured. "I was going to cut your toenails but never mind."

Thick, crooked, and purple, Dink's toenails looked as if they had escaped from a petri dish. Only someone who truly loved Dink would stoop to such a chore. Tulip dropped the pink nail clippers into her purse.

"Either you're a jinx, or God hates me. Which one do you think it could possibly be?"

Robbie J stayed staring at the televisions. He was accustomed to the dynamic between Dink and Tulip. I wasn't, and it made me nervous when Dink raised his voice during their fights.

Dink stopped yelling and threw one of his battery-operated singing hamsters at the television set. It landed near my keyboard. I picked it up and pressed its tummy, trying to diffuse the awkwardness, but I regretted it the moment the thing started singing.

Take. Me out to the ball game. Take. Me out with the crowd.

"Oh my God, shut that fuckin' thing up. Thing gets on my fuckin' nerves already," Robbie J said.

I knew there was no off button; still, I looked for one.

Tulip remained standing with her purse over her shoulder. "God doesn't hate you, honey," she said, mildly. "Admit you're powerless over baseball and that your life has become unmanageable. It's the first step."

"You think it's funny. I'm gonna lose this winter and we're going to have to sell the house."

"You say that every winter."

"But this winter I know. Trust me. We're going to go broke. It's going to sneak up on us, quietly. Quietly broke."

It hadn't always been like this. The year Dink was in the halfway house, he had such good luck that Tulip never saw any of his temper tantrums. It wasn't until they moved to Vegas that she witnessed what happened when Dink lost. One afternoon she arrived home from a matinee. The moment she stepped out of the car, she heard yelling. Fearing that her husband had gone into cardiac arrest, she ran into the house. There was Dink, stripped to the waist, writhing around on the floor and pulling his hair with both hands.

"What is going on!" Tulip screamed.

"Cocksucker, motherfucker!" Dink cried. "WHY did he BUNT? Why, why, *WHY*?"

Tulip ran upstairs and into the bedroom. She turned on her stereo, but even *Rubber Soul* on high volume couldn't drown out her husband's yelling. So she packed an overnight bag and drove to the office. She fell asleep on the couch reading about fantasy vacations in *Sunset* magazine.

"Dinky, he takes you to all the funerals and none of the weddings," his friends often said, shaking their heads. But it wasn't just the funerals that bothered Tulip. Dink didn't do anything husbandly. At the gas station, he stayed in the driver's seat, glued to his sports ticker, while Tulip pumped the gas. He didn't know how to rent a movie. His idea of grocery shopping was going to the 7-Eleven and buying baloney and American cheese. In all the times they visited his mother in Queens, Dink never once took Tulip into Manhattan for a day trip to Central Park or to visit a museum. It was strictly Shea Stadium, the track, and lunch at the Georgia Diner on Queens Boulevard. If Tulip asked Dink to do a simple task around the house, he'd panic. "I make the money," he'd argue. "You change the lightbulbs." Her first husband was so much more competent. David used to take her Jaguar in for tune-ups. He always pumped the gas and opened doors. When David lost races, he never would've imagined blaming it on his wife. He never would've called her a jinx.

Dinky, Dinky, Dinky. He was such a child. But Tulip never wanted kids.

Dink continued to scream and punch himself in the head. Without saying good-bye, Tulip closed the door so quietly that it took Dink a moment before he realized she was gone.

"I know something that'll make you feel better," I said.

He covered his face with his hands. His voice weakened.

"A bullet?" Dink said.

"Chinese poker!"

I grabbed the deck from my backpack and sat in the empty seat beside him.

"My wife is a jinx. I deal with it as best I can." He stuck a pen in his mouth and chewed on its end. "Best out of three," he said. "You shuffle."

Beneath the banquet table, amid kinked computer cables and tangled telephone cords, our knees touched.

I came home to a message slid under my door by the motel manager. "Your father called," the note read, "wondering if you're still alive."

I had yet to tell either of my parents about my new job. I felt that my mother, who was living in Ohio, recovering from her thirty-two-year marriage to my father and the long, bitter divorce that followed, was better off not knowing what I was doing. It would just cause her worry. But Dad never worried. Working at a dealership in Fort Myers and playing blackjack every weekend on *The Big "M"* (he referred to the casino boat's high-limit table as his office), Dad is—and always has been—a very lenient man. Other than the casual remark that I'd make a good car salesman, he never pushed me down any career path. As long as I wasn't "headed to the slammer," Dad was proud. I put Otis on his leash and we walked to the corner pay phone.

"A collect call from *BETH*. Will you accept the charges?"

"Yello . . ."

"Dad!"

"Beth Raymer. You alive?"

Then the question that always followed:

"You workin'?"

"I'm working for a professional gambler!"

"Professional *who-what*?"

"Sports gambler," I said. "I help him make his bets."

I leaned my back into the phone booth and gazed across the street, inside the 7-Eleven. Its glass front doors were wide open and welcoming. Native Americans played the slot machines that lined the walls. Their free hands gripped necks of bottled beers. One of my neighbors, a Filipina hooker, came on to an elderly tourist in an electric wheelchair. Her long black hair sank into his lap as she leaned down and whispered in his ear.

"How much you make to do that?" Dad asked.

"Twenty dollars an hour, under the table!" I said. "Plus vacations and bonuses."

"See if ya can get your old man a job. I got fired."

This was not unusual. As a kid, if I walked home from school and saw my dad's car in the driveway, I knew he had been fired. He sold cars seven days a week, from nine in the morning until nine at night. Under no circumstances, other than being fired (or quitting), would his car be in the driveway during daylight hours.

Through the sliding glass doors, I'd see him, drifting around the pool in the white styrofoam lounge float, Miller Lite tallboys jutting out from each of the built-in cup holders. In my bedroom, I'd quickly change into my bathing suit, run through the house, cannonball into the deep end, and ask him why he got fired. "That's the car business, Beth Anne. Bunch of assholes." Looking like her entire world had just collapsed, my mom stood in the shade and asked how we were going to afford groceries. Dad would finish one beer and crack open the other, while I spun him around in circles as though he were the guest of honor in a water parade commemorating unemployment. In the days that followed, I'd sit Indian style on the driveway and watch him work on the Corvette. A matinee at the dog track, a few games of catch in the street, a couple evenings watching *Benny Hill* reruns, then came the inevitable morning. The smell of Old Spice and drip coffee, and Dad in his dress pants, a button-down, and a tie. The classified ads tucked in his armpit. "Where are you gonna work this time?" I asked on his way out the door. His answer was always the same: "Who knows, Beth Anne. Some asshole fired me. Some asshole'll hire me."

I asked if he was serious about working for Dink.

"See what he says. I'll get a room at the Mirage. I'll get 'em to forward my unemployment checks there. Me and Brenda Baby'll move to Vegas."

Brenda Baby was my father's most recent girlfriend, a skinny-legged blonde whose augmented breasts were out of kilter with her petite frame. The first time she invited me to her house for dinner, I brought Otis along and when she bent over to pet him, the weight of her chest propelled her forward and she fell. During my parents' divorce, my father drained his 401(k) and took off with Brenda Baby to the Bahamas. They lived in a suite atop the Crystal Palace Casino for a month. I'm not sure what went on there, how much money Dad won or lost, but eventually they returned, unharmed, and moved in together. I liked the thought of Dad living down the street at the Mirage. Perhaps Dink could take Dad under his wing and teach him how to gamble responsibly. And if Brenda Baby belonged anywhere on this planet it was Vegas, baby.

"When you and Tulip first started dating, was she curious about what you did?" I asked Dink one evening as we shopped for music at Best Buy. He was buying me so many CDs we needed a shopping cart. As a mentor, Dink believed that grooming my musical taste was just as important as teaching me the nuances of sports betting, if not more so.

"Minorly. She knew I had money. Here. The Ramones, *Road to Ruin*. Excellent album."

I tossed it into the cart. "But what did she think of you being a gambler?"

"You and your questions," he said. "Here. The Replacements. Great band."

"I don't think Tulip likes me."

"She just doesn't know you. Why don't you two do something together?"

"Like what? Shop for overstuffed chairs for the living room?"

I snatched up the Gram Parsons anthology, gasped, and pulled it close to my heart. Dink took it out of my hands and placed it in the top area of the cart, where the important, delicate things go— like eggs and children.

Down Rainbow Boulevard, Dink swerved in and out of traffic. We had stayed at Best Buy for too long. Now we were going to miss Monday night kickoff. I unwrapped the plastic from my CD cases and inserted *Sacred Hearts and Fallen Angels,* disk 1. I slipped off my flip-flops, slouched deep in the leather seat, and dangled my feet from the passenger side window. "Sing with me!" I shouted over the wind. I smudged the side mirror with my toes.

"I don't know the words," Dink yelled.

I turned up the volume. Everyone knew "To Love Somebody." It was a standard.

I watched Dink begin to sing and keep rhythm by tapping his ticker against the steering wheel. What a perfect companion I had in him. For three months we'd been spending nearly every moment together and each day I could feel my heart becoming lighter. I loved Dink's stories and generosity, his taste in music and how we made each other laugh. Having Dink in my life was the plain difference between spring break and incarceration. He looked over at me, gave a quick smile, and looked back to the road. I could feel in my throat the desire to say something serious. I pulled the ticker from his hand and played with his fingers. At the red light, I brought my palm to his palm and let my fingers fall in between his.

We held hands through the Monday night football game, in which Tampa Bay beat the Rams outright, and afterward, beneath the blackjack table at the Golden Nugget. The next night, in the dark of the Hilton sports book, we sat close, my head on his shoulder, and rooted for Gonzaga to dribble out the clock. It was a blowout game between two little-known college teams that no one cared about, except for the coaches, the players, perhaps their parents, and, thanks to the invention of the point spread, a Vegas wiseguy and his young apprentice.

"I like him so much," I told my friend Jamie, from the pay phone across from the 7-Eleven. "Do you think I should confess my love and see if he'll leave his wife and run away with me?"

"Who's this again?"

"My boss."

"The guy you said always has tuna stuck in his teeth?"

I pressed my thumb into a chunk of hardened bubble gum stuck beside the coin slot.

"Yeah," I said. "Him."

CHAPTER SIX

Between Us

Most nights after Tulip went to bed, Dink and I met for dinner at the ESPN Zone. Dink presented me with stacks of CDs. Donovan and Joe Jackson were my newest undertakings. As we sat across from each other in the booth, I read song lyrics while Dink watched the late hockey game on the miniature television attached to the end of the table.

"We need the Bruins and under. Our root is for no one to score. But if someone must score, we want it to be the Bruins." He brought a fork heaped with mashed potatoes to his mouth.

I ordered another glass of wine. A friend of Dink's once lectured me on why I should never order wine at a sports bar. It was the kind of crap that caused headaches and stained lips, the guy said. It was unsophisticated. Embarrassed, I had switched to rum and Coke. Now, alone with Dink, I was free to drink the ESPN sauvignon. The wineglasses ESPN used were as round as cereal bowls and the bartenders poured to the rim. The waiter returned with my new glass. I used my tongue to pick up the pieces of cork that floated on top.

After dinner we went to the arcade and took turns on the virtual reality boxing game, which included real boxing gloves to wear. I never liked video games but I loved the feeling of letting my hands go and landing punches. I loved the explosive sound effects that came each time my glove smashed into my opponent's face, which was now covered in blood. Goateed frat boys gathered in a half moon around me and began cracking jokes. They broke my concentration. In a blink I was on my back and my opponent was dancing around me, arms raised in victory. Game over.

"My turn," Dink said. He struggled to put on the boxing gloves and his phone rang. Too-lip, he mouthed, before answering. She yelled so loud that Dink had to hold the phone away from his ear.

"There's no *fucking* reason you should be out so late with her."

I cocked my head and checked Dink's wristwatch. Late? It wasn't even ten.

"Every night you go to bed at nine o'clock," Dink yelled back. "Now, because I have a new friend, you're forcing yourself to stay up just so you can tell me what I can't do."

She hung up on him.

"No more boxing. I gotta go. She's losing it."

"One more game," I begged. "Come on, one more game."

"Fine. One more game."

The next morning, the day of my first pay and collect, the three of us sat beside each other in icy silence. Dink dumped a heap of cash from his duffel bag, I sipped my coffee and doodled, and Tulip sat between us. Tight-jawed and nostrils flaring, she snapped back the pages of a magazine, far too angry to actually be reading. And God knows she wasn't working. She was nothing more than a chaperone, hanging around to make sure we didn't flirt.

I tried to act uninterested in Dink but I couldn't. Two cups of coffee and the huge stack of money made me giddy. Dink owed a bookmaker in Costa Rica eighty grand. The bookmaker owed the same amount of money to Yitzhak, a customer of his from Tel Aviv who happened to be visiting Vegas. To make everything easier Dink would give Yitzhak the money he owed the bookie. That's where I came in.

Using just one hand, Dink counted the money. The stack lay in his palm and with a flick of the thumb, he shot the bills onto the table like cards from a deck. He kept count of eighty thousand while simultaneously reading the USA *Today* sports section. Veteran gamblers talk a lot about *feel*. They say that with time they get a feel for the market, the lines, the money. I felt like I was watching feel in action. Dink was so cool.

"I understand it's a little weird, bringing this kind of cash to some stranger," Dink said. "But you get over it. After two or three times you trust I won't send you to some mob casino manager in the back of a Dumpster somewhere."

He handed me the package. "Count and make sure it's all there."

On the floor, I sat on my heels and put the bills, all of them hundreds, into neat stacks of ten. Eighty thousand. Check. I scooped the piles up with one hand and, like a bouquet of roses, brought them to my nose, inhaled, and smiled.

Tulip's face contorted in disgust and she grabbed her car keys. Watching her storm toward the door, I noticed she was pigeon-toed.

"Okay," Dink said. "Yitzhak, Israeli, short. He'll be at the roulette table at the Paris. Go."

"Wait," I said, stuffing the money into my backpack. "So, I just go up to him and say, 'I have your money'?"

"The whole thing seems weird until you realize the stranger's just like you. You know, goofy stranger."

"Goofy, like awkward?"

"Goofy like harmless. Goofy like he probably enjoys smelling money too. If you want, we can meet in the Stardust parking lot afterward and go to lunch." He smiled, bashfully, and handed me three dollars for the valet's tip.

It was just past nine a.m. Inside the Paris casino, cocktail waitresses in skimpy French police uniforms hurried past me, delivering Bloody Marys and cups of coffee to hungover tourists at the blackjack table. The jingle of coins beat an unsteady rhythm from the rows of slot machines. A casino employee dressed as a peasant sold eight-dollar pastries from a wooden cart. Next to the roulette table two middle-aged men in Ohio State sweatshirts drank thirty-two-ounce strawberry daiquiris from Eiffel Tower–shaped glasses. Beside them stood a short guy in his late thirties. His bangs were black and slippery. The collar of his pink polo was folded up.

I tapped his shoulder.

"Yes?" he said. His bright brown eyes met mine.

"I have your money," I said. He was cute. I giggled nervously.

His hands dug into his pockets. "Okay, we go to the suite to count." His head motioned toward the elevators.

Dink had mentioned nothing to me about going up to Yitzhak's suite to count the money. But in the two seconds I considered it, it seemed like normal procedure. How did he know I didn't skim some bills off the top between the time I left Dink and arrived at the casino? How did I know he wouldn't take the money from me, pocket some, and then call Dink and say that the package was short? Plus, Yitzhak was five-foot-seven and wearing pink. He certainly didn't come off as a threat.

The elevator climbed to the soundtrack of *A Chorus Line*. One singular sensation and the doors opened to a four-thousand-square-foot suite with wraparound panoramic windows and a domed ceiling painted sky blue with a fresco of fake clouds. Israeli men sat at a lavishly decorated banquet table, feasting on smoked salmon, tomatoes stuffed with scrambled egg, and poppy seed pastries. In the center of the table, atop a silver tray, a cow's tongue unraveled over red apples and celery stalks. At the other end of the table sat two black guys in oversized jeans and sweatshirts. White desert light shot over the mountains, through the window, and reflected off the tops of their smoothly shaved heads. Stacked on the china plates in front of them were Belgian waffles doused in syrup and snowcapped with powdered sugar.

The group's personal cocktail waitress welcomed me with a mimosa.

"Everyone," Yitzhak announced, "meet Bar."

"Beth," I said, to the maraschino cherry at the bottom of my champagne glass.

I took a seat next to the Israelis, who talked among themselves in Hebrew. Shiny black chest hair curled out the top of their unbuttoned golf shirts. On their fingers were huge gold rings set with bright jewels the size of jawbreakers.

As I finished my mimosa, I heard bills spitting through an electronic counting machine. Across the room, Yitzhak stood in the doorway of the hall closet. With one hand on his hip, and a pointer finger hooked over his bottom lip, he stared at the machine conscientiously, as if it might steal some bills for itself if he took his eyes off it.

Approaching him, I asked if everything was okay.

"Bizarre, your line of work, no?" he said. His eyes stayed fixed on the machine. "Do you get nervous meeting strangers, carrying so much money?"

I didn't mention that this was my first pay and collect. I repeated the line Dink had said to me earlier, that the people I met were just like me, harmless.

His Adam's apple moved up and down as if it too were watching the bills in motion. "You are a very friendly girl," he said. "You would be a great asset."

I did not ask the obvious question: *to what?* Instead I blurted out, *"Really?"*

The last bills shot through the feeder and the neon blue counter blinked 80000.

"I'll walk you out," he said.

Outside the casino, we stood by the Fontaine des Mers replica. An elderly man posed next to a sculpture of a mermaid holding a large fish that sprayed water from its mouth. A woman with a camera shouted, "Say Vegas!" and the elderly man smiled.

The wind picked up and blew warm across my face, bringing with it Yitzhak's spicy cologne. To escape the glaring sun, he moved a step closer. Our shadows collided. "Kiss him," I said to myself.

"My friends you met upstairs. We travel from many casinos.

Prague, London. We use lasers to operate tables, to see hands of dealers."

I sensed that his smile was a way of pretending that he was joking, just in case I threatened to call the cops. You couldn't work among Las Vegas gamblers without meeting people who tried to take advantage of casinos. Some of the successful card players in Dink's circle of acquaintances started their careers as "peekers," meaning they sought out inexperienced blackjack dealers who held their decks carelessly, making it easy to peek at the next card. There wasn't any more to it than that. Then there were guys who used shaved coins to trick slot machines into awarding credits. One guy was known to use a powerful magnet hidden in his cigarette pack to manipulate slot-machine wheels. But I had no idea what it meant to "operate tables" and I never heard of anything like using lasers to see through cards.

"If you're making this up you better tell me now," I said. "I hate when people make up stories just to see if I'll believe them."

The lasers, he said, were planted inside their rings. The black guys were decoys.

If I understood correctly, and I think I did, Yitzhak and his crew were doing the kind of thing that landed one in jail. Or, more to the point, got one killed.

"How much money could I make?" I asked.

"I think you'd have much success," Yitzhak said. "A no-sweat, no?"

A teenager with acne and a clipboard interrupted us. "You guys got a second to save Yucca Mountain?"

"No," Yitzhak snapped. "We do not *got* a second."

The teenager dropped his head and wearily made his way toward the elderly couple.

"Am I so rude?" Yitzhak said, smiling. His lips were full and his teeth crooked in the most perfect way.

"You're not rude," I said. I found his arrogance attractive. His accent too. And he smelled so good. Who cared if Yitzhak was robbing the casino? I liked being close to him. I wanted to hear him talk more. But I also felt that Dink might be worried about me and that it was time to meet him.

"I have to go," I said, then waited to see if maybe he'd ask me out. He put his arm around me and I felt my face blush.

"Okay," he said, softly. "Maybe you don't mention this. At least that we promise each other?"

He scribbled his phone number on a piece of paper.

"Call me," he said. "I am really interesting in your thoughts."

It was such a beautiful day that I left my car with the valet and walked along Las Vegas Boulevard to the Stardust, my head swarming with fantasies. Yitzhak *was* interesting in my thoughts. Operation Yitzhak was so much more glamorous than Dink Inc. I had never been to Europe, let alone casinos in Prague. With Yitzhak, I could spend my days poolside, drinking vodka infusions. At night, I'd have sex with him and his Adam's apple, then slip on a black silk gown, my ruby-red laser ring, and walk gracefully down the mahogany spiral staircase and onto the busy casino floor. In between heists, in our tiny European flat, we would sit, shoulder to shoulder, and count the money. Then make love on the money, fulfilling one of my earliest sexual fantasies.

A swoosh of pink, white, and blue stars twinkled. The Stardust sign loomed above the parking lot where Dink's Altima was parked. His big, curly head was silhouetted against the afternoon sun. How could I leave Dink? Prague, I'm sure, would be amazing, but nothing could be better than wandering around the arid desert in jeans skirt and tank top, meeting sexy casino cheats, assisting Dink with his affairs. Vegas is where I belonged. Where I was known, simply, as Dink's girl. I ran across the street, excited to tell him about Yitzhak and the lasers.

"Israelis are always behind things like that," Dink said, unfazed by my story. "Pay and collects can be brutal. I'm sorry . . ."

"Don't be sorry," I said. "I love when things like that happen."

The windows were down and we could hear the roar and screams of the roller coaster down the street. I reclined the seat and hung my feet from the window.

"Where are we gonna eat?" I said.

"No," Dink said. "I'm sorry, but I have to fire you."

He dropped a letter-sized envelope into my lap and severance pay spilled out. I never knew money could look so terrible.

I brought my feet back into the car. A lump the size of a bingo ball began pulsing in the center of my throat. I mustered a wispy "I'm sad," which I said to people just before I cried. A kind of heads-up in case they couldn't or didn't want to deal with it.

Dink's voice rose with emotion. "Beth, no crying. It's been fun but this is not good. I can't have Tulip start drinking again and that's what she's threatening to do. You're young. You're bright. You'll find another job."

My tears dropped.

"She says you're coming between us," he said. "And she's right. Do yourself a favor, take the money. Let me know if you need more."

"Why don't you do yourself a favor," I hollered, "and get rid of your miserable fucking wife."

Screams from the roller coaster.

"Okay," Dink shouted back. "Outta the car." He put his hand on my shoulder.

"I was gonna ask you to hire my dad," I said. "I want him to move here." My tears flew in every direction. I tried to look at Dink but it hurt to open my eyes. I snapped a piece of hair from my scalp.

"Stop eating your hair and take the money!" He leaned over me and pushed open the door. "I'm not hiring your father. I only hire people I can boss around. No crying. Out!"

"Stop being so mean!" I screamed, stepping out of the car. I wiped and wiped my eyes, but the tears wouldn't stop. Snot trickled into my mouth.

"I'm married! What does that mean to you?"

I bit my tongue. I wasn't a threat to their marriage. I was a threat to her lifestyle. She wasn't afraid of losing her husband. She was afraid of losing her meal ticket. What did that mean to *him*?

"It means nothing," I said, trying to reason with him through the window. "Pay her alimony. She can live in the guest room."

"Beth," he said, exasperated. He rested his forehead on the steering wheel and spoke to the floor mat. "It doesn't always help when someone thinks you're the greatest and you don't think you're the greatest."

"What's that got to do with anything?"

He mumbled, "Just give it time, all right?"

Inside the Stardust, at the entrance of the Wayne Newton Theater, I sat Indian style and counted the money from the envelope. Seven thousand dollars. The last bill was a fifty with a yellow Post-it attached. "For Otis," it read, with a drawing of Otis, his fuzzy ears sticking out of a Yankees baseball cap.

I got out of bed, pushed play on my boom box, and then got back underneath the covers and snuggled with Otis for comfort and consolation. His snores and the hiss of the swamp cooler gave way to Gram Parsons's "Dark End of the Street." Upstairs, doors slammed. The steel stairway creaked. My neighbors were returning home from their graveyard shifts. A knock at my door and Otis jumped off the bed and ran in front of me, *woofing* in his deep baritone.

"How many times you gonna listen to that song, baby girl?" my neighbor asked. A clip-on bow tie hung from the collar of his unbuttoned tuxedo shirt. "It's a pretty song and all but I don't need you to be playin' that again all mornin' while I'm tryin' to get some sleep." He bent down to pet Otis and Otis dodged his hand.

"Sorry," I said. "I'm grieving."

"I'd say," he said.

We turned our attention to an overweight streetwalker hobbling by in her bare feet. The sling backs of her red high heels dangled from her fingers. Her large, dark nipples shone through her white lace unitard like coffee stains on a tablecloth. My neighbor whistled through his missing teeth.

I read the paper in the bathtub. The local story of the week was that Sandy Murphy, who was serving time for the gruesome murder of her boyfriend, gaming heir Ted Binion, was having an affair with her cellmate, Jessica Williams. Jessica was a twenty-one-year-old stripper with a genius-level IQ, who smoked pot, took Ecstasy, and later crashed into a clean-up crew on a Las Vegas highway, killing six teenagers. Now, she and Sandy had been spotted "cuddling up together, laughing, talking, whispering all night." It made me happy that Jessica had found love—or at least intimacy—inside the Clark County Detention Center. Our ability to adapt; it's what I love most about humanity.

I tossed the paper aside and slid deeper into the tub. My expenses—car payment, gas, rent, Otis, food and entertainment—came to twenty-four dollars a day, seven hundred twenty dollars a month. Seven grand could've lasted me close to ten months. But what then? My inability to work toward a goal was getting on my nerves. I forced myself to consider the future and make a plan.

I applied for a job as an assistant to a knife thrower. When that didn't pan out, I applied to film school in Savannah, Georgia. I copied the résumé of my most successful ex-boyfriend—the one who complimented me on the stories I made up for my Web site—and wrote my own glowing reference letters. Still I doubted I'd get in. I thought of calling Yitzhak. His number was on my nightstand. But if I ran off to Prague, what would I do with Otis? Otis didn't want to move to the Czech Republic. And on second thought, yes, Yitzhak *had* been rude to the Yucca Mountain teenager. I blamed the early morning mimosa for my hasty crush, but it wasn't the champagne's fault, it was my nature. One minute I could be so excited about a guy, complimenting the restaurant he'd chosen, telling him how nice he looked. The next minute I could become so bored or disappointed by his conversation that I'd grab my purse, excuse myself to the restroom, walk past the hostess stand and out the front door. I did this often while at college, leaving my roommate, Jamie the actress, to deal with the distressed phone call that always followed. Holding the receiver tight to her chest, she'd ask me what she should say. "Don't tell him I'm here!" I'd whisper back. "Just tell him I do this a lot. Tell him it's because I'm adopted. Fear of abandonment, so I abandon first." Never one to pass up even a bit part, Jamie recited her lines, perfectly.

With my ears submerged beneath bathwater, I willed Dink to stop by. It was nine on Sunday morning. He'd be at the office all day. But there was a small chance he could visit before driving over to the Den of Equity. I closed my eyes and tried to imagine seducing him. I had tried to do this before but my imagination was never able to build up enough momentum for a complete scene, let alone a narrative. Behind my eyelids, images and story lines stuttered and cut to black, as the movie projector in my head kept breaking down. There was so much I admired about Dink: his sense of humor, taste in music, ambition, generosity, and confidence. But I couldn't imagine him naked and it frustrated me that I felt nothing animalistic toward him. No heat, no rush of blood.

Ah, but wait. That wasn't true. Flash back to the '70s, turn up the klieg lights, and zoom in on Dink, in color, age twenty. One afternoon I had snooped through his wallet and came across his Queens College ID card from 1973. I definitely felt lust for the boy in the picture. The tips of his brown curls were sun-tinted blond. His face was thin and tan; his features sharp. With his head tilted to the side and his pale pink lips slipped into a sexy smirk, he looked like a young, pompous drug dealer. I wanted to be in bed with Dink age twenty. I stared at it, mesmerized, until Dink, age forty-eight, came along and snatched it from my hand. His double chin, bouffant hairdo, and flaccid arms made my stomach flip. "Good-lookin', huh?" he said, sliding the ID back into his wallet. I felt cheated and it showed. For the rest of the day Dink kept asking me what was wrong.

I stayed in the bathtub and sang "Dark End of the Street" to myself until the drain swallowed the last drop of water. Then I turned the faucet to the left and filled the bathtub once again. I felt a little better, but I still wanted to hit something. Which is how I ended up at Johnny Tocco's Boxing Gym.

*   *   *

Resisting the urge to scribble my name into the steamy mirrored walls, I stood in the corner and kept my hands at my sides. But Johnny Tocco's was so small that no matter where I stood, I seemed to be in someone's way. Men threw medicine balls into each other's stomachs and combinations into the heavy bags. Others callused their knuckles by punching sand inside a bucket. Their grunts resounded. To make room for a boxer to do push-ups, I stepped up onto the corner of the ring. Drops of dried blood were splattered like raindrops across its blue canvas. The buzzer ended the round. Jump ropes stopped smacking, torsos stopped crunching, and the hypnotic triple beat of the speed bag came to a halt. Something warm and wet splashed against my forearm.

"Don't stand so close to the spit bucket," a boxer said.

I asked if girls were allowed to box here.

With the help of a translator, Señor Morales agreed to be my trainer. In the weeks that followed, I reported to the gym every day at six p.m. Facing the steamy mirror, I assumed my fighting stance and lowered my chin to my chest. For the next two hours I practiced throwing my jab and snapping it back. Humidity turned my curls to frizz. Sixteen-wheelers roared down West Charleston, rattling my reflection. In the ring behind me, a pair of lightweights sparred. Breathless and glistening, they circled one another before exploding into battle. Trainers stood to the side, white towels spotted with blood slung over their muscular shoulders. Put 'em together, they shouted. Use your left. Your other left. Think!

Dink's absence and rejection had created a void. And looking back, I think that what led me to Johnny Tocco's that evening was my instinctive need to find someone in my life who could provide me with guidance. Lucky for me, I found so much more than that. Boxing was the most challenging thing I'd ever done. It gave me the discipline I had been craving, since I had no professional life to speak of. I felt a natural affinity to the boxers and their rugged individualism. I enjoyed developing a style and expressing myself

through rhythmical punches. And unlike the day-to-day at Dink
Inc., gym life provided me with a substantive goal to work toward,
a reason to look forward: a fight!

Eso, eso, Señor Morales encouraged. Concentrating on staying
loose and quick, I threw my jab and snapped it back.

Tulip's cheeks had swelled up and over her eyes. Her bloated neck
was propped against a white silk pillow. Pink, purple, and blue
bruises camouflaged her face. Grease oozed from her pores. Long
staples protruded from in front of her bandaged ears. Her hairline
had receded an inch, maybe two.

The face-lift had been a success.

But Dink didn't think so. He was out forty-five grand and his
wife's face looked as though Barry Bonds had just used it for bat-
ting practice. He regretted having agreed to the surgery. She didn't
even need it, she was cute the way she was. It disturbed him that
she had put herself through that much pain voluntarily. He didn't
like that she moaned so much. Was that normal? Yes, Tulip's sister
assured him, it was normal. She massaged Tulip's face with a Zip-
loc bag packed with frozen peas.

Many adults notice the progression of time through the growth
of their children. Dink considered his hamsters children but they
had a maximum life expectancy of only three years, not exactly a
full measure of time's passing. Dink had the same lifestyle he'd had
when he was in his twenties. Now, as then, his days revolved around
sports, money, and friends. As he stood over a battered and bedrid-
den Tulip, it became clear that time had indeed passed. The best
years of his life had been lived and now he was old.

If Dink could be granted one wish it would be this: every morning he'd wake up to a shoebox full of money falling from the ceiling. Without answering to anyone, he'd spend the cash—and his
day—however he pleased. That's what his life was like when he
was a bookmaker in Queens and that's when he was happiest. Now
he felt stuck. He didn't enjoy gambling as much as people thought

he did. It was just the only thing he knew how to do to support himself. If he could make book from his house, he would, but he couldn't, so he gambled, which was a lot more pressure. He felt he had passed the point in his life when he could be successful at other things. For a moment, he considered opening a bagel restaurant or a rock club. No, he told himself. Now it's too late.

He felt squeamish. Looking in the bathroom mirror as he brushed his teeth, he saw that his tongue was turning green. He didn't want to keep this ailment to himself; he was in need of consolation. But when you gamble for a living, you learn early on that civilians are quick to judge. It didn't matter the condition—stomachache, headache, fatigue—they were all attributed, immediately, to "your gambling."

Jyrki the hamster sleepily made his way to the cuddle spot inside his five-star hamster hotel. The last game of the day ended and Dink graded his work. He had spent the last thirteen hours sitting in a chair, working, and he still lost for the day. He was falling behind in his hockey handicapping. He didn't think he could do this anymore, or at least do it well. He thought about the smart and successful gamblers he knew when he was in his thirties. Most of them were now selling their homes to pay off debts. Would he be the next one to fall? Smarter people had fallen because they risked too much and didn't realize their earn was over. He was tired of worrying about going broke and he didn't want to be sick anymore. Maybe he was allergic to the floor cleaner the housekeeper used. Or maybe he'd been sick for so long that parasites were beginning to take over his body. He counted out the bankrolls and rubber-banded them in the middle so they'd be ready for the runners in the morning.

Lying in bed, he couldn't stop thinking about an earlier game. *Why did Syracuse foul when they were down eight with six seconds left? The game was over. There was no hope to win. Why foul? It wasn't even a bad mental error. It was a stupid, irrelevant situation that occurred for no reason and it beat me out of a bet.*

Which reminded him: *Canucks, under. Better go bet it now.*

He returned to the computer and punched in his bet.

If he thought about me, he never let me know.

For weeks I had imagined my phone ringing and Dink being on the other end. When the moment came, his voice lacked the emotion I was hoping for. I could barely understand his mumbles. Long stretches of silence were filled awkwardly with horse racing commentary blaring from his television. After a long tirade directed at the seven horse, Dink grumbled, "You can have your job back, if you want. There's a Dink Inc. field trip on Tuesday to Costa Rica."

I jumped up and down and screamed as though I were a lucky contestant on a game show. "Yes, I want to go! I miss you! Why did it take you so long to call me?"

Dink had mentioned Costa Rica before, in passing. Over the last couple of years many of his friends and acquaintances had moved to San José, the country's capital, to set up online sports books and cash in on the Internet gambling boom. The legalities were hazy, but for the time being, bookmaking was legal there. More than half the bookmakers we placed our bets with were based in San José. I always thought that if Dink moved to Costa Rica and started a business, he'd make billions. With all of his connections, and knowledge and good name, how could he not?

"Don't get too excited," he said, raising his voice over mine. "I just wanna see the environment. I just wanna see if it's a place where I can make money and obtain fun."

"Of course we'll be able to obtain fun!"

"Consider it a fact-finding mission," he said. "Pick me up at ten. Fuckin' seven horse! Why'd he ever leave the farm?"

I felt uneasy arriving at Dink's house on the morning of our flight. I hadn't a clue if Tulip had agreed to Dink's decision to re-hire me, or if she even knew that I was accompanying him to Costa Rica. Dink greeted me at the door and, in a whisper, told me of Tulip's face-lift. He made it clear that he didn't want me sneaking a peek at Tulip but I did anyway. I waited until the sister left Tulip's side for a beer break by the pool, listened for the patio door to slide shut, then let my curiosity guide me down the hallway.

Tulip's room was golden yellow and enormous. Windows overlooked the ninth hole, partly shaded by swaying king palms. On the nightstand, beside bottles of prescription medication, lay travel magazines, worn and tattered. Tulip was delirious on painkillers. Her blood-speckled eyelids flickered and she gazed up at me. Her milky eyes watered like an elderly dog's. Cupping my hand over my mouth and catching my breath, I made no secret of my shock. She closed her eyes and she looked dead. I reached out and snapped my fingers beside her ear, something I did to Otis when he was a puppy and I feared he was deaf. She lifted her hand and clumsily groped the damp curls trapped beneath the industrial-sized staples in her head.

"Don't get old," Dink whispered, as I walked into the den. He held Jyrki close to his heart and gently stroked his fur.

Out of habit, I searched the couch for change before falling onto the cushions.

"Does she know we're going to Costa Rica together?" I asked.

"She knows. She wants you to return the severance pay."

"Not gonna happen. Tell her I lost it playing Flip It."

"We have a layover in Miami. Florida's a felony registration state. So remind me, I have to check in at the Felony Motel and Laundromat. It's on Collins at 41st Street. Right near the Fontainebleau."

"There's a Felony Motel and Laundromat?"

"Still as gullible, I see."

"I missed you," I said.

He put Jyrki back into his hamster hotel and shut the miniature door.

"Say you missed me too," I said.

"I missed you too," he said. "Friends?"

I placed a pillow on top of my nose and hugged it to my face. Any way I could keep him in my life, I would. If it meant being friends, so be it. "Whatever," I said.

When we arrived at the Miami airport and checked in for our flight, Dink really did have to show his felony card to the attendant behind the counter. The expression on her face changed as she read the words: "Douglas Heimowitz, Convicted Felon."

"Thank you, sir," the woman stammered, returning the card.

I snatched it from her hand before Dink could take it back. It was the size of a business card and as pink as a valentine. I slipped it into my back pocket, for a keepsake.

CHAPTER SEVEN

Obtaining Fun

Disco blared from the cabs and electronics stores. Skinny drug dealers in tight jeans roller-skated around the main square, selling joints. Two-door Datsuns with flame decals on their hoods spewed exhaust onto the narrow streets. Our cabbie didn't bother to stop for pedestrians.

Dink hardly fit into the taxi. He pinched his nose to avoid the fumes. "We're headed for the eighties," he hollered nasally over the driver's Bee Gees tape. "I can't do it again."

There were no street signs or addresses in Costa Rica. Directions were given in relation to landmarks, some of which had been destroyed by earthquakes long ago. Thankfully, Big Tim, our sportsbook tour guide in the passenger seat, knew where to take us. Big Tim used to work for Dink in Vegas. But in 1997, when online sports books began popping up in the Caribbean and Central America, he headed south in search of employment. We picked him up at the Hotel Del Rey, which Fodor's travel guide described as "the city's most notorious gambling establishment . . . swarms with prostitutes . . . avoid it." But to Big Tim, who rented a room there by the month, the Del Rey was home.

I leaned back against the headrest and inhaled the smell of

burning trash. Though it was common knowledge that there were about three hundred Internet gambling parlors operating outside the United States, the practical details of the insular world remained a mystery. Dink and I had no idea what to expect. En route, Tim briefed us. Other countries, Antigua, Australia, Curaçao, and the Isle of Man, were also friendly to online gambling. But none of them could compete with Costa Rica, which combined low start-up costs with reliable telephone and Internet service. In San José, office space was cheap and abundant, as were bilingual employees willing to quit their jobs as dentists and teachers to work for four dollars an hour sitting in front of a computer screen, taking bets from moody gamblers. Government fees and licenses, if one bothered to apply, cost less than eight thousand dollars, compared to the six-figure sums needed to open in the Caribbean. The Isle of Man had the misfortune of being situated in the dreary climes of the Irish Sea, and Australia was too far away. Costa Rica, conveniently located in the same time zone as Chicago, could be reached in three hours from Miami, Houston, and Atlanta. Going home was no problem; but why would a gambler want to? Prostitution was legal and McDonald's delivered.

Stocky goons armed with machine guns motioned our car through the sports book's gate. Surveillance cameras followed us from the parking lot to the receptionist's desk, up the elevator, and along the hallway, where more armed guards stood one after the other.

Inside, the betting floor resembled your typical offshore call center if it were designed for a porn film. Just-out-of-college Latinas in tube tops, miniskirts, and platform heels sat cross-legged behind computer screens. "*Me-jammy* Heat, game two twenty-four, minus six," they enunciated into the microphones of their headsets. Between calls they brushed their long hair and applied fruit-flavored lip gloss. The few male employees took up seats in the far back row, beside the foosball table. The nonstop ringing of telephones and clerks confirming bets ranging from ten dollars to ten thousand dollars sounded the book's success.

Beeber, a red-faced American in his forties, ran the place. He sat at a metal desk in a back office enclosed in bulletproof glass. Dink knocked on the glass, interrupting the animated conversation Beeber was having with himself. His bodyguard stood at his side. Beeber had no patience with small talk. If Dink was serious about opening up offshore, he said, wiping sweat from his sideburns, he ought to know a few things going in. First and foremost, there had been some kidnappings. American bookmakers and their families had been kidnapped and held for ransom. It was wise to have bodyguards. Ex-policemen made for excellent protection. They could also help get you a gun. You should be packed at all times. Second, the electricity went out constantly and employees were never on time. Many of them had drug problems. If you had high blood pressure, *Fuggetaboudit*. Extortion attacks, another major problem. Russian computer hackers were sending e-mails threatening to take your Web site off-line the morning of the Super Bowl. You had to Western Union the cocksuckers forty grand to get them off your back. Not fun.

"I think he's paranoid from doing too many drugs," I whispered to Dink as Beeber and his bodyguard walked to the men's room. "He's got, like, specks of cocaine all over his face."

"I think that's dandruff," Dink said. "I really don't think the stuff he's saying is that farfetched."

"He sits behind bulletproof glass fifteen hours a day! Who does he think is gonna come gun him down? The dude across the street selling oranges from his oxcart?"

"Maybe he has poor relations with some bad people back east, who knows," Dink said. "Save it 'til we leave. There's cameras everywhere, people can probably hear what you're saying."

"Russian computer hackers?" I whispered.

The second sports book we visited was a sleek four-floor operation that employed a thousand Costa Ricans and offered free on-site day care. There were no bulletproof windows or bodyguards in sight. Framed photographs of players from the New York Giants and a wedding picture of the bookie's mother and father hung from his office walls. Leonard, the owner, seemed more levelheaded than Beeber. I asked about the Russian hackers.

"Well, we're guessing they're Russian; they asked that the money be wired to St. Petersburg," said Leonard. But the hackers, in his opinion, should've been the least of anyone's concerns. The biggest enemy was, still, the U.S. government, which did not approve of Costa Rica's cozy relationship with the betting industry. Try as they might to escape the United States' antigambling laws, offshore bookmakers still worried that the U.S. government would find ways to prosecute them. Bookmaking might be legal in Costa Rica, but the fact that most customers were American meant that, in the eyes of the United States, they could still be tried under American law. The specific law, the gambling community had recently found out, was U.S. Code Title 18, Section 1084, commonly known as the Wire Act. Born of then attorney general Robert Kennedy's efforts to break the Mafia's violent grip on American life, the 1961 law made it illegal to use phone wires to place bets across state and international lines. But it remained a matter of opinion whether the law could be applied to the highly unregulated world of the Internet. The bookmaker who would become involved in the precedent-setting case was a U.C. Berkeley graduate with a degree in nuclear engineering; a self-proclaimed "nice Jewish boy from Long Island" named Jay Cohen.

Everyone in the gambling world had heard of Jay Cohen and everyone shared the same worry: if they can bust Jay, they can bust anyone.

In 1996, Cohen was a twenty-eight-year-old options trader in San Francisco who figured that opening an Internet sports book would be good business but wasn't sure it was legal. His lawyers didn't see any problems provided all the company's employees and bank accounts existed in a jurisdiction that allowed gambling. One year and six hundred thousand dollars later, Cohen and his partners moved to Antigua and launched World Sports Exchange. Soon, Cohen had two thousand customers and was booking as much as two hundred million dollars a year.

The rise of online gambling and the media attention it received angered social conservatives, who cautioned that the Internet made it too easy to turn into a degenerate gambler. No longer would you have to go through the trouble of finding a bookie. If you felt the sudden urge to bet the Eagles two minutes before kickoff, you could do so from the privacy of your own home. You could "bet with the click of a mouse," which was the very phrase World Sports Exchange used to advertise its services.

This didn't make Las Vegas casinos and certain states very happy, either, since they were equally bent on protecting local gambling monopolies. Professional sports teams, though they relied on gambling to develop their audience, did not want to be associated with shady operations and threatened legal action against online gambling sites using their trademarked logos.

Jay Cohen probably would have survived the increased legal scrutiny surrounding online betting had he not made one mistake. He couldn't resist speaking to the media. It was the sort of hubris that revealed his inexperience in the world he had taken by storm. Seasoned gamblers knew that even where their profession had the stamp of legality, such legitimacy was tenuous at best. Gambling was loathed by many and always under public scrutiny; it was best to keep a low profile. That's why successful gamblers leased their cars, always paid in cash, and instructed their kids to say that Dad worked in "consulting." You never knew when or how you would be pulled down.

Cohen, though, felt confident that his business was totally aboveboard, and he said so in the pages of *The Wall Street Journal* and *Sports Illustrated* and during prime time on *60 Minutes*. He explained that he modeled his business on another sports book, one that was completely legal and operated freely in New York State. This was Capital OTB, the off-track betting corporation that served as the state's bookie for horse racing. And just like World Sports Exchange, Capital OTB took bets by phone from bettors anywhere in the United States. If Capital OTB was legal, how could WSE, doing the same thing, be illegal?

Cohen's media crusade turned his brown eyes and baby fat into the public face of offshore Internet gambling. But once gambling had a face, the government had a target.

In 1998, the United States charged Cohen in a criminal complaint with violating the Wire Act. As Attorney General Janet Reno said at the time, summing up the government's position: "You can't go offshore and hide. You can't go online and hide."

Cohen did not view himself as some mobster in hiding. He was a law-abiding employer based in Antigua. The Wire Act did not apply. To prove his point, he returned to America to fight the charge, surrendering himself to FBI agents in New York City.

When the trial began, the government attacked Cohen's arguments in straightforward terms. It wasn't enough that his company operated wholly in Antigua. By using phone lines to book American customers, the company had clearly violated the Wire Act. Signaling its intent to establish a precedent, the government said it didn't matter that the Wire Act only referred to phone lines, which had been the traditional means of getting down with your local bookie. Had the Internet existed in 1961 it too would have been included in the law.

Cohen was found guilty on eight counts of violating the Wire Act and sentenced to twenty-one months in prison. After losing his appeal, he served his time at Nellis prison camp in Nevada, twenty-five miles north of the Las Vegas Strip.

"And all that bullshit was before September eleventh," Leonard said. "Now the government is propagandizing that bookmakers in Costa Rica may be funding terrorists. They're saying there may be a link. That we may be wiring our winnings to Al-Qaeda. They're using that as an excuse to shut us down."

"The government's retarded," Dink said. "People were bookmakers in the United States. They were never anything *but* bookmakers. Then they made the laws too tough so the bookmakers moved to Costa Rica. And now the bookmakers are funding terrorists by taking some bet on the Cubs from a guy in Chicago?"

Congress, criminal complaints, prison camps: these were just abstract words to me. The money was what stuck. The two-hundred-thousand-dollar days; the fifteen-*million*-dollar months. The numbers these men were netting were as supersized as their chauffeur-driven

Hummers, eight-thousand-square-foot compounds, and Costa Rican girlfriends' newly implanted double-D silicone breasts. House parties were thrown nearly every night. The beginning of baseball season, a finalized divorce: there was always a reason to celebrate.

The faint light of the moon led guests up a stone path to a bookmaker's mountaintop estate. Hookers from the Del Rey dipped their toes into the heated infinity pool that overlooked three volcanoes. Friends visiting from the States snacked on the smorgasbord of sushi laid out around the teakwood deck. The air was cool, the plants and trees rain-rinsed. Lightning bugs flashed near the Jacuzzi where the bookmakers gathered. In velour tracksuits, sipping rum from highballs, they discussed the conversion of European hockey odds and rated each other's fantasy basketball teams. The Costa Rican clerks—and their friends, siblings, cousins, and uncles—passed joints and took turns on a guitar. Arpeggios floated into the rustling mango trees until sunrise, when they yielded to birdsong.

After such a party, my enthusiasm soared. On hotel stationery I would list potential employees for Dink's offshore headquarters. My dad would make an awesome sales manager. Newly single (Brenda Baby had broken his heart), he'd been looking to flee to a foreign country to escape alimony payments to my mother. During my parents' marriage, my mom never had a job, a result of my father's old-fashioned attitude. On the grounds that *she* left *him*, Dad refused to pay alimony, leaving Mom, at fifty years old, to support herself on a minimum-wage retail job. Mom raised my sister and me and I felt she deserved alimony. It was the only thing my father and I argued about. "You know I love you kids," Dad was fond of saying when I confronted him about Mom's situation. "I just don't want to give your mother any money." If I offered him a job at Dink Inc. International, I could give him a high salary, then dock his paycheck a couple hundred bucks and send my mom some of the payment she was entitled to. And if my sister ever got clean, she might be right for a clerical position. It would be a win-win situation for the entire Raymer family.

At the hooker bar inside the Del Rey, while waiting for Big Tim to chaperone us to our next excursion, I listed the estimated start-up costs. I learned that online sports books required the same licenses as the country's hot dog vendors. If we wanted one, we should talk to some guy named Enrique, who offered them at a discount.

Mosquitoes swarmed around my ears and ankles. The sweet smell of the cabbie's cigar clashed with his pine-scented cologne. Or was that a leak in the oil valve? I pressed my cheek against the sticky window and watched a malnourished rooster peck out litter floating in a flooded gutter. I began to see why the gamblers compared Costa Rica to the Wild West.

Still, I kept my enthusiasm alive. Even when we visited bookmakers who admitted they were on the verge of bankruptcy, whose betting floor was as quiet and morose as a living room of mourners sitting shiva, I could only see potential. Their office space was orderly and centrally located. If they went out of business, we could take over their lease. Tactlessly, I asked how much they planned to sell their computer servers for.

Dink, meanwhile, was miserable. It was his first time out of the country and it became obvious that he was more than a homebody—he was Rain Man. Without his daily direct feed of NHL games, chocolate milk, and fried potato knishes, his mood was agitated and at times he became hysterical. Realizing that his ticker didn't work overseas, he banged it against his head. There wasn't a satellite in the country that picked up hockey games, and each night Dink sat on the edge of the hotel bed, inches from the TV, repeating the word "brutal" with each click of the remote. He refused to sip Coca-Cola out of a little plastic bag, Central American style. When he ordered a pizza and it came topped with coconut, he refused to eat it, even when I volunteered to pick off the slivers, piece by piece. Losing patience, I threatened to punch him. He growled—actually showed his teeth—and marched out of the restaurant. From that evening on we ate our meals at the Denny's by the airport and I never felt another twinge of romantic love for

Dink ever again. And, ordering the "Moons Over My Hammy" sandwich for the third night in a row, I realized I had been wrong about Tulip. It wasn't just money that kept her in the marriage. It couldn't be. No amount of money could compensate for Dink's stubbornness and constant self-loathing. She was a patient, loyal wife, and Dink was exceptionally lucky to have her.

Just beyond the polluted, billboarded city of San José, voluptuous green hills peeped through wispy white clouds. If, just for one day, Dink left behind the noisy, air-conditioned sports books and the relentless talk of money won and lost, I was sure that his mood would improve and that he could reflect clearly on the endless possibilities of this new and exciting venture. I arranged for a day trip to the Tabacón resort, where we would soak in hot springs at the foot of an active volcano and have a heart-to-heart.

It was Valentine's Day weekend and lovers from all over the world shared flirty glances inside steamy thermal pools in the center of a tropical rain forest. Rushing waterfalls clapped against shiny black rock. In the high fog, tent bats slept inside banana leaves. Holding my Lava Flow mixed drink above water, I doggie-paddled to the center of the pool.

"I can't!" Dink shouted over squabbling parakeets. "I don't know how to swim." He cringed as if the act of breathing fresh air caused him great pain.

"It's four foot deep!" I shouted back.

Hoisting his swimming trunks high over his marshmallow-white belly, he descended unsteadily into 106-degree water. His glasses fogged and he pulled them from his face. Without them, his small eyes darted and he looked confused. He walked toward me, slowly, his outstretched arms cutting through the steam. I thought he was pretending to be a mummy. I laughed and stirred my drink until, suddenly, I realized that Dink was truly scared and I rushed over to guide him to the sitting area. I cleaned his glasses underwater and dried them with a stranger's towel. He slid them over his ears. They instantly fogged.

"Can we please move here," I said. "It's time to take Dink Inc. to the international level. I'll take care of all the start-up headache stuff. Just please let's move here. I want to make a million dollars. I want the best of it!"

He swayed his head and shoulders side to side, a mannerism of his that indicated uncertainty. He always swayed two minutes to post. "I don't think this is the best of it," he said. "I thought it would be easier. I thought it would be like working in Queens."

"This is as close to Queens as you're gonna get," I said.

"No it's not. In Queens there wasn't anyone at my door with a machine gun."

"We don't have to have the guy with the machine gun."

My naïveté hit a nerve. Potential dangers shot from Dink's mouth like a string of firecrackers. Kidnappings, bodyguards, unreliable drug-addicted clerks, computer hackers, jail time. Dink was already a felon; if he were arrested again he would serve time in prison. When would I understand that? he asked, turning away from the sunburned couple French-kissing beside him. When would I understand how tough this business was?

No bookmaker or gambler expects to get paid in full by everybody, every year. And that was just one of the job hazards. Personal masseuses will lift a few grand; betonsports.com will go bankrupt, have a fire sale in the middle of the night, and run away with whatever is left in their customers' accounts. The real problems come when the FBI knocks down your door, freezes your bank accounts, and cleans out your security boxes. When you go before a judge and hear the words "conspiracy" and "racketeering." Even more demoralizing were the inside jobs. Hand a casino runner one hundred grand to make bets every day and at some point the temptation will be too much. How many afternoons had Dink listened to one of his casino runners invent some phony robbery? *I went to the mailbox, I had your money in a fanny pack, and I was held up at gunpoint.* Nineteen grand, gone. *Look, Dinky! See? I got punched in the face.* Eighty grand, gone. Some of the employees didn't even bother to concoct a lie. Bernie confessed to stealing ten grand to pay his mortgage. Fishman, while working as a runner, robbed Dink of twenty thousand. He claimed the money fell from his pocket, and then admitted that he lost it betting baseball. "Like an idiot he bet the biggest underdog in the series!" Dink said, growing more agitated with each recollection. "I told him, 'If you're gonna rob somebody, lay the favorite. You have a better chance of winning. Why would you take the underdog? You're robbing! Bet the most likely winner so at least you can say "I won!" ' "

Dink rushed through the sinister side of the business as though it were the part of a graveyard where the sun doesn't shine. There was a casino runner who once claimed to have accidentally flushed three hundred thousand dollars' worth of poker chips (the ones he was supposed to bet sports with) down a toilet inside Caesars Palace. Dink looked at me: could I even fathom how all that felt? And then to have all those fingers shaking in your face, saying they told you so. Your wife calling you stupid for trusting the scumbags with that much money. And then she goes shopping. She has nothing to do so she spends. A fight about money ensues. Why doesn't she do something to help with the monthly nut? Why doesn't she go to real-estate school? Because she's a woman of leisure. Those are her exact words. *She's gonna end up like her women of leisure friends,* you say to yourself. *Fifty-three, divorced, and working behind a makeup counter for nine dollars an hour.* The door slams and you're alone. Finally you can shake the computer monitor and throw it against the wall. You can pace the floor and punch the air and get lost in your daydream of revenge. Calming down, you watch TV. The pageant's on. You have five hundred dollars on Miss Israel and she doesn't even make the top ten. And how can it be that Miss Sweden is black? What's the world coming to? The three hours you sleep that night are marked by hysterical nightmares of losing money. The day's first thought is of revenge. Everyone cheats. Everyone else is a liar. You're only as good as you were yesterday. You'll overcome this. It's a high-risk, high-reward business. You'll be rewarded. One day. One day. One day. It becomes your mantra.

Dink looked at me through a long pause. Clear-winged butter-flies fluttered around our heads. "I'm telling you this because you're gonna get old, you're gonna get sick, and you're gonna die. So you gotta have fun while you can.

"Actually," he said, reconsidering, "you have more fun than any-body I know. I guess I was telling that to myself."

The trip to Costa Rica wasn't a fact-finding mission. It was a spiritual mission for Dink to come to terms with how he felt about the business. Why would he invest offshore and run the risk of having even more employees rip him off? It was a shitty business no matter what the geography was, and now that he realized that, we could go home.

Not three weeks later, I was in the office when Tony, our casino runner, called.

"No, you didn't," Dink said, pressing his palm to his forehead, feeling for a fever. "You didn't get robbed. Come back to the of-fice."

"I'm not coming to the office," Tony said. "I'm gonna kill myself. Tell my wife I love her."

"Don't do that," Dink said. "Don't do that. Let's just try to work it out. Come back to the office. We can work out a payment plan."

Tony hung up.

"He threatened to kill himself?" I asked. I couldn't believe what had transpired. Just two minutes before, we were playing gin rummy, waiting for Tony to call and tell us what basketball bets he had made. Robbie J avoided eye contact. He gave in to every itch and fidget.

"I can't have that," Dink said. "I can't have that over my head. He's my . . ."

And here his breathing became hard and he couldn't say the word "friend" that would have completed his sentence.

"Get out, NOW!" he yelled. "Everyone OUT!"

Standing outside the office door, I heard a computer hit the wall. "I can't FUCKING do this," Dink yelled. I could tell he was crying. The real-estate agents and accountants passing by as they left work for the day rolled their eyes, wondering what the guy in Suite A was raving about now.

CHAPTER EIGHT

Damage Prevention

Tony didn't kill himself. He bought a Mercedes-Benz and took off to Reno. Robbie J quit to become a full-time gambler. Otis was fired for barking. Lonely, depressed Bruce was recommended by the Den of Equity host. Dink offered him a job and bought him a brand-new moped for transportation. Bruce lost Dink's bankroll shooting craps, then called from a pay phone and threatened to kill himself.

Exasperated, Dink closed his eyes and stuck out his tongue. "Is it green?" he asked.

Tulip leaned over the table and for a long moment examined its bumps and ridges. Aside from the few bleach spots dotting her jaw line, her face had fully recovered from its lift. Her skin was smooth and golden. Clear gloss accentuated her plumped-up pout. She looked like a thirty-five-year-old babe, vivacious and nubile. Thrilled with her looks, she admired her reflection in every window and stainless-steel appliance she came upon. Even the gloom of the office and her husband's wretchedness could not sink her high spirits.

Dink retracted his tongue and swallowed hard, wiping the spit from his chin.

"My body's rejecting me," he said. "The parasites have disrupted things and now I'm turning green."

"Baseball makes you crazy," Tulip said. "Why don't you quit for a little bit?"

"No one believes me!" Dink snapped. "You think I want to be this miserable?" His voice changed, as though he was going to cry. "I want to have fun like everyone else! All I do is foot the bill! But no more!"

Dink whipped a remote at the TV. "We are officially operating on damage-prevention mode. Tulip, YOU NEED TO GET A JOB!"

Tulip tossed on a floppy, wide-brimmed hat and round sunglasses with pink pearl lenses. Exuding newfound self-confidence and sex appeal, she coyly tilted her head to the side. "Honey," she purred, "if you don't respect money, why should I?"

Tulip had a point. For thirty years Dink had made his living gambling and yet he couldn't even begin to estimate how much he'd won or lost in any given year. For someone so savvy in assessing the value of odds, of home-court advantages and changes to pitching rotations, Dink failed to respect the value of hard cash. I can't tell you how many times Dink arrived at the office, wondering aloud what he'd done with the forty grand he'd picked up the day before or complaining that he had "misplaced" sixty thousand. He said this in front of his employees, who were busting their asses to help him make that money—for a salary of six hundred dollars a week. I often wondered if his blasé attitude toward huge amounts of money had anything to do with how often people ripped him off. If he blew off the money, he could pretend that he hadn't been openly defied and utterly disrespected. His self-esteem, it seemed, was worth more to him than his weekly take-home. Or maybe it was just the gambler's mentality. Just as my father used to say on family casino vacations: money is no object.

Whatever it was, somewhere along the way, I adopted it too. Instead of a bank account, I kept my money rolled in an empty coffee canister inside the fridge. I loaned money to friends, grossly overtipped waiters and valets, and bought fancy gifts for my family.

And come those excruciatingly hot midsummer days, when air-conditioning added extra appeal to high-end department stores, I'd treat myself to money-blowing extravaganzas. I'd buy four-hundred-dollar bikinis and thirty CDs in one pop. Then I'd grab my road atlas and Otis and I would go on trips to Arizona, Utah, Colorado, and California. We'd stay at luxurious spas with hot springs and private mineral pools, and then return to Vegas, funds depleted, but enthusiasm for the job restored.

But whether cause or symptom, the tongue fungus killed fun in the office. Everything changed. The ugliness and wildness of the business had gotten ahold of Dink and wasn't letting go. Fun was now the ultimate sin. If you made the mistake of smiling or expressing joy in Dink's company, he asked you to leave or he fired you. Dink demanded loyalty, and there was no better sign of solidarity with the guy than sitting in front of your computer and looking as miserable as he did.

Not until I was chin down, hands up, in the sweltering heat of Johnny Tocco's did I feel a sense of relief. Having grasped jabbing and footwork, I graduated to sparring. My sparring partner was a two-hundred-twenty-pound black woman named Regina whose social worker introduced her to the gym in hopes that boxing would help her recover from an abusive marriage. Regina outsized me by five inches and one hundred pounds; the only way to create equality was to give her a handicap. So after our trainers buckled our headgear and smeared Vaseline over our noses, they took a moment to duct-tape Regina's right glove to her breast.

The electronic bell dinged. Out of nervousness, I clamped down on my mouthpiece and hummed, low and steady, while circling Regina. One side of her face was disfigured. She never mentioned anything about the scars (Regina was an aloof woman), but the skin on her cheek looked melted; it wouldn't surprise me if her husband, in a fit of rage, had once pushed her face into a hot burner. When she shadowboxed in front of the mirror, I felt sorry for her.

But in the ring, I cast all pity aside. With her overhand lefts coming at me like blades on a windmill, she became my sworn enemy. I attacked relentlessly, throwing short, quick jabs and double jabs. But I had yet to grasp the importance of bobbing and weaving, and after snapping her head back I stood, stiff and satisfied, waiting for a receipt, as Señor Morales would say. A solid smack flashed like heat through my ears and in that instant I finally understood what it meant to fight someone with heavy hands.

Practice ended with Señor Morales's fighters gathering in the ring and throwing twenty-pound medicine balls into each other's stomachs. Throughout the drill, I kept one eye on the ball and the other on Rodrigo, jumping rope in the corner. From snippets of conversations I overheard while wrapping and unwrapping my hands, Rodrigo's background emerged: he and the other illegal Cuban immigrants made money by building cages for the Las Vegas Zoo. His mother worked as a maid at the Stratosphere casino. He lived with her and his five brothers and sisters. His goal was to be a titleholder.

With each whisk of the jump rope, Rodrigo's forearms bulged. I watched him bounce, double-bounce, skip, jog, knee-up, and fall back gracefully into his boxer's shuffle. Sweat streamed over his stomach muscles, which were brown and cut like a Hershey bar. In the last thirty seconds of the round, he tossed the jump rope aside and dropped to the ground for push-ups. He had the last-minute endurance of a champion.

After our showers, I asked if I could walk him home. I loved the way the soap smelled on his skin and trying to make him laugh made me deliriously happy. Neon lights at the hourly motels buzzed overhead. On the curb outside the 7-Eleven, next to all the panhandling teenage runaways, Rodrigo smoked cigarettes. At five-foot-nine, 132 pounds, he constantly needed to suppress his appetite to keep weight. Across the street, floodlights illuminated a billboard of two women wearing lace G-strings. The brunette's breasts pressed into the blonde's as they made out. The ad had something to do with loose slots. Rodrigo pulled his Spanish-to-

English dictionary from his duffel bag. Sitting close, we talked about our dogs.

The new strategy was to hire people who were not degenerate gamblers, which proved difficult. First, Dink hired Jake, a brash, bigoted Mormon. When I found him cheating on the office basketball pool, I demanded his termination. But it took an offhand remark about hamsters not being allowed through the gates of heaven to force Dink's hand. An upbeat lounge singer named Stephanie quit her Starbucks day job to work at Dink Inc. Her knowledge and love of music made her fun to have in the office, but her fundamentalist Christian values soon came to light and her pro-Republican rants became unbearable. She was so thankful for the job, coming from Starbucks, that Dink couldn't bear to fire her. After two weeks of training, she still had no idea what we were doing and Dink demoted her to "lunch girl."

Joe came to us after being laid off from a respectable electronics firm where, for ten years, he wrote and directed video games. The contrast between the professionalism of his career at the studio and the loud unruliness of Dink Inc. appalled him.

"We should demand hazard pay," Joe griped as we fled the office, the shouts and groans of Dink's latest tantrum trailing behind us. We slammed the crash bar across the fire door and rushed into the sunshine like inmates in their first ecstatic moments of escape.

Joe flipped down his shades. "What does that man live for? The drama of winning and losing and throwing the ticker?"

Heat from the asphalt seeped up through my flip-flops. Happy to be out of work early, I walked along with my eyes closed and welcomed the sunshine's intense red through my eyelids.

Joe continued. "Such stupid amounts of money! He's a millionaire and he's the most miserable man I've ever met. I hate having to come in to that pigsty every day, surrounded by all that hypochondria . . ." He seemed to reflect for a moment. "Although, shit, man, I think that fungus eating his tongue might be real."

At the height of Dink's tantrum that day, he fired the entire staff, an increasingly frequent form of catharsis that lasted until he hired us all back. Joe, however, never returned.

But guess who did?

Lonely, depressed Bruce. I walked into the office one day and there he was, only two months since he had stolen from Dink. AND DINK REHIRED HIM. I soon found out that forgiving thieves and taking them back was normal procedure for Dink. Tony, it turned out, had stolen money a year earlier. He'd "lost" $40,000, claiming it fell out of his car at the Jack in the Box drive-thru. Still, on the afternoon I heard Bruce nagging Dink to hurry up already and order lunch, I snapped.

"We should have you killed, you fat fuck!" I yelled.

Dink intervened. "We can't kill Bruce just because he robbed my gambling money."

"I cannot, I *will* not, stay in this office and sit across from some fat fucking degenerate thief who makes the same amount of money as me," I vented.

Bruce laughed at me, the tartar on his teeth yellow as pus on gauze. Dink did nothing. I stood there, smoldering, undercut by the very guy I was trying to stand up for. Feeling the disdain flowing through my body, I looked to Dink in anger and disappointment. Forget all the gambling psychology you've ever heard. The only thing you need to know is this: every gambler is a neurotic with an unconscious wish to lose. And as for the rare professionals who are talented enough to beat the house, rest assured they will go to whatever lengths necessary to surround themselves with people who will lose their money for them.

In an attempt to make peace and keep me out of the office and away from Bruce, Dink rehired Otis and appointed me casino runner. With a cash-stuffed backpack hanging from my shoulder, I started my route at eight a.m. Rodrigo lived right behind the Stratosphere, my third casino pit stop, and I found myself stopping by to say hi, to smell his musk, to kiss him, and then finally, to set aside the Spanish-to-English dictionary and have sex with him on the kitchen floor. It had been a long time since I found myself attracted to someone so young, sexy, and strong and I could feel lust's slow poison work its way through my body and damage my common sense. The Wee Kirk o' the Heather wedding chapel was just a block from his house. If we got married, he wouldn't have to fear being deported. We could split our time between Havana and Vegas and have sex with each other every day. These were my thoughts as Rodrigo undressed me and I moved my lips down his smooth, warm chest.

"The Duke game!" Dink shrieked. "What's the line on Duke?"

Flying down the interstate, I held the cell phone as far from my ear as I could. Puzzled by the loud, screaming voice piercing through the front seat, Otis tilted his head.

"Horrible traffic," I said. "I'm sorry."

I could almost hear Dink's blood pressure rising. Then came the screaming rant about how broke he was and how it was my fault because I didn't care about his bankroll. Feeling too good to care, I hung up on him, rolled down the windows, and turned up the radio.

Just when it seemed that I would never care for another co-worker, Dink hired Grant Durrett. A twenty-six-year-old budding gambler, Grant snooped around ATMs for receipts with high balances, which he would scatter across the dashboard of his car in hopes of impressing dates and luring one-night stands back for more. Grant charmed me with his skewed vision of the world, undoubtedly shaped by his father, a thief who had served time in Leavenworth for drug trafficking. After not seeing his dad for ten years, Grant finally got a call from him. Freshly out of prison, he wanted Grant to come live with him in North Vegas and for the two of them to be "father and son" again. Grant, having always wanted a relationship with his father, was happy to comply and immediately dropped out of his Arizona junior college. Father and son played cards, drank beer and got to know each other. Within months of their reunion,

Papa stole the ten thousand dollars Grant had stashed in his bedroom and used the money to gamble and pay off his bar tabs. Grant moved out and swore off his dad forever. Unfortunately, his mail was still delivered to the trailer and his dad, Grant Durrett Sr., pounced on the opportunity to steal junior's identity, leaving his dear son another twenty grand in debt. When Grant realized his credit had been ruined, he returned to the Pair-A-Dice Trailer Park, white-knuckling a nine iron as though it were a battle-axe and expressing hopes that his father's future included equal parts recidivism, denied parole, and ass-rape.

Grant had been on the periphery of Dink Inc. for some time. Years before he ripped off Dink, Tony had been Grant's mentor. On their first day of working together, Tony instructed Grant on what teams to bet and handed him thousands of dollars. Grant, who had never seen that much money in his life, stuffed the cash in his front pocket and immediately got an erection. On the afternoon Tony stole Dink's money, Grant was supposed to meet him for lunch. Tony was Grant's hero, and he never saw him again.

Grant's overplayed bravado, though at times hard to stomach, served him well in gambling. To make extra money, Grant began taking bets from players he met at sports books. At casinos along the Strip, he approached out-of-town players and offered them his services as a bookmaker. That way, when their Vegas vacation was over, they could return home to Newport Beach, Brentwood, Santa Barbara—places that had no sports books—and continue to gamble. All they had to do was call Grant. During my time in the business, Grant Durrett, Patron Saint of the Screwed Over, was the only person I met who physically threatened his customers when they failed to pay. He'd wait for them outside the casinos they frequented, follow them to their cars, then bang their heads against the hoods. If they didn't have the cash, he stole their credit cards and went on shopping sprees at the Fashion Show Mall.

When Grant wasn't admiring his new threads, threatening to murder someone, or sharing every sordid detail of his latest threesome, he was at the office, trying to buy penicillin over the Internet. His mom had told him his dad was allergic to it and Grant desperately wanted to get his hands on some so he could mix it into the old man's food one day. Leaning on one elbow, I'd watch him consider the sites, his thick veins pulsing at his temples. His lips were red and always wet with spit. His mouth hung open naturally, giving the appearance of perpetual bewilderment—a misleading expression, for Grant was unflappable, making him the perfect confidant.

"Do you think it's weird no one ever gets punished when they steal?" I asked.

"Very," he said, without taking his eyes off the computer.

"Do you ever feel, like, when you have a hundred grand in your pocket and Dink's being an asshole and you pass the airport on the way to the Hard Rock, do you ever feel like just taking the money and running away?"

"No."

"I do."

"Yeah, me too."

"Where would you go?"

"Reno, chill with Tony."

"Would you make up a lie that you got robbed or would you just run away?" I asked.

"Run away."

"We should make a pact," I said. "If one of us ever loses willpower and steals a bankroll, let's promise to support one another. That no matter how much money we took, it's still not that bad."

"Whatever you want, Bethy," Grant said, which I happily took as a yes.

The time had come, but I didn't think I was ready. I chewed at my thumbnail until I tasted blood, and then moved to my pinky.

"This will be her first fight too," the translator assured me, referring to my opponent. Señor Morales nodded.

"All I know how to do is jab," I said. I realized I was whining and stopped talking.

A boxer known as the Psychotic Grasshopper joined the conversation. Bouncing on the balls of his feet, he threw uppercuts. "Oh, so is 'at it, girl? You wanna train but don't wanna fight?"

Female boxers love to train and hate to fight. This is their reputation. They are more dedicated, scrupulous, and less ego driven than their male counterparts, making them model students. When talk comes of an actual bout, though, most women demur and once their reluctance—whether rooted in pacifism or fear—is made clear, their trainers, who simply don't have time for anyone who treats boxing merely as a form of exercise, ignore them.

Saturday afternoon I weighed in at a gym in northern Las Vegas. Mine was the twelfth amateur bout and the only female fight on the card. For the next two hours I waited, resting against the same wall as the gurney. One hundred or so spectators arrived. Until Dink walked in, face scrunched behind his ticker, with Tulip and several Dink Inc. employees of yesteryear in tow, I had been the only white person in the crowd. I waved from across the room. "Get her!" Tulip yelled. Now that her husband no longer enchanted me, the tension between us had eased. It was refreshing to be on her good side.

Squatting beside me, Señor Morales cupped his hand on the back of my neck and swiveled my head away from Tulip. My eyes tracked the crowd. A group of kids slapboxed near the snack stand. Mexican moms dandled their newborns. Old men in cowboy hats kept to themselves. EMT workers shook hands with a policewoman. Twenty minutes later I saw the same policewoman wearing a sports bra and silk shorts embossed with a Puerto Rican flag. Only then did I understand that Señor Morales had pointed out my opponent.

No one told me that fighting at the Police Athletic League gym meant that I'd be fighting an actual cop. "Fuck," I said, winded, even though I hadn't left my place against the wall. Wrapping my hands, Señor Morales extended his neck and puffed out his bottom lip—*don't be a baby*. "Oh, this is stupid," I muttered, and that was the last thing I said until my fight was over.

In the center of the ring two heavyweights in bloodstained shorts staggered like drunks. Neither had the energy to keep their hands up. I spotted Rodrigo, ringside, studying the fight with a murderous expression. I was wearing his boxing trunks. Inside the waistband, scribbled in permanent marker, his last name pressed against my queasy stomach.

An official motioned me toward the ring and my insides froze up. I turned my attention to the cement floor and followed Señor Morales to the red corner.

The sight of two women in the ring hit the crowd like a shot of tequila. Their whoops and whistles embarrassed me. In the opposite corner, the cop, Giobanna, loosened her shoulders. Close up, she appeared less intimidating. She was shorter than me, no more than five feet tall, and so chunky that everything was dimpled—cheeks, knees, and elbows. When Giobanna's name was announced over the loudspeaker, she pumped her gloves in the air. The referee looked at me in my corner, Giobanna in hers, and shouted, "Box!"

Giobanna came at me so aggressively that my instinct was to call for a time-out. In amateur boxing, cornermen aren't allowed to speak to fighters during rounds. Luckily, English-speaking boxers from my gym yelled instructions from their seats. One-two, Beth! Straight down the middle. Use your jab. Stick! I stuck once and did little else.

By round two, Giobanna's mouth hung open, showing the black of her mouthpiece, the first sign of fatigue. She moved around, all whomperjawed, as though her entire left side had seized up. Dominating the center of the ring, I did the only thing I knew how to do. I jabbed. When the crowd screamed for real punches, I jabbed. When Giobanna swayed back, far out of my reach, I jabbed. Even after the bell—jab! My one attempt at throwing a straight right ended up as more of a bitch slap across Giobanna's face, a move the crowd mistook for showboating and which prompted the referee to give me a warning. Psychologically, though, it broke what little determination Giobanna had left, and for the remainder of the fight she stumbled toward me, her distended nose smashing into my glove like bug to windshield. God, I thought, I loved punching her face. I felt free, strong, and in control. The only thing that caught me off guard was the final bell.

The referee raised my glove in victory. Someone pushed a trophy into my arms. Its engraved marble base declared me CHAMPION.

The adrenaline stayed in my blood for weeks. I couldn't sleep; I had no appetite. It felt a lot like falling in love. Every morning at five, as the silvery stars faded, Rodrigo and I did our roadwork at Red Rock Canyon. As we kept pace with one another, our sneakers crunched into the desert sand. Sometimes we came upon wild donkeys, gray ones with white noses, roaming the wide, empty spaces of the Mojave. Seven miles later when we reached the picnic tables, we caught our breath and lay on our backs, looking up at the planes drawing racing stripes across the sky-blue sky.

My brain stalled in confusion. I fell backward onto the bed and reread my film-school acceptance letter. As my eyes retraced the word "Congratulations!" I felt neither excited nor proud. Three months had passed since I'd applied, long enough for me to completely lose interest. Film school had been nothing but a passing fancy and it was hard for me to pretend otherwise. Still, it was in my nature to take advantage of absolutely every opportunity to celebrate anything—even the most unmerited achievement of my life. I grabbed some cash from the coffee canister and returned with a bottle of champagne.

Days passed before I finally told Dink.

"I'm not going," I said, handing him the letter. "I only applied 'cause you fired me and I was in a bad mood."

"Beth, go. Do something with your life. You don't wanna be making bets at Arizona Charlie's when you're forty years old."

"Yes I do," I said, sincerely. Despite how much Dink and I had been arguing and how short-tempered I'd become with his self-pity, I was not ready to say good-bye.

Dink raised his eyes from the letter and looked straight at me.

"No you don't. Go to school. If you don't pick a profession, it'll pick you. "

*   *   *

It was impossible for me to ignore Dink's words. He was right: it was time for me to start planning a future, a real one. I called the school and accepted my offer of admission. Once I allowed myself to commit, my frame of mind shifted and I was able to see things more clearly. There was no sense in considering a long-distance relationship with Rodrigo. Our thing had been going on for two months now, which was quite a stint for me. Suddenly, he seemed less like an ideal husband and more like a dazzling hazard sign blocking my new stretch of highway. On the afternoon of his fight in Bakersfield, I walked him to the bus station. The closer we got to the hisses and groans of bus brakes, the more eager I was to not have him in my life anymore. This is how I was with men. As easily as I fell in love, I fell out of it. And most of the time I didn't even bother to break up or say good-bye. I simply disappeared and hoped they wouldn't hate me. My lips touched Rodrigo's for the last time and I retreated. Standing arm's length away, I wished him luck, and promised I'd see him as soon as he returned.

My going-away party, sponsored by Dink Inc., took place at an Irish pub. Boxing friends brought their good humor. Gambling friends brought presents—purses, clothes, jewelry, and cash tucked into cards—which I ripped open the moment they were handed to me. Salt-rimmed tequila shots circled the waiter's tray like numbers on a clock and by the time the main course arrived most everyone was smashed. The increasing sincerity of each slurred toast made me feel like a fraud.

"You guys," I said. "I'm not going to be a success. My application was a complete lie."

"Totally normal," a gambler's wife replied, and the party carried on. One card read: "Your loser ass friends will miss you." Everyone was so kind. I laid my head on the table and cried, "I don't want to go."

Someone said: You're drunk.

Someone said: Where are you going, again?

Someone said: Don't go. Move to New York. Fight in the Golden Gloves.

I lifted my head.

"She's going," Dink countered. He and Tulip were the only sober ones in the room.

Tulip raised her glass of sparkling water. "I'll miss you, Beth." Her voice was small. "You were the best buffer against a husband a wife could have." Blushing and giggling, she glanced lovingly at Dink for his reaction. His face was buried in his ticker.

"To buffers," I said, and clinked Tulip's glass.

Toward the end of the night, Dink presented me with a gift wrapped in notepaper scribbled with old wagers: SF 1st Half ↓22 −130 50. In drunkenness, I saw skillful origami.

"Wow," I said, breathlessly.

"It's not wow. Open it."

I unfolded the sides, revealing a dozen poker chips. Five thousand dollars' worth. Trimmed in gold, they looked good enough to eat.

"I know you didn't save any money," he said.

I hadn't felt this taken care of since I was a child. I slumped my face into his soft Buddha belly.

Along the Strip, a paradise of twinkling lights poured through the streets and raised my spirits. The chips slid around my palm, which had turned sweaty from holding them so tight. At the New York–New York casino, I strolled over the Brooklyn Bridge replica and followed the cobblestone streets lined with fire hydrants and one-hour parking signs. Past Helen Yee dry cleaners, I found the casino cage and cashed in my chips. The cage girl counted the money into my hand and something in the way the bills fell into my palm made me seriously regret my decision to go to film school. To me, money meant gambling, not security. Adventure, not school. Studying film was the last thing I wanted to do with my life. I had known this from the moment I opened the letter. What kind of sad trick was I playing on myself? Who in their right mind gets five grand and moves to *Georgia*? At twenty-six, I understood I'd never have this much spending money ever again. What I wanted now, most of all, was to box. Feeling light-headed and courageous, I decided to move to New York and fight in the Golden Gloves. I'd read a book about it. It was the country's premier boxing tournament. Champions Cassius Clay, Sugar Ray Robinson, Mike Tyson, Oscar De La Hoya, had all competed in the Gloves during their amateur careers. If I made it to the finals, I got to fight in the legendary Felt Forum at Madison Square Garden.

"Winners!" a sign read, and beneath it were photographs of people holding enormous cardboard checks written out for millions of dollars. "They got their piece of the Big Apple, are you next?"

It took me twenty-five minutes to stuff my life belongings into brown paper grocery bags and pack up my truck. Otis jumped up into the passenger seat and put his paws on the dashboard. I checked the road atlas, tucked it in the console, and turned the ignition. It was senseless. But a windfall of cash and the chance of even greater thrills could make me that way.

CHAPTER NINE

New York, New York

Mud-splattered taxis bullied each other down Broadway. Hordes of gray-coated pedestrians rushed past me, squinting against the blowing sleet. Gusts of wind rang through my ears and my numb fingers could barely push the numbers on the keypad.

"A collect call from *BETH*. Will you accept the charges?"

Through the static Dink mumbled and then put me on speaker-phone. "You know better than to call the office on a Saturday," he said. "There's five hundred sixty-five games about to go off. I'm having a hard time maximizing my gains and there's a rash under my left armpit. Make it quick."

"I want my job back," I said. "I wanna come home." In the winter chill, my sobs came out as thick as cigar smoke.

"Beth, no. Stop with the dead-end jobs and do something with your life. You're gonna fall behind and you're not gonna be able to catch up."

Dink's warning came too late. I felt like I *had* fallen. Compared to Johnny Tocco's, my new boxing gym in the West Village was a disappointment. My truck had either been towed or I had forgotten on which of a thousand streets I'd parked it. Out of curiosity, I got in touch with a cute Israeli guy I'd met on an airplane a few months earlier. At some point over dinner we came to the realization that while on that plane we had, in fact, experienced love at first sight and for reasons I still can't fathom, I moved into his Upper West Side apartment. It was a stupid move and now I was paying for it. He did strange things before bed.

Worse than any of this, though, was my homesickness. New York's confinement and biting cold were inescapable and I longed for Vegas's wide-open spaces and merciless heat. Each morning, awaking to the noises of the city, I felt oddly embarrassed. As though by leaving Las Vegas, I had skirted some kind of obligation. It had never occurred to me that one could feel guilty toward a place, but that's exactly how I felt.

I stomped feeling back into my feet. "Make me junior partner," I said, shivering. "I'll catch up later."

In the background Grant taunted: *Beth-y can't make it in New York. Beth-y can't make it in New York.*

Hearing his voice made me even sadder. "I miss you guys so much," I said. "Are you eating breakfast? Who gets the bagels now that I'm gone?"

Dink raised his voice: "Beth! You had the opportunity to go to a good school and do something long-term and then you got drunk and took off to New York. Do yourself a favor. Pick something reasonable and focus. Not a boxer, not an in-home stripper . . ."

"Hey!" I said, offended. That was supposed to be a secret.

". . . I mean, tomorrow you could learn how to run a Roll-n-Roaster franchise and within two years if you work hard I imagine you could probably have one of your own. That'll do well! All you have to do is find the guy who's successful at running his Roll-n-Roaster franchise and emulate his success."

Wordless, I slid the toe of my shoe across a patch of dirty snow. Beside me, Otis whimpered and chewed at the lumps of rock salt stuck in his paws.

"Anyway," Dink continued, "your position's been filled. I hired Angelo."

"Hi!" said Angelo.

Dink may have no longer been my boss, but he was still my mentor. And it was his advice that sent me worn and weary into a Sixth Avenue Kinko's where, for the first time in my life, I attempted to write a real résumé.

"Significant Work History," I typed. And there I stayed, slumped in the chair, long past sundown, staring at those words. I'd been out of college for five years and I had not one job to put on my résumé. I'd always wondered what gamblers would do, what jobs they would have, if they didn't have gambling. Now I was wondering that about myself. At first, I tried being honest. I thought maybe if I used my imagination I could create something impressive out of my past jobs. But no matter how much I cut and pasted, I couldn't spin what looked more like a rap sheet into a résumé. I felt like a juvenile delinquent trying to figure out what the judge wants to hear.

The more frustrated I became, the more I pined for Dink Inc. As discouraging as working for Dink sometimes was, I never had to pretend to be someone I wasn't. Sitting beneath the quivering high-wattage lights, diluting my life until it was as colorless as dishwater, I felt like a fraud.

I pressed my finger down on the delete key and held it there in defiance, erasing bullet point after bullet point. I didn't come to New York to do the Long Island commute and work as a secretary at Citigroup. I wanted to work for a gambler. I wanted to box. And other than that, I wanted to be left alone.

A twenty-inch snowfall confined me to the Israeli's apartment for two of the longest days of my life. In the shadows of his living room, he played Israeli fight songs on his Casio keyboard. On day two, I was jumping rope in the hallway when the phone rang.

"I'm only doing this because I'm concerned for your near future," Dink said. His cheerful tone signaled that he had, indeed, found a way to maximize his gains. I couldn't believe I had actually followed his advice and tried to get a legit job. His big Roll-n-Roaster-franchise lecture hadn't even been sincere. He was just in a bad mood because the Patriots weren't covering the spread. When would I learn?

He gave me the phone number of Bernard Rose. A "harmless maniac" Dink had known since he was a teenager, Bernard had a gambling and bookmaking office on Long Island.

Without hesitation I hung up on Dink and dialed the number.

"Right, right, Dinky's friend," Bernard remembered out loud. "You like pizza? You been to Ronkonkoma? The. Best. Pizza. Famous for its pizza. Take the railroad to Ronkonkoma and look for the most miserable guy driving a limo. That's Mikey."

As the morning sun pushed the temperature up from the negative into the single digits, I hightailed it through the Long Island Rail Road parking lot and jumped into the back of Bernard's stretch limo. It was warm back there and had a greasy smell, which seemed to fit with Mikey's surliness. Navigating the slushy streets, he kept a running monologue under his breath. *Like hell I'm gonna let yuh in. Nice blinker, tough guy.*

Through the tinted windows, I watched people wave to me from their cars. Parents pointed me out to their kids. They thought I was famous.

In the back of a pizzeria, at a red-and-white-checkered table, the three-hundred-seventy-pound Bernard Rose sat splay-legged, the lower half of his belly hovering just a foot or so from the floor. Gripping a chocolate éclair the size of a hoagie, he smiled to himself as he read the paper.

"Today is the most beautiful day in the history of the world!" Bernard beamed. His black, unruly eyebrows curled into glittering blue eyes. The gray at his temples glistened with perspiration. "Cher is coming to Madison Square Garden!"

"Ah, Christ," Mikey said, disgusted. "Well guess what? I ain't drivin' yuh there." He plopped into a corner booth, where he sat, bemoaning his existence for the entire afternoon.

Bernard offered me a seat and poured me a glass of root beer. "I had the weirdest dream last night," he began, creating instant intimacy. "I was real aggravated yesterday. My wife was mad at me. My parents came over so I'm trying to hide my gambling. They pick a time to leave and it's halftime of all the four o'clock games. Torture! I can't leave the computer to tell them good-bye so I pretend to be stuck in the chair . . ."

Across the room, a waiter delivered food to an elderly woman lunching alone. Bernard cupped his hands at the corners of his mouth and shouted, "Vera! How come you're getting served before me?"

"Because, Bernard," said Vera, "I'm special."

"That's my weakness," Bernard whispered. "Women with a lot of personality."

Waiters arrived at our table, balancing pizzas, bowls of spaghetti, Caesar salads, baskets of garlic knots, and French fries. Bernard took one last bite of his éclair, set it on top of his cell phone, and tucked a paper napkin beneath his third chin.

"Meatballs make me so happy it's scary," he said. "Anyways, yesterday. Lots of aggravation. Very rough sleep."

He wound pasta around his fork until it resembled a fat spool of yarn. "So, my dream. I was dead. Dead! I was watching my own funeral and I could hear everything everybody was saying. My wife was telling somebody that she wanted me to come back to life. That she loved me and she was upset that she never told me. Are you tasting this marinara?"

With each colossal bite, Bernard's fat cheeks and bulbous nose grew rosy with delight. His greasy lips had a hard time keeping pace with his racing mind and rapid speech. He was looking to get into the pineapple import business, the ice-cream-cone business, the popcorn-machine business. He dreamed of starting up his own premium-rate telephone service: 1-900-BAD-BEAT, a number gamblers could call when they suffered a heartbreaking loss and needed to vent. "Ninety-nine cents a minute. Think of the advertising! 'If you need assistance with debt consolidation please press one.'

"I'll trade you," he said. "My pepperoncini for your garlic knot."

For Bernard our meeting was probably just a favor to Dink, a chance to get out of the office and order a few more items off the menu without the guilt. But for me, it was the first time since leaving Vegas that I was sitting across from someone, enjoying myself. Watching him smile and chew, the afternoon light coming in through the frosty picture window behind, I was seized with the urge to crawl into his lap and rattle off my Christmas list.

"Dinky says you're an independent thinker," Bernard said. "I like that. Let's think of a job for you."

"Make her get her Class B license," Mikey said from the booth. "Make her drive the limo."

"I'm good on the phones," I said, ignoring Mikey. "And I like going on pay and collects."

"Ah, Christ. Who doesn't?" Mikey said.

With the last garlic knot, Bernard soaked up the grease from his plate. "Got it! Hows about you pick up the donuts in the morning. Love Boston creams. Addicted! What we'll do is, you'll be my girl Friday. Girl-Friday-dream-therapist. That's you."

Leaning in closer, he whispered, "I'll pay you forty dollars an hour. It's more than Mikey makes."

Double what I made at Dink Inc.: "Perfect," I said.

Surrendering to the empty baskets and pizza trays, Bernard removed the napkin from his chin and set it gently atop his plate. He slapped his hands together, cleaning the crumbs from his palms. "Done," he said. "Let's go get a pedicure."

I moved out of the Israeli's immediately and into the second floor of a brownstone in Brooklyn, walking distance to the Flatbush Avenue LIRR terminal. Five mornings a week, the stretch limo waited for me outside the Ronkonkoma station. Grudgingly, Mikey set aside the sports section and drove me to Dunkin' Donuts, where I'd pick up a dozen Boston creams and two large black coffees in styrofoam containers and bring them to Bernard's office.

Named after Bernard's favorite sandwich, BLT Inc. was on the fourth floor of a characterless building overlooking the Long Island Expressway. The "rent-a-space" was a tiny, windowless room with access to a lobby that supplied a copy machine, a stapler, and Sarah, a communal secretary with a matronly bun and obvious crush on Bernard. BLT shared the floor with three other businesses. But they weren't really businesses. They were just divorced men past forty who didn't have a lot going for them. One of the guys lived in his rent-a-space, a secret Sarah was kind enough to keep to herself. On Fridays, as an end-of-the-week goodwill gesture, Bernard ordered BLTs for everyone on our floor, which I delivered, courtesy of BLT.

From the moment I met Bernard, I understood why Dink called him harmless. But it wasn't until the door to BLT closed that I witnessed the other half of Dink's description, *maniac*. How the man generated money through booking, betting, hedging, arbitraging, middling, and scalping, the way he pinched pennies and shaved points and chopped numbers. It wasn't gambling. It was cannibalism.

Unlike Dink, who handicapped games and employed a crew to search for weak lines, Bernard had no raw handicapping skills and he worked alone. He was, however, an exceptionally gifted mathematician who was utterly confident in his unique arbitrage system. The strategies he used in his sports betting—scouring the market, placing big bets on small discrepancies between bookmakers' lines—were no different from the strategies hedge funds use to exploit small deviations in commodities prices or foreign-exchange rates. Sixteen hours a day, seven days a week, he sat in front of his computers booking bets, making bets, calculating sixteen-team-if-reverse-round-robins in his head and taking advantage of the very large, very liquid, no-risk betting opportunities created by the Internet. He referred to his gambling style as "grinding," and fellow bookmakers around the world knew him as the Industrial Sander.

"Charting, it's alls about the charting," he'd say. Though I never once saw him *chart* anything. Nor did I see him use a calculator. The amount of money that moved through BLT on a daily basis made Dink Inc. look downright conservative. Even when Dink found a very cheap price on a matchup he absolutely loved, I never saw him bet more than seven thousand dollars on a game. When Bernard found the best of it, there was no limit to what he bet. No matter how marginal the mathematical advantage, he would keep betting and betting and betting—*hundreds of thousands of dollars*—until the kickoff, tip-off, or first pitch took the game off the board. Only after the game started did Bernard consider how much he had riding on it.

It was shocking. Sitting at my little desk directly across from his, I watched Bernard frantically scribble on the backs of paper plates the hundreds of bets that he placed and booked. "Should I lay the sixteen minus the oh-two to get a take-back of plus seventeen minus the oh-nine?" he'd ask the office goldfish, while overfeeding it. The day's climax came at six p.m., when the folks in China were just waking up. Their action came flying over the Internet gambling sites, creating awesome scalp and middle opportunities, or, as Bernard called it, "steam."

"We're steaming!" he'd holler, giving off a faint whiff of custard filling. "Complete bedlam! Bet, Beth, bet! Get on the phone! Steaming!"

Bernard was involved in every imaginable facet of gambling and bookmaking and I'd guess that about twenty-five, maybe thirty, percent of what he was up to was illegal. Point being, he should've been a little more discreet. As if the limousine and the yelling and the ever-ringing telephones weren't enough to raise suspicion, each day, around noon, Wombat, Guppy, the Battler, Bernie the Bartender, and other gambling clients or "famous guests" that Bernard booked or went to the track or synagogue with staggered into our sweltering little office. Polite conversation quickly devolved into how much was owed to whom and when it could be paid. One of my girl Friday responsibilities was to make phone calls to see how we could move the money, calling Dookie's guy who wanted to get paid in Yonkers and Scooter's guy who needed money in Newark, confirming that Chinese John had a package ready for pickup at his restaurant in Flushing and Lenny Smalls was good for sixty dimes. Once the pay and collects were arranged, Bernard settled into his chair. With the famous guest at his side, he shared stories of what the guest was famous for.

"Totally famous. Invented the handoff. Put the money he owed you in a fancy Lord and Taylor string shopping bag and instead of saying hello, he walked past you and swung it right into your hand. Very graceful. Very athletic.

"Notoriously. Famous. Three ex-wives. All sued him for mental cruelty.

"Unbelievably famous. Super Bowl Sunday, 1981. Bet sixty thousand on the Eagles. Midway, first quarter, Eagles are down fourteen nothing. They were favored. He had no chance. All of a sudden, comes flying down the stairs with a dozen eggs, cracking them over his head. He was overheating. I said, 'Drink water!' but no. He rubbed egg all over his face. Fourteen nothin'. Famous."

I would not be lying if I said these famous guests were the most socially inept misfits I'd ever met. Dink's friends in Vegas . . . sure, some were a bit odd. But these guys still lived with their *mothers*. Watching them watch Bernard as he lifted their inadequacies into the heightened world of legend, I saw the faces of men who had never before heard anyone say something nice about them. Their smiles were so unnatural they looked more like agony. Bernard was an exceptional storyteller, but his real gift was his vulnerability. Sharing his unabashed love for Cher and pedicures was just the beginning. He talked freely of his visits to his "pill doctor," his struggles with his weight and obsessive-compulsive disorder, and the gloom he felt when he argued with his teenage son. The guests listened to Bernard in wonderment, as though they were waking up to the realization that they weren't the only ones with such problems. I think Bernard was their only link to humanity.

"They all want to be your best friend," I said, after a famous guest left.

"When you're doing good everybody wants to be your best friend," he said. "When you're doing bad nobody wants to know you. That's in any business in any part of life. If you live long enough, you'll see what I mean."

*　　*　　*

Like most people who have suffered a traumatic event, Bernard split his life into two categories: all that came before and all that came after what he referred to as the "1983 Broke."

Before the 1983 Broke, Bernard was thin, boyish, and profligate. Growing up in Sands Point, on Long Island, Bernard had as neighbors the power broker William Shea (whose eponymous stadium was the home field of the New York Mets), the CEOs of MGM and Pfizer, and the singer Perry Como, who, on Halloween, handed out silver dollars in lieu of candy. Still, it was the Rose residence that the neighborhood kids flocked to. At Bernard's, they could eat sandwiches and play cards with the gregarious mathematical prodigy who, at three years old, began beating his mom at her own game—gin rummy—while keeping score in his head. When the Roses went grocery shopping, Bernard rode along in the cart and kept a running figure of each item tossed inside. Arriving at the checkout line, he'd announce the grand total, tax included.

Though everyone in the Rose family enjoyed a good card game, there was something in the way Bernard played poker at age twelve, the way he thrived in the high-action environment, that made his mother uncomfortable. Returning home from the office one afternoon, she found Bernard hosting a poker tournament at the dining room table. For his friends' refreshment, he had put out an impressive spread of crackers, cheeses, and deli meats served atop a polished silver tray garnished with fruit. Hand after hand, he was fleecing every single one of them.

Bernard's interest shifted from poker to sports gambling when he was fourteen. Working weekends at his father's beer-and-soda store, Bernard noticed the unkempt customer who, no matter the weather, wore a bright red fireman's jacket. Bernard assumed Barfy was homeless. But then he noticed his father bought stuff from Barfy. Football parlay sheets.

"You can bet whatever team you want?" a mystified Bernard asked his father. "You don't have to have someone bet against you?"

Bernard and his friends loved football and they always tried to bet each other. But every Sunday they all agreed the Jets would win and that was the end of it.

"Nope," his dad said. "That's what a bookmaker's for. Lay fifty-five dollars to win fifty and it's no problem. "

For Bernard, this information marked a true awakening. Barfy, football sheets: life was beginning to make sense. Crunching sports statistics gave Bernard the intellectual stimulation he craved and by his senior year, he was making enough money from cards and betting Barfy to buy his own custom-made leisure suits. Textured and four shades of brown, just like the kind Perry Como wore. Bernard couldn't wait until he had to give the lunch lady a couple dollars so he could pull his huge wad of cash out in front of everybody. The pull of money was very strong. Just feeling the weight of it in his pocket gave Bernard a shot of libido.

Bernard's popularity was such that at sixteen, when he started booking, he quickly out-customered Barfy and even Dinky, who was four years older. Not wanting to be an accomplice to her son's illegal activity, but loving him too much to throw him out, Bernard's mom rented him a caretaker's cottage on a nearby country estate. Nestled among evergreens and a lily pond, the cottage was the perfect cover for the illegal high-stakes gambling taking place inside. Free from the oppressiveness of home and school, Bernard became the renegade scientist of bookmaking. Carrying out erratic mathematical experiments in the forms of live betting and reverse parlays, he laid off with other bookies, booked people against each other, and cross-booked six different racetracks.

To his friends, he was a god. And to this day, they still remember the afternoon in 1977 when they first discovered just how much Bernard was worth. Overhearing him on the phone, taking five- and ten-thousand-dollar bets for over an hour, a friend finally asked, "Bernard, how are you dealing that high?" With some persuasion, Bernard revealed his bankroll. He had made two and a half million dollars from gambling. He was nineteen years old.

Mesmerized, his new entourage tagged along with him everywhere he went, which of course included Roosevelt Raceway. Most of the entourage had never spent time at the track and it seemed to them a very strange place. There were a lot of different cliques and within each huddle there seemed to be a lot of secrecy going on. Bernard navigated each group effortlessly, leaving his entourage to eat SuperPretzels and pretend to understand the exacta board.

One evening, Bernard returned to them. He looked electrified. "You see that guy?" he whispered, nodding toward a kid just a few years older than them.

Certain that the kid had given Bernard a tip that would make them all rich, the entourage gathered in closer.

"That guy," Bernard said. "He's married!"

That Bernard viewed matrimony as big, inside information revealed the second gulf widening between him and his peers. His broke-ass friends were getting girls and Bernard wasn't. Young, rich, gifted, but chronically love-shy, unable to even mutter the word "date," Bernard, at nineteen, still called them "things." He knew plenty of guys who went on "things," but what impressed him most were the guys who were married. It seemed so nice to have a wife to spend money on and care for. But he was getting ahead of himself. God forbid he ever got lucky and found himself on a "thing" with a girl, let alone getting married. Deflated, his entourage rolled their eyes and Bernard let his thoughts drift back to long division.

Finally an older, very mature guy from the track (G.B., age twenty-four) became Bernard's romance mentor. Offering Bernard guidance on how to adequately spend his money, G.B. helped him move out of the cottage and into a thirty-second-floor penthouse with a five-bridge view. He decorated and stocked the penthouse with all the items Bernard needed to draw in the girls: marijuana, every type of pill imaginable, Commodores albums, disco lights. To ring in 1978, G.B. threw a party, inviting everyone from the track. From behind the glass-beaded curtain, a dozen nineteen-year-old girls emerged, one after the other, like ducklings from tall grass. "Gentlemen," G.B. announced, "meet the Swedish Connection!"

The Swedish, Bernard thought, make excellent meatballs.

None of the girls was actually Swedish, by the way. They were just trashy blond-haired girls from far Long Island. Not that it mattered. Across the room, Bernard watched as they giggled and did the hustle. Quick, quick, slow, slow, their hips swayed rhythmically inside their flare-legged jumpsuits. G.B. dropped Quaaludes into Bernard's shirt pocket. It was at the height of the disco era—this was not the generic stuff. The pill kicked in and Bernard found the absence of compulsive thought soothing. Disco bulbs glowed red like meteorites sailing through the night and Bernard discovered he could be quite charming on Quaaludes. A raspberry-freckled Swede sat beside him on the davenport. Feeling that something was expected of him, he played with her hair. Between his fingertips, her dry, damaged split ends felt like crushed silk. The room pulsated.

Alas.

In the same way a gentle kiss leads to more passionate kissing, that night's party led to more refined partying, until it was no longer a party but a lifestyle. The Swedish Connection doubled. Bernard bought a water bed. The penthouse became a magnet for every addictive personality on Long Island trying to escape his wife. Friends on benders walked through glass patio doors and kept walking. They flipped their cars in the condo's parking lot. Everyone lusted over the Korean hooker who came over to give massages, except for Bernard, who fell in love with a beautiful lost soul named Natasha.

Miraculously, as drugs dragged his friends through gutters or turned them into arrogant jerks, Bernard kept his wits. On any given night at Roosevelt, twenty-one-year-old Bernard, now Long Island's most illustrious bookmaker, could be seen with his young wife, Natasha, in their matching his-and-hers full-length fur coats, just like the kind Joe Namath wore.

His glitz, however, did lead to unwanted attention. One morning, after a busy day of pay and collects, Bernard was just inside his front gate when he heard a noise. Turning around, he saw two men jump out of a car. One pulled a gun, the other a knife. It happened fast. Bernard was scared.

"Special police unit!" yelled the man with the knife. "Get in the car!"

In the front passenger seat, Bernard felt the weight of the man behind him, leaning over the headrest, holding the knife to Bernard's throat. Watching the exit signs whiz by as quick and vivid as a life review, he tried to anticipate their plan. The images in his head terrified him. He didn't have much money on him, just thirty thousand in his pockets and forty thousand in his briefcase. Would they be mad there wasn't more? Mad enough that he should risk jumping out of a car going sixty on the Union Turnpike?

In a chain-linked dirt lot, in an area nobody lived in, the robbers patted Bernard down and took the money from his pockets. They took Bernard's Louis Vuitton briefcase, dumped the cash out, and then politely returned the case to him. "Minus the knife," Bernard later recalled, "those guys were a real class act."

Six months later: same place, different robbers, less class. Bernard felt the brunt of an object smashing the back of his head. When he opened his eyes, he was on his stomach. Change rolled from his pockets. Another blow and the robbers fled, with the briefcase.

Somebody was setting Bernard up and he didn't want to stick around one more second to find out who. Bequeathing his penthouse to the Swedish Connection, he and Natasha, in her fringed-suede hot pants, took off for a safe, faraway place where nobody would know him and he could make book without worrying about getting killed. Another country? Well, maybe another zip code. On the corner of 60th and Columbus Circle in Manhattan, their new building had a rooftop swimming pool and a European bank just one block away.

From his desk, overlooking the horse-drawn carriages along Central Park South, Bernard made calls to friends and associates. "I'm somewheres far away," he said, raising his voice for emphasis, as though the international connection was giving him trouble.

"But I'm still open, I still want your business. I'm still taking bets, high as the sky. Just on the lam, that's all."

Bernard adapted quickly to big-city gloss. Looking svelte and stylish with his close-cropped hair and leisure suits, he walked to the European bank every day to visit his money. The concierge led Bernard through the marbled, gilded hallway to his safe-deposit boxes. With the concierge's help, Bernard had figured out how much money could fit in each box. Using hundred-dollar bills, and depending on how much breathing room one felt the stacks needed, they guessed roughly six hundred thousand dollars. Bernard had six boxes.

Bernard took high tea at the Plaza most days, surrounded by crystal hurricane lamps and Park Avenue ladies setting aside their fur muffs. Keeping to himself, he ate cucumber finger sandwiches and admired whatever extravagant purchase he'd made while killing the hours between the bank and teatime. On one particular afternoon, this meant a five-foot-tall eighteenth-century cast-iron coat tree. The saleslady said it was famous and Bernard couldn't resist. He finished the last of the petits fours. Awash in the sound of the harp's weeping tune, Bernard enjoyed the straight sugar rush.

On the evening of January 30, 1983, Super Bowl XVII, Bernard felt a thrill in his belly. It was as though he'd been waiting his entire life for this very kickoff. Many of his customers' teasers had carried forward—about nine hundred thousand dollars' worth—and all he could do was hold on to their action and hope like hell that the Dolphins, who were favored by three, lost to the Redskins. His work spread on the coffee table before him, Bernard called the penalties in his favor, "Pass interference, Blackwood," before the officials did.

With the Redskins down by four going into the fourth, pacing, mumbling Bernard looked just as agonized as the coaches on the sidelines. Feverish, he felt an overwhelming desire to symmetrically arrange the sodas in the refrigerator. A Quaalude slipped the world into C minor and gave Bernard the power he needed to endure the game's pivotal moment when Washington, with time running out, ran its trademark play, the I-Right 70 Chip.

He'll hand to Riggins. Good hole! He's got the first down to the 40, the 30 . . .

Bernard's kneecaps melted.

HE'S GONE, HE'S GONE!!! TOUCHDOWN, Washington Redskins!!

At game's end, Bernard graded his work. Nine hundred thousand dollars richer, he flopped on the couch, let his jaw drop open in disbelief, and then smiled at the ceiling. On that cool, exhilarating evening, as light rain pattered the window and Natasha snuggled beside him, Bernard could not have foreseen that he would soon become obsessed with winning nine hundred thousand dollars every night, that he would immediately start dealing way too high, that his mathematical formulas would fail him, that he would see the piles of money go below three million, two million, and down to one point six, that desperation would send him chasing until the last pile of money had quickly dwindled down to the height of a book of matches, that within three weeks—three weeks!—of his legendary Super Bowl triumph he and Natasha, scared and stone broke, would be fighting in a roadside motel off I-95.

Greed is not a virtue. This wasn't news to Bernard, he had guessed as much. But what he hadn't guessed was that when his money left him, Natasha and his friends wouldn't be far behind. Or that he would find himself twenty-three, divorced, hundreds of thousands of dollars in debt, and working for his father. The people Bernard owed money to thought it was a cover. But it wasn't. Bernard had gone straight and was now in the wholesale candy business. Truffles and coconut clusters, maple-nut goodies and Lindt Swiss classics—Bernard used food to soothe the heartbreak and depression. The waists on his brown and gray work slacks continued to grow: forty inches, forty-six, fifty-two. He slid the hangers, searching for something, anything, that might fit, stopping just short of the full-length fur coat hanging, shredded and dead, in the very back of the closet.

"Hello, I'm a wholesaler," Bernard said to the store owners. "The products you sell, I have, so if you need anything, here's my card."

Squishing himself back into his Pontiac, he'd continue his commute.

With time, Bernard took the candy business from $185,000 a year to $18 million in volume. Eventually he remarried. After Natasha, his new even-tempered, dedicated wife was a blessing. They had a child and bought a home in suburban Long Island. Bernard enjoyed being a father; he liked coaching his son's sports teams. His parents, racked with worry when he was gambling, finally looked happy for him, and that made him feel good about himself. Everything was turning up wholesome; a strange twist to a life already marked by so many soaring highs and suicidal lows. At times, when he yearned for his gambling life, so charged with limitless possibility, he watched the movie *Trading Places*.

"Nothing you have ever experienced will prepare you for the absolute carnage you are about to witness," says Dan Aykroyd, during Bernard's favorite scene. "One minute you're up half a million in soybeans and the next, boom, your kids don't go to college and they've repossessed your Bentley. Are you with me?"

Watching the film gave Bernard hope and encouragement. He became a strong believer that people had the power to change. Human beings needn't worry, they will adapt to whatever situation they find themselves in. No matter how big the swing, the sensations will pass and the mind will adjust.

It was by accident, really, the night his wife brought home a computer and he stumbled across an Internet sports book. Oddly, the casino was based somewhere in Antigua and you could click on it. Bernard sent in three thousand dollars. For the first time in fifteen years, the harmless maniac made a bet.

*   *   *

"We're not cautious," I said to Bernard as I regained my composure.

I had overreacted to a loud crash in our neighbor's office. It was Maintenance doing construction. I thought it was a battering ram.

Working in the business, I sometimes imagined what it would be like if I were caught in an FBI raid. In my daydreams, I always had the luxury of seeing the police cars in the parking lot and having time to prepare myself. But BLT had no windows. I didn't like that at all. It made me jumpy.

"We're semi-cautious," Bernard said.

"Nuh-uh, Bernard. I saw you had Sarah making copies of our who-owes-who-what sheets. That's not cautious."

"You're making me nervous," Bernard said. "Let's change subjects."

He continued humming along with the Cher tape crackling from the boom box and I prepared our take-out Chinese lunch. After spooning fried rice onto his plate, I topped it with Hot Lover's Chicken and crispy noodles. A feast for a general, just the way he liked it.

"So," I said, sitting back at my desk, legs crossed. "Did you have any dreams last night?"

CHAPTER TEN

Infighting

The more you sweat in battle, the less you bleed in war. That's an idiom often heard in boxing gyms and one my teammates and I had in mind as we warmed up each evening by greasing our bodies with Albolene makeup remover, Saran-wrapping our waists, and shadowboxing in the ring. With each punch our breath quickened and by the end of the first round, our clothes were soaked.

Over the past three months my Golden Gloves journey had taken me to Coney Island rec centers and the blue-lit basements of Staten Island churches. Along with twenty other women, I would wait in bleakness for two, three hours while officials flipped through our boxing books, trying to arrange bouts according to weight and experience. Finally, a trainer, fellow boxer, or volunteer would explain that because our opponent had suffered an injury or a nervous breakdown or didn't make weight, or because there was no opponent to begin with, we had won! Hollow victories were embarrassing, but with limited competition what could one do? Such was the state of women's amateur boxing in 2003.

But at the semifinals, things changed for the better. Inside a rundown high school gymnasium, in front of a sparse crowd, I defeated my opponent so badly that her nose busted open, leaving her blond hair streaked with blood. Two weeks later I would be competing inside Madison Square Garden's legendary Felt Forum in the finals of the Golden Gloves.

I was ecstatic. This was the best thing that had happened to me in a long time and it felt good to have something big to look forward to. A teammate of mine was a Golden Gloves champ and he wore his gold (plated) Golden Gloves pendant around his neck everywhere he went. Once, he let me try it on. The miniature gloves felt cold and heavy against my chest. If I won a pair, I thought to myself, I would never take them off.

Ray, my trainer, eyed each of us and barked out instructions. "Yo, Felson, no good. Let your hands *go*. Anna, no good. Turn your waist. Yo, Raymer . . ."

Wanting to impress him, I picked up the pace, letting my hands go and turning my waist. His studious expression morphed into a look of concern. With the fat of his palm, he eased out the wrinkles in his forehead. "Outta the ring," he said.

Ray stepped on the two bottom ropes, pulled the top two up and I ducked through the opening and hopped onto the gym floor. "There's something I want to talk to you about," he said. Cupping his hand around the back of my neck, he steered me toward the mirrors on the back wall. He looked at me hard. "The woman you're going to fight. *Do-ming-a*."

On paper, my opponent, Dominga "La Tormenta," was twenty-six. In reality, she was thirty-one and was rumored to have fought professionally in the Dominican Republic before immigrating to New York. She'd been fighting on the amateur circuit for as long as Ray could remember, knocking girls out in all five boroughs, kissing her biceps while her vanquished opponents squirmed on all fours.

"This gorilla lands punches and believe me, the entire room feels 'em," Ray said. "I've only seen a few women make it past round two with her. That's not to say you couldn't do it. But what do you think about what I'm telling you?"

In his own subtle way, Ray was letting me know that I could forfeit the match and he would understand. Mismatches were one thing. A mismatch with a ringer in front of five thousand people and television cameras was something else.

I expressed to Ray the embarrassment I felt for making it to the finals after winning only one fight. If I won the gloves by beating the two-time defending champ, I would feel as though I'd actually earned something. Plus, I said, winning is a lot more fun when you beat someone good.

"You got it," Ray said. "Just wanted to give you a heads-up." He tightened the laces to my boxing gloves.

Looking for just a little more insight, I asked Ray to describe Dominga's fighting style.

"Thunderous," he said.

Over the next two weeks, fear sank its claws into the pit of my stomach and never let go. The feeling stayed with me during my lunch break when I ran laps in BLT's vast parking lot, and lingered throughout my nightly workouts, making me feel as restless and jumpy as the double-end bag after a good whopping. Lying in bed, I imagined myself in the ring with Dominga. Pivoting, ducking, slipping around her, landing body shots to her rib cage. Exhilarated by my imagined finesse, I'd hop out of bed and run to the bathroom so I could watch myself shadowbox in the reflection of the medicine cabinet mirror. Jab cross hook. Jab cross hook. And finish with the jab.

Dominga stood on the scale, naked. Around her, girls with buzz cuts ate energy bars. I usually found comfort in seeing my opponent's naked body at the weigh-ins. I could evaluate their muscle tone, and draw conclusions from their tattoos or stretch marks or C-section scars. Dominga's skin was flawless and she was built like a Mack truck. A vein the width of an earthworm started at the tip of her widow's peak and ran down the center of her scowling brown eyebrows, along the side of her neck, descending into her armpit and jutting out again, ending, finally, on the highest point of her biceps, which was as hard and round as a navel orange. Dropping my skirt, I reminded myself that boxing is the science of controlling fear.

"Remember, keep your right *up*," Ray said. He sat across from me and wrapped my hands. "Bang and bring it back. *Move.* Bang-bang. Not bang . . . bang. Bang-bang."

My cut man rubbed my shoulders. "Feelin' strong, kiddo?"

I wanted to say something, but I feared that if I opened my mouth I would vomit. My knee bounced up and down. I cursed myself for not calling immigration and having Dominga deported. She'd be on JetBlue by now, leg-cuffed and *la tormenting* someone else.

"We're losin' her," Ray said.

"You're not losing me!" I said. "I'm here! I'm thinking positive thoughts!"

An official peeked his head into the room and told us to start making our way to the ring.

In the hallway, waiting for the summons, I scanned the near-sold-out crowd of five thousand screaming, bloodthirsty fans squished into stadium seating. An amplified voice buzzed incoherently and for one fleeting moment, I felt the sudden excitement of having arrived at the place I'd dreamed of. I was smack in the middle of Manhattan, about to fight in one of the most famous boxing venues in the world. It was staggering. And I started to think just how awesome it would be if I actually won. Sure, Dominga had more experience than me, but I doubted she'd be in better shape. I was running seven miles a day and training six days a week. Pumped with sudden hope, I did a quick little bob and weave. Middle section, center right, I spotted my dad, Dink, Bernard, and Mikey, sitting side by side. They came all the way from Florida, Vegas, and Ronkonkoma, respectively. It was a big deal and I couldn't bear the thought of letting them down or embarrassing myself in front of them. Just the thought of it turned the swells and rolls of my nervous system into tsunami-sized waves and, once again, fear overshadowed all else. Now I understood why most boxers didn't invite anyone to their fights. The official motioned us toward the ring. "Here we go," Ray said. He continued shouting in my ear, but his words were lost in the raucous crowd.

In the gold corner, in vivid, living color, Dominga threw upper-cuts into the air and talked smack in rudimentary English. My breathing ceased.

The referee called us into the middle of the ring and spoke the ritual phrases. I rolled my head from shoulder to shoulder, a nervous tic more than anything else.

Back in my blue corner, head lowered, I stared at the canvas until I heard the ref shout, "Box!"

The first round served its purpose, allowing me to gain control of my nerves and even throw a few punches. Unreal, considering my gloves felt as heavy as anchors. It was round two that Dominga's haymakers began to come down on me. Another one, another one. Flush now. They connected with a dull thud, roughly the sound of a Mack truck hitting a cow.

When I returned to my stool in the corner, there didn't seem to be enough air. My top lip was so fat it was plugging one of my nostrils. I tasted blood. A lot can happen in two minutes.

"Open your eyes," Ray said, removing my mouthpiece. His voice was gentle. "Don't close your eyes in between rounds."

My eyes wouldn't open on their own. I raised my eyebrows to help them out. Still, only one of them opened all the way.

The heat from the TV camera light felt as hot as Vegas summer sunshine on my face. My cut man cold-pressed the eye that was swollen shut. "You're not throwin' enough punches," Ray said. "Stay in close and bang her up. Forget the head. Go to her body."

In the final round, Dominga's switch to southpaw came as an unwelcome shock. Solid smacks were followed by *ooohs* from the crowd. My hands began to droop. I felt heartbeats behind my eyes and all over my head. Out on my feet, but too in shape to actually go down, I heard the hollow, rushing sound that comes when you place your ear to a seashell. It's not the sound of the ocean, after all, but the sound of a boxer's brain swelling in a ring far, far away.

*　　*　　*

The early morning was gray and cloudy. At least it was to me. Walking up Flatbush Avenue to catch the 7:39 to Ronkonkoma, I was grateful to have a coffee in my hand and the fight behind me. Pain had hindered my sleep and I was just now beginning to feel the fight's fatigue. Parts of my face shined eggplant purple. With one eye swollen shut, my vision was too impaired for me to sprint across the intersection in front of approaching traffic as I normally did. Amid the hyperactive schoolchildren and the angry cabbies shouting from car to car, I waited for the signal, patiently.

"Ho-ly!" said one of the construction workers. The rest of the crew turned, looked at me, and snapped their heads back. The same guys had been working on the corner since I moved into the neighborhood. Every day they waved and smiled, complimenting me on one thing or another. But today there were no compliments. I waved.

One of the crew walked toward me. His orange hard hat roofed sweaty, concerned eyebrows. "Give me his address," he said. "I don't need no name, no description, nothin'. I'll know the monster when I see him."

In the time it took me to grasp what he was getting at, he pulled a pencil from behind his ear and jotted his phone number onto the napkin wrapped around my to-go cup.

"You don't want to tell me now, no problem, I understand," he said. "You call me when you're ready and I'll be there."

"Thanks," I said, stuffing the number into my pocket. You never knew when an offer like that could come in handy.

As usual I was the only person in the train car, worming out to the Island while millions of others bustled their way into Manhattan. Resting against the window, one eye open to the burst of blooms and greenery, I tried to think of anything else I had to look forward to now that the big fight had flopped.

My father's deep tan, lazy pace, and genuine crocodile-skin boots set him apart from the flows of midtown professionals passing us on the sidewalk. But what really pinned him as a bona fide Floridian was his surprise reaction once we walked inside the bar.

"Where's everybody at, Bethananna?" he said, looking around the dark, empty space. It wasn't even noon. But back at his hangouts along Fort Myers Beach, the bars would already be packed.

He held up two fingers and shouted "Beer!" to the bartender.

It was Dad's first time in New York and he wasn't impressed. He found the women stuck-up and the city loud, overpriced, and cold. He was disappointed in me, he said. Not because I had lost, or wasn't doing anything long term with my life, but because I was choosing to live "in the snow." Twenty years ago, my parents made many sacrifices to move their young family from a small coal-mining town in eastern Ohio to the sunny climes of Florida. Dad understood my move to Las Vegas. Who wouldn't want to live in Vegas? But to leave him and the Sunshine State for New York was a flagrant act of betrayal. Our backs to the street, he lectured me.

"Winter's for poor people, Beth Anne. You have money, you get out. You can waste an entire life shovelin' snow. You and Mr. Otis need to come home."

The bartender set our beers in front of us. I pressed the frosty mug to my puffy cheek and held it there, like an ice pack.

"Dad, there's nowhere for me to work in Florida. I like my job here, with Bernard."

"You got a college degree. Use it. Be a teacher."

"Dad." I turned to him, slowly. My neck was sprained. "Do I look like I have anything to teach?"

"Don't matter. Florida schools, they'll take anybody."

Nothing. Silence. When his shoulders wilted and he cast his eyes downward, I understood where this conversation was headed.

"Your sister's back in the slammer," he said.

My sister's problems had existed for so long that declarations such as these no longer came as a surprise. What pained me, though, was bearing witness to the ongoing misery her problems caused my parents. After the divorce, my dad went through a lot of changes. He lost weight and grew a beard. He began drinking cosmopolitans and smoking Virginia Slims menthol cigarettes. An attempt, I think, albeit unconscious, to get in touch with his feminine side. And it worked! For the first time in my life, I had a father who actually signed birthday cards (instead of just sending them off in the mail, blank), and spoke about his feelings. Sometimes he was only able to mutter one sentiment at a time—Sad. Hurt.—kind of like a caveman. But other times he could be very emotional. Now was one of those times.

"The daughter I know is gone. Poof!" He twisted the corner of the cocktail napkin. "I've tried to get her work at dealerships, she used to be great on the switchboard, but she can't hold down a job anymore. I'm scared we're gonna lose her."

"Dad, I'm sorry." I touched his arm. "Is bail going to be expensive?"

"I don't know what else to do for her. Those rehabs don't give a shit about people. They just want money."

"Dad. Rehabs can work. The trick is, you have to stay awhile. She checks in and by lunchtime she's gone."

"She don't need any more doctors putting shit in her head, Beth Anne. She needs family. You're her sister, you should be helping her. But, hey, if you'd rather stay in the cold with the terrorists and get beat up, it's up to you."

The guilt trip worked. They usually did, even though I knew better. After all, I was the only one on speaking terms with everyone else in the family. My sister didn't speak to my mother and my parents didn't speak to each other, and since I spoke to everyone, I was well aware of their worries and struggles. Dad still wasn't paying my mom alimony. Knowing she spent most of her time pecking at a calculator, living in paralyzing fear of an unexpected bill, Dad would call her, drunk, and tell her about his young date and the surf-and-turf dinners they enjoyed out on the gambling boat.

And then there was my sister. When she wasn't waking up in jail cells, she lived with an abusive drug addict who had a Lee Press-On Nail for a front tooth. I was so scared of him and their dreary living conditions that I no longer visited her. Accepting her collect calls at two in the morning, I'd listen to her cries turn to howls as she pleaded with God to give her the strength to blow her brains out and put an end to the paranoid nightmare that was her life.

She could stay in manic states like that for hours, her screams coming through the receiver and piercing my eardrums as though she were being stabbed to death.

Coming down, she'd say how much she loved me. Later, when the drugs were gone and withdrawal set in, she'd threaten to have me killed unless I sent her twenty-eight dollars, Western Union.

Between the three of them, my loyalties and anger would get so confused that I didn't know who to be mad at or who to pity, who was lying or who was telling the truth, who to send money to, or who to spend Christmas with. And though my father's tormenting of my mother and endless promotion of the guilt trip gave me plenty of opportunities to put him in his place, I rarely did. Because, as the years went by, it became more and more obvious that out of all of us, it was Dad who missed having a family the most. After the divorce, and post–Brenda Baby, he moved not into a beachfront condo like he'd been telling everyone he would, but into a sturdy three-bedroom house he named the Raymer Ranch. Everything he bought for the house was family-sized: the couches and pool floats, boxes of cereal and shampoo. It was as though he believed he was holding down the fort until whatever misunderstandings passed and we all returned home.

And after the evenings spent eating lobster with his latest girlfriend and the drunken, mean-spirited phone calls to my mother, Dad would settle into the little corner of his three-piece sectional couch and watch home videos he had shot when we first moved to Florida. With the remote resting on his belly and the side of his face nudged into a pillow, he'd fall asleep to the family sounds of "A Raymer Christmas, 1983."

I understood that my father's guilt trip was really a plea for me to come home so that he wouldn't be alone. At moments like these, when I was forced to admit to myself just how defeated and broken my family was, how absolutely alone each of us were, I felt a violent hacking through the center of my brain, like a butcher's knife, digging in and dividing my thoughts, leaving half of me desperate to make my father's, my mother's, and especially my sister's life easier, to never leave them again. The other half demanded I pack up my shit immediately and run.

My mood was now so low I found it hard to keep my head raised. Noticing this, Dad nudged me: his way of apologizing.

"Forget about it, Beth Anne. Don't let your sister get you down."

"She didn't get me down. You got me down."

We looked at our beers, not each other.

"Your old man's just depressed, that's all."

"Dad, I'll come home."

"When?"

I tried to imagine when I'd be truly ready to return to Florida and help, once and for all. At what age did life begin to seem unspectacular? Forty-three, I decided.

"In 2019," I said.

"We'll all be dead by then," he said.

"Nobody will be dead. Just old. I'll be the caretaker." I'd never heard myself sound more depressed. "Do you have money for the jukebox?"

He tossed his wallet onto the bar. It, too, was made of crocodile skin.

"We're staying here all day," I said, pulling out a fifty-dollar bill.

"Fine with me, Bethananna."

To everyone's astonishment but my own, I continued to box. At twenty-six, I understood that boxing should've been an exciting, healthy *supplement* to my life as opposed to its centerpiece. But to me, and every other woman over the age of nineteen who was involved in the sport, it served as the ultimate distraction from life's dilemmas and complexities. I cherished it for that reason.

The one thing I had in my life that I did look forward to was returning home from a long day of gambling in Ronkonkoma to find my roommate standing over the stove, lovingly whipping up an exotic dessert—some *Brigadeiro,* some zabaglione—while reading Sartre in French or translating poetry from Portuguese or watching a film in Italian. The daughter of a Brazilian United Nations officer, Carolina had traveled all over the world and lived, it seemed, in most of it. As a result, she was fluent in six languages and spoke with an unrecognizable accent. I had met her four years earlier, in Las Vegas, where she was a student at Nick's Blackjack School. To work as a casino dealer was one of her secret fantasies.

At night in Brooklyn, Carolina and I listened to bossa nova records from our rusty fire escape while planning exotic vacations. She brought the cigarettes, the South American maps, and fascinating stories, and we devised a road trip from northern Chile to Rio de Janeiro. "Let's just make sure we end up here," I said, adorning Ipanema Beach with a doodle.

I would've been very happy to spend every evening on the fire escape soaking my sore knuckles and studying Brazilian road maps, but on occasion Carolina and I did venture out of the apartment. One night, while visiting a friend of hers, the three of us smoked pot and watched his collection of music videos from the sixties. Suddenly, the most gorgeous man I had ever seen appeared on the screen. His thick, dark hair was slicked back and he was dressed as a sailor. In the beat just before he began to sing, he smiled, shooting a primal energizing force through the room. Opening our mouths, Carolina and I let out the high-pitched screams of oversexed teenagers.

"I've never felt this way before!" I said, barely finding the energy to finish my sentence.

"Who is this," Carolina gasped, ". . . *god* of a man?"

"Frank Sinatra Jr.," said the friend, unimpressed.

"What do you mean?" I said, confused. "Is Frank Sinatra Jr. . . . Frank Sinatra?"

"No," said the friend.

"He must've had a son!" Carolina said. And to this realization, Carolina and I embraced and fell backward onto the bed. We were so stoned.

"What's up with the Beatlemania?" said the lean figure standing in the doorway. His blue eyes shined as though they were lit from within. I watched him situate himself in the corner chair and roll a cigarette. His messy, nut-brown hair and long lashes added softness to his angular face. I liked his freckles.

Sliding his fingers toward the middle of the rolling papers, he gave the tobacco a final twist. One smooth lick and the cigarette was taken care of. He shook the fire from the match and noticed I was staring.

"I'm Jeremy," he said. "The roommate."

Jeremy was in graduate school at Columbia, studying journalism. He'd been in the room next door, grappling with his thesis, until our screams disrupted him. He only stayed long enough to finish his cigarette and make some jokes about the videos, which made me laugh. Leaving the apartment that night, I walked past his bedroom. Looking a little depressed, he sat on his bed. Head tilted and pout tense; he played bluegrass on his acoustic guitar. He impressed me without meaning to.

From that night forward, I tried to stay in Jeremy's life. I left awkward, giggly messages on his cell phone, inviting him to my fights. He didn't come. I left more messages, inviting him to parties. He didn't show. In the month after his graduation, I'd heard that he was recovering from shoulder surgery and I invited myself over. Taking cues from Carolina's sophisticated tastes, I put together a gift basket of Belgian beers, dark chocolates with orange bits, and a CD of my favorite songs. Propped up on a pillow and tucked into crisp white cotton sheets, Jeremy lay, glassy-eyed from painkillers. Because he couldn't move his arm away from his body, or wear deodorant, the room smelled strongly of body odor. Not an unpleasant smell.

I set his gifts on the nightstand. As he looked up at me, his long lashes touched the tips of his bangs.

"Can I massage your shoulder?" I said.

"No," he said.

And that was the extent of our romantic dialogue.

I probably—*probably*—would've stopped imposing my feelings at that point. Except, on occasion, Jeremy did call me. I sensed in his voice and well-mannered conversation that he was open to getting to know me. Or maybe he just liked being so enthusiastically adored by me. Either way, over the next year, something sweet happened. We became friends. At first, it seemed, he called or stopped by only when he was feeling downhearted. Like when a job interview didn't go well or a story he pitched had been rejected. Otis won him over, however, and soon Jeremy was stopping by even when he was in a good mood. Like when his date with a pretty Korean reporter ended with a sunrise tryst inside a phone booth.

I wasn't put off when Jeremy spoke about being with other women. In fact, I often initiated the more intimate talks. His last two relationships had ended quite badly, leaving him brokenhearted. I thought, maybe, if I knew what went wrong, I could make it better. "And what is it about her you like so much?" I heard myself saying as we sat at the cozy kitchen table, Otis at our feet. I listened to the details of his failed love life as carefully as an intruder listening for footsteps.

Over the passing months, even more miraculous than my continuing ability to keep my feelings to myself was the fact that Jeremy never bored me. Which confused me, because he was incredibly steadfast and rational—virtues I had always (wrongly) considered dull. But his moods, as constant as daylight, separated him from any other person I'd ever had or attracted into my life. My family, friends, ex-boyfriends, bosses, not to mention my lifestyle and the kinds of jobs I'd always gravitated toward, had one thing in common: precariousness. Jeremy's dependability was so far removed from my life that I found him exotic.

Friends thought it was strange. I was after a cute Jewish kid from Pittsburgh who studied religion at Vassar, traveled from the Terai to the Himalayas, became fluent in Tibetan, and now daydreamed of returning home, buying the *Pittsburgh Tribune-Review* from Richard Mellon Scaife, getting control of the editorial page, and then announcing his candidacy for the Senate.

But for now, Jeremy was just a lowly cub reporter, and sometimes Otis and I tagged along while he did his reporting. Standing to the side of the double homicide-suicide crime scene, I watched him question the detective. Beside the smashed noses and bald heads of the *Daily News* and *Post* reporters, Jeremy looked young and sweet, though his demeanor was just as aggressive. Wearing black corduroys and a frayed sweater, he took notes and names in his reporter's notebook and it occurred to me that I had never met someone so ethical. Not once did I hear Jeremy tell a lie. He didn't even exaggerate. When he was four years old, he helped himself to a pack of Hubba Bubba from the grocery store. It was the only time he ever stole anything and twenty-five years later he couldn't repeat the story without blushing. His interest in social justice led him to journalism, which he viewed as a creative way to serve the community.

"Wow," Jeremy once said, as he watched me prepare for a pay and collect. "You're so quick at counting money."

He found my gambling jobs intriguing even though, for a long time, he couldn't grasp exactly what it was I did. Trying to understand, he bombarded me with questions, but I was so unaccustomed to articulating how the gamblers made money that everything I said sounded like gibberish.

"Okay, let's take it a step back," he said. "Tell me what *you* do. How do *you* make money?"

"I told you. I get the donuts."

Unconvinced, he looked at me. "Is that code for something?"

"No. Every morning I get Boston creams. A limo picks me up."

"But how come you go to doctors' offices with thick rolls of money?"

"Because I'm paying and collecting."

"Beth," he said, switching to his professorial voice. "I'm going to ask you a question and don't get mad. Will you please let me help you get health insurance?"

Practical, intelligent, kind, and adventurous, Jeremy certainly had a lot going for him. But, to be honest, his positive qualities weren't what held my interest. What drove me absolutely crazy with determination was his extreme criticalness and aloofness. I never seemed to please Jeremy and it was hard to make him laugh. As our friendship developed, I don't know how many times I pulled a newspaper from his face or stood in front of the television, blocking *The NewsHour with Jim Lehrer*, and demanded his attention.

On the night Jeremy presented Otis with his very own press pass, I went to sleep thinking, for certain, that he was the love of my life.

Then I changed my mind.

We were on the Q train during rush hour, standing clear of the closing doors, standing so close that if I'd lifted my nose, we could've kissed.

"I went on a date last night," I said, over the stagnant smell of urine.

"How was it?" Jeremy said. He admired a young woman softly singing with her iPod.

"Fun," I said, though it hadn't been fun at all.

"Did he ask you to go home with him?"

Jeremy's question took me by surprise. As much as we talked about flings, it was always me asking him about his love life. Until now, he had never asked about mine.

"No," I said. "We had a late dinner and then he put me in a cab and I went home."

He looked at me. His blue eyes shined against the monochromatic sludge of shoulder-to-shoulder beige raincoats.

"He put you in a cab? How'd you finagle that one?"

I knew there were things about me that got on Jeremy's nerves. My intellectual shyness made it hard to have in-depth conversations. I had no interest in politics or current events. He often felt that I laughed *at* him, as opposed to with him, which was true. But it never occurred to me that he didn't even find me worthy of cab fare. Something told me he would never have said that to his women friends from Columbia. As I was taught in elementary school, I took a deep breath and counted to ten. Not that it helped my anger subside.

"I didn't have to finagle it, fuckhead."

"Beth, calm down."

"You're an asshole. You really are."

Jeremy sucked in his cheeks, hesitating before he spoke. "You're taking it the wrong way."

"No I'm not," I said.

Off the Q and up the steps, back across the platform, trains rumbled overhead, and I dwelled on all the things I absolutely hated about Jeremy. At the apartment, I bad-mouthed him to Carolina. He called the next morning. I would've poked my eyes out if he hadn't.

He asked that I meet him at the Metropolitan Museum of Art. Eating our lunch on the museum's steps, the smell of honey-roasted peanuts cooking from a nearby street cart, Jeremy didn't bring up our subway tiff and I was glad. Watching him gently unwrap the snacks he had made for us, it occurred to me that I probably had taken his comment the wrong way. Interpreting it the way I had probably said more about me than it did about Jeremy.

"I had a vision while walking in the subway tunnel between Eighth and Seventh Avenue," Jeremy said. "I pictured a mad gunman pulling a pistol out and pointing it at someone. Everyone ran, except for me." He handed me a cupcake.

"You made these? For us?" I said.

"Yeah."

"Jeremy! I love them!"

"Well, why don't you taste them first?" He continued with his story. "So, I kicked the gun out of the guy's hand just as he shot it and I saved the other person. The gunman and I fell to the floor and I pried the gun from his hands. Then the cameras came and I was made a superhero. The mayor cut me a check for ten grand and I put it in savings."

"You put money in savings even in daydreams?" I said.

An affectionate couple with a radio sat beside us. Overhearing the last licks of a Led Zeppelin rock block, I felt no desire to go inside the museum and admire still lifes with apples and oranges.

"It'll be boring inside," I said. "Let's stay out here and talk about hopes and dreams."

"We can't," Jeremy said. "There's someone I want you to meet. Zoe. She'll be here in a few minutes."

"Zoe?" I said with a wince. Thinking if that was not the most obnoxious yuppie name on the face of this planet, I didn't know what was.

"I think you'll like her," Jeremy said. "I hope you'll like her."

Then came Zoe, in newsboy cap, emerging from the windy afternoon with puckered kisses. I pulled myself to my feet as Jeremy introduced us. Like Jeremy, Zoe was underweight and lightly freckled. In the gray light of the winter sky, her northeast-pale complexion reminded me of oyster meat. Her teeth were sharp.

"Zoe's in design," Jeremy said, initiating conversation.

"Like, T-shirts and coffee mugs?" I said.

"Uhm . . . no," she said.

"Beth has some great logo ideas for T-shirts," he said to Zoe. Then to me: "Tell her about your ideas."

I would never understand him, I thought. "I have no ideas," I said.

Jeremy smiled numbly. An actor working alone. I did not sympathize.

"Beth works for a professional gambler," Jeremy said to Zoe.

"Yikes," Zoe said.

A prolonged silence followed. Zoe in design cocked her head to the side and brushed Jeremy's bangs from his eyes. Something I'd wanted to do all day.

Goose-bumped from the cold, I untwisted the scarf from my throat and sank helplessly into my work chair. Bernard whirled an electronic nose-hair clipper inside his nostril. His long, loose cheeks wavered from the vibrations.

"I'm running away," he said over the gadget's faint buzz. "I'm getting the fat person's surgery then I'm running away."

Bernard had just returned from Curaçao, an island in the Caribbean, which he jetted off to every few weeks to work as a bookie-in-residence at Pinnacle, one of the most successful offshore sports books. During the visit, Bernard had made a mistake while setting odds for a college basketball game. At tip-off, the owner of Pinnacle angrily realized that if Columbia happened to beat Penn, a 26-point favorite, he would lose half a million dollars. At the first score of the game—2 to 0, Columbia—Bernard got so scared he ran out of the place. Penn ended up winning by thirty, but the owner, infuriated with Bernard for leaving, punished him by moving him to the NASCAR department.

"NASCAR!" Bernard said, switching the clipper to the other nostril. "Trading NASCAR is, like, the biggest snub in the face ever! I can't work for that guy anymore."

But Bernard reveled in the carefree Caribbean lifestyle, and was looking for any excuse he could find to stay in Curaçao. So the plan he came up with was this: after undergoing gastric bypass surgery, he would open an offshore sports book of his own. In Curaçao, right down the street from Pinnacle's headquarters. For an investment of six hundred thousand dollars, he had already secured computers, bandwidth, and a license. He'd rented a ranch house for the American employees, complete with a maid and cook.

"I'd like you to be part of the venture," Bernard said. "Part of the team."

I looked at Bernard as though I had just witnessed a lion jump through a hoop of fire. Life! One minute you're lovesick and a little queasy from the early morning commute. The next, you're offered a job in the Caribbean. Six grand a month, under the table, all expenses included.

With the mention of money, everything became possible again. It wasn't Ipanema Beach, but I *was* getting closer. Immediately, I decided I'd buy the most expensive, shimmery Brazilian-cut bikini I could find to celebrate my good fortune. And as far as New York was concerned, I was happy to leave. More and more I saw the city not as a place where big dreams come true and no one sleeps, but as an exceptionally diverse prison under constant riot control. I hugged Bernard with the enthusiasm of a criminal who had just beaten a life sentence on a technicality.

"Aren't you excited?" I said, sinking into his hot, soft body. "You're going to be skinny! Why didn't you tell me any of this earlier? Why are you so secretive? It's not like you."

"My mind-set's a little different these days. It's set on a ledge, my mind." He talked quickly and looked anxious. I flattened myself against the wall so Bernard had more room to pace the floor of our tiny office. "I don't know if I'm going to make money, lose money. If I'll be able to enjoy fat-free, sugar-free pudding. I haven't told my wife that I'm going to Curaçao and I don't think I'm ever going to."

As the countdown started to his surgery date, Bernard called gambling clients. "I'm going to be the new MGM," he said. "Anything you wanna bet, any amount, you bet with me. I'm gonna have the best, most juicy odds in the business."

He blackened the boxes on his desk calendar. Ten more days until the new you. Nine more days until the new you.

It would be easy, here, to simplify my relationship with Jeremy by saying I was infatuated with him, he ignored me, and then all of a sudden, we fell in love. What's missing in that narrative is that I never knew what he saw in me. But as the time grew closer for me to leave, we began quarreling like the lovers we weren't and making up with impulsive kisses like the lovers we were slowly becoming.

"I am so fucking bored with the women I'm dating," Jeremy said during an atypical moment of self-disclosure. "I could never be friends with them. All I do is compare them to you. I'm always interested in what you have to say."

"Jeremy, that's kind of weird," I said, nervously, feeling that perhaps at some point I had accidentally misrepresented myself. "I'm not smart."

"I don't know why you say that," he said, pulling me onto his lap. "Maybe you're not book smart, but I don't think book smart is appealing. You're wise. Not about everything. But when you're an old woman you'll be wise about a lot of things."

He made me feel intelligent and interesting! I loved him! We held hands along the river and through Chinatown's dingy alleyways. At tables for four we sat side by side exchanging childhood stories and confessing every secret. I brought up the subject of my in-house stripping at Nightmoves. Beginning the conversation delicately enough, I got a bit carried away while explaining the intricacies of performing for one of my favorite customers, a polio victim.

Finishing my story, I looked up from my shrimp dumplings just in time to see the blood race from Jeremy's face.

"That, I feel, is very disgusting," he said.

"You said you liked my detail-oriented stories," I said.

"Well, not that one."

"It's not disgusting, Jeremy. If you ever got polio, wouldn't you like to call someone and have them come over and hang out with you?"

"I just didn't know that about you, Beth. I didn't suspect that about you. But, I guess it's always good to have your assumptions challenged."

"Much better. I hated you and now I like you again."

"It was insensitive, I'm sorry. I'm very confused by this whole topic. Let's order more dim sum."

And this was very typical of Jeremy and me. One second, love fest; the next, love dispossessed. Quick, fiery overreactions closely followed by apologies. No grievance that couldn't be laughed or kissed away. I'd never felt as happy as I felt with Jeremy and the feeling wasn't leaving. Three whole weeks of being romantic with the same person and the feeling was not leaving.

"I'm worried you're going to be arrested," he said, looking forlorn on the morning of my flight. "You're going to go out one night and have fun only to be arrested in the morning."

"I'm pretty sure that won't happen," I said, packing my suitcase.

"I'm worried your car is going to go off a cliff. Are there cliffs where you're going?"

Killing time as we waited for the taxi, Jeremy played me a bluegrass song on his guitar. He sang in a voice high and lonesome. Something about a sad good-bye and a maiden longing for a home that is no longer there.

CHAPTER ELEVEN

All Serious Action Players

The air was so moist you could drink it.

Trade winds stirred the fronds of tall, leaning palms and whipped through the rolled-down windows of our company car, a Lincoln Town Car, long and white as a speedboat. Bernard navigated the washed-out roads lined with cacti and I found it hard not to stare at him. His pillowy chest and the loose flesh of his face and neck had vanished. He was almost thin! Yet he seemed only dimly aware of his body's resized dimensions. Still assuming a seat belt wouldn't fit, he didn't wear one. To accommodate a doubling stomach that was no longer there, he had the seat reclined as far as possible and the steering wheel tilted to its highest angle. He hadn't even bothered to buy clothes that fit. His oversized T-shirt slipped off one shoulder and he kept his shorts up by gripping the waist in a bunch.

Tanned Dutch girls in bikini tops zoomed by in rental cars. In the shadow of a dilapidated Colonial mansion, paint shedded from the fluted columns like bark from a tree and Rastafarians played dominoes. "My favorite nail salon!" Bernard said, pointing to a sun-scorched bungalow. "Wish we had time for a mani pedi." He held out his hand to check on his cuticles. "Are you seeing how skinny my fingers are? This surgery's been good for me. Except for last night. I blew a game and couldn't eat anything to make myself feel better. Just had to sit there like a normal human being. Torture! But I notice I have more stamina for gambling, so I can't complain."

The road curved and I caught my first glimpse of the Caribbean Sea. Its glistening turquoise roused me like a forceful, unexpected kiss. "I can't believe we live here!" I said. Then, louder, over the wind: "How do I get to the beach?"

"No idea," Bernard said. "But I'm sure you'll find it."

Bernard had been on the island for nearly a month. Except for his left arm, glowing crimson from hanging out the driver's-side window, his skin was as white as a fresh Ronkonkoma snowfall.

"I want you to enjoy your life down here," he continued. "There's a lot of bosses out there who want you to be miserable. It's a bit of their strategy. Like when I sold the candy business in '93, I went to work for this company selling gourmet nuts. My boss couldn't stand that I was happy. And I wasn't even happy! Oh my God, look. The animals."

I thought Bernard was being racist until I looked over and saw wild goats grazing a church parking lot. Bernard locked the doors.

"I know you like your adventures. You're like my first wife. As long as there was some degree of thrill she was happy. Just make sure you're at work by eight o'clock. I depend on you to get everything set up. Other than that, there's really no whaddayacallems."

"Rules?"

"Yeah, no rules. Girl Friday, dream therapist, thrill seeker. That's you."

Bernard named the sports book ASAP, for All Serious Action Players. For months I'd heard the acronym being tossed around in abstract ways. As in: *A-sap is going to deal very thin, with special emphasis on alternate spreads.* Or, *Where most sports books deal a money line three hundred, come back two-fifty, A-sap will deal it two-eighty-nine, come back two-sixty-one.* I thought of ASAP more as a pattern of firing synapses in Bernard's brain than an actual place of business. So it took me a few moments to respond to the charming two-story house covered in bougainvillea that was, in fact, ASAP.

Up the quarried marble stairs and through the French doors, I followed Bernard into an outbreak of nervous fluorescent lights, a dizzying number of ringing telephones, and high-definition blue emanating from dozens of flat-paneled computer screens. At ten minutes to post, it was the busiest time of day. Wiseguys scrambled to protect their bets and squares wanted action on the televised games. News broke of a thunderstorm in Florida and Bernard dashed for his desk. Briefcase bouncing at his side, free hand gripping his waistband, flip-flops falling off his feet, he made low buzzing sounds as he lowered the Marlins total. Keeping true to his nickname, the Industrial Sander increased his voltage.

Behind a long curving desk lined with keyboards and monitors sat the "Italian crew," a moody, thickset, elbow-to-elbow syndicate of Tonys, Vinnys, Genos, and Jimmys from Philly and far Long Island. In front of them stretched rows of Afro-Caribbean clerks sitting at individual desks. Sufficiently tall—the Dutch genetic imprint—with the upright postures of aristocrats, the clerks gracefully switched from one phone to the other. They shouted questions and the frenzied Italian crew shouted back. The rushing and the accents led to some confusion.

"Do we want de Dollars or de dog?"

"Youse guys gotta listen up! The Dollars are the dog! "

"I don't understand shit what dis Chinese mother *focker* is askeeng me. I don't know if he have no teeth or what."

"Transfer him, line three."

Once everyone fell into rhythm, voices were only raised to ask Bernard for counsel. Staring slack-jawed at the projection screen hanging in the middle of the room, he watched color-coded bets roll in from over the Internet: one thousand, five thousand, and ten thousand dollars in red, white, and blue.

"Pepe de Cuban looking for Milkmen *on*der seventeen, *on*der for one-nine dimes."

"Howie Pork Chop crying my *fock*ing ear off. Wants Gringos minus run and a half minus forty. Say he don't give a *fock* if it's forty-tree."

Even though I knew there were other sports books on the island and that most of our clerks came to ASAP with several years' experience, hearing them throw around bookie jargon with such aplomb made me smile. For most of them, English was their fourth language, a technical language they used to earn a living, but along the way they'd invented their own patois. On this barren, thirty-eight-mile-long rock in the middle of the sea, the Dodgers were the Dollars, the Yankees the Gringos, and Milwaukee the Milkmen. It was exciting to see a whole new group of young people stretching my language and making it theirs. In my head, I picked out those I hoped would be my friends.

"Dookie say he knowed de peetching changes," said a young man in the front row. "Asking for twenty dime on *Tom*pa Bay over de yo."

"Yo" is actually a craps term for the number eleven. Despite his "Jesus Is Lord" baseball cap, the clerk had clearly been around a lot of gambling.

Abruptly, as though a ghost had snuck up from behind and spooked him, Bernard jumped into motion: "Check on Motown! Check on the Cuban! Give HPC . . . fuck, we're buried on that game. Give Pork Chop five dimes minus the forty. Now! No one talk for two point two seconds. Complete silence! I need to know right now who's sweating the Cubbies? Who's my sweater?"

Generally speaking, gamblers can be very superstitious. But it seemed to me that Bernard was steadily becoming insane. He believed that watching games brought bad luck so he turned off the TVs hanging from the ceiling and hid the remotes. A strong believer in the power of telepathy, he took the most incompetent employees and, instead of firing them, established a team of "sweaters." While everyone else answered phones, took bets, and made bets, the sweaters were paid (eight dollars an hour, plus benefits) to sit in silence, stare at yahoosports.com, and telepathically root for the need. The only time the sweaters were permitted to speak was when the game ended and they reported the score. God help them if they didn't say the winning team first.

An older, unhurried gentleman raised his hand. "I sweating de Cobbies, Mr. Bernard."

"Ronald, yesssss!" Bernard said, pumping his fist. "Guys six and oh in sweating preseason. Keep up the good work, Ronald. ONE MINUTE TO POST!"

Over the course of the next minute, the telephones must've rung seventy times. Sweat trickled from Bernard's hairline and his breath came in short gasps. "And quick, before I suffer a brain hemorrhage. Everybody meet Beth. She works here. Her laugh is on a ten-second game delay so don't feel bad if she doesn't get your jokes right away."

The clerks looked at me, intrigued. They'd seen plenty of gringa wives and girlfriends come to visit. But only the men came to work. I think they assumed I was either Bernard's daughter or mistress. When they greeted me, contorting their faces, it looked almost painful for them to pronounce the *th* in Beth, so we settled on Betty.

First pitches took the games off the board. Three-quarters of the room headed for the smoking porch, unlit cigarettes dangling from their lips. Fifteen-hour workdays were not uncommon, thus the crew's only breath of fresh air came filtered through a Marlboro red. Jaundiced yet relieved, Bernard collapsed into his chair. He washed down Xanaxes with lukewarm Nescafé and dripped Visine into his eyes. In Bernard's mind, ASAP was a five-year project. Five years of high, high intensity, then he would sell it, perhaps to Pinnacle, our competition down the street. But as I watched his eyelids sink, lower, lower, as slow and fluid as a bottle drifting to the bottom of an ocean floor, I wondered how he'd be able to last that long. Five years in the vacuum of high-stakes offshore gambling is like thirty years in any other line of work. After all, Internet gambling doesn't close on weekends or holidays. It exists 24 hours, 365 days a year. A mere two weeks into preseason baseball and already Bernard looked sickly and spent. I never dreamt I'd say this, but he needed to put on some weight.

By the four o'clock games, he'd recovered. His eyes, as wide and clear as those of any expert in his element, darted from one game to the next. He formulated mathematical probabilities and barked orders no one dared question. At a moment of peak intensity, the forty, fifty bets that came in *per minute* were the size of mortgages and yearly salaries. In the midst of the commotion, drunk on the adrenaline-testosterone cocktail—the house specialty—everyone managed to keep their head. Inspired by the sheer absorption, I sidled beside the Italian crew, grabbed a phone, and joined them.

We lived in a house so fancy it had a name: Quinta Cindy. Quinta Cindy's walls opened to a lush garden landscape, allowing in the breeze and yellow-bellied birds looking for places to nest. Sunshine covered every square inch of the mahogany floors, and from the hammocks on the wide veranda you could smell the sea, just one mile away. I shared this lovely, tranquil spot with the Italian crew, who in their paranoia briefly believed I was a private detective working on behalf of their wives, and Lionel, a McDonald's drive-thru clerk Bernard hired one morning on the fly. Highly self-conscious and quick to criticize, Lionel had the squat build of a wrestling coach and shoulders like granite boulders. He wore sapphire pinky rings, chain bracelets, and a heavy gold necklace from which hung a fist-sized horse medallion. It thumped against his chest as he walked. You could hear Lionel coming before he turned the corner.

Bernard brought dozens of characters over from the mainland to work at ASAP, but one thing stayed the same: I was the only woman. Having spent the last four years working in sports gambling (not to mention my boxing and in-home stripping), I felt I had spent enough time in the company of men to become inured to their waywardness. But I hadn't. In the States, desires pushed up against social mores and familial responsibility. Fear of the law tempered the scope of their gambling and drug use. They could cheat on their wives, sure. But they still had to be home by eight to tuck in the kids. In Curaçao, I witnessed complete unbridling of these desires. The heat's sensuality; young, exotic women, topless beaches, the soft swells of buttocks; Heinekens served in seven-ounce pony bottles, the perfect size for ensuring cold beer to the last drop; inexpensive, high-quality cocaine and hookers: the lifestyle was all set up. All you had to do was get there.

The looks the men exchanged made it clear. They couldn't quite believe their newfound freedom. The money Bernard offered them was so astronomical that even their wives couldn't say no. But had their wives actually said yes? Had the words *Go, honey. I'll take care of the kids* really crossed their lips?

They had. And once the men overcame their initial shyness and stopped brooding over their receding hairlines, their inhibitions broke free like long-awaited exhales. Most waitresses, and any Venezuelan hooker, totally unhinged them. Loud, grunting, wild sex. They'd almost forgotten what it was like to participate in it, and not just stare at it on a screen. Returning from their lunch breaks flushed and dazed, lost in a mélange of body scents, they splayed across the carpet and stared at the ceiling, as though they had just plunged down a sloping field of wildflowers and needed a moment to recover.

But no one—no one—fell harder for a woman than Bernard Rose fell for Maritza de los Santos.

ASAP happened to be having a meeting at Club Havana—the cheap open-air strip club where all executive decisions were made—the night Maritza first took the floor. Her nervous, unvarying dance moves made it clear she was new. More comfortable facing the concrete back wall than the sparse crowd, she spent most of her stage time shaking her backside to an impossibly fast Shakira remix. When she did turn to us, through an uncoordinated twirl, her barrette unclipped, and her thick black hair spilled over her smooth brown shoulders and small, unsupported breasts. The slight disruption turned her forced smile sad. She lost her rhythm, her poise. Her song was not yet over when she bent at the waist, retrieved her clip from the floor, and walked offstage.

In an instant, Bernard jumped to a standing ovation and

searched frantically for a translator. "Someone! You. Anyone. Please help me! Find her and ask if she'd like to join our table for an iced tea!"

Wearing little more than a sheer sarong and wooden banana earrings, Maritza approached our table. Up close, moonlight accentuated the shine of her hair and the whites of her big brown eyes. By midnight, Bernard had paid off Maritza's boss and freed her of the club's ninety-day contract. Passing the travel-sized English-to-Spanish dictionary from hand to hand, Bernard gazed into Maritza's eyes as though he relied on them to breathe.

Three days later, Bernard resurfaced. Wearing inside-out pajama bottoms and his oversized, off-the-shoulder T-shirt, he looked another twenty pounds thinner, unshaven, and disoriented.

"Bernard. We've been worried about you," I said.

Though Curaçao is a Dutch colony, tulips and tolerance it is not. If anyone at ASAP had picked up a copy of the *Vigilante* that weekend, they would've seen a front-page colored picture of a young black man, lying sideways in a weed-choked alley, the seat of his jeans blood-soaked from a gunshot wound to his sex organs. He'd been cheating with a girl and her boyfriend shot him in the balls.

"From now on," I said, "you call."

"I'm sorry. It won't happen again." His speech was sluggish. "I'm in love. Buried in love! Why do we have so much on the Expos run line?"

"Because when you're not here everything goes to shit," I said, and handed him the activity reports. "We lost eighty-eight thousand dollars on the early games. We got middled on everything. Sorry."

Uninterested, he set aside the report. "Beth, I'm in trouble. I look at Maritza, I smell her hair, and all I can think is I want her to have my baby. Baby Bernards. All over the island!"

Bernard's obsessional love spread through the office like an epidemic. Hardly a day passed without some heavyhearted soul searching the Internet for advice on postnuptial agreements or reverse vasectomies. They took chances on new wardrobes, bought cologne, and attempted exercise. Computer passwords changed from Lombardi, Soriano, and Barkley to Vivianna, Magdalena, and Beatrice. I didn't speak up until talk turned to a serious discussion on polygamy.

"You guys. Can't you just enjoy these experiences? Can't you just appreciate your dirty secrets and be happy? Do you really have to go straight for the full-fledged double life?"

"Yes," they said unanimously.

Divorce was too expensive, not to mention risky. "Christ, Beth," they said, annoyed by my naïveté. "Who do you think out there actually *calls* the friggin' FBI hotline?"

Ex-wives, that's who.

Days later, during a typically busy shift, a clerk called to me from across the room. "Betty?" she said. "The lady on my phone is very *op*set and cryeeng. I do not understand what she says. May I transfer her to you?"

Perplexed, Bernard looked at me. Save for the ringing telephones the room fell silent. Then, speaking on behalf of every man in the office came a quiet, defeated voice. *Oh my God. It's my wife.*

My line flashed.

"Sports," I answered.

A sad female with a high voice began to cry and I tried calming her. The guys couldn't stand the suspense. Their whispers flew at me.

Beth! Say bad connection and hang up.

Beth! No matter what, I'm not here.

Beth! "He had to fly to Santo Domingo. Big banking emergency." Say it!

I held up my hand to shush them.

"I'm just not sure what you're asking me, " I said to the woman. "What is it you want me to do?"

I pressed mute and looked up to a sea of watery, pleading eyes.

"It's a customer's wife," I said. "She says her husband has a gambling problem and wants us to shut down his account."

Oxygen returned to the room. Worried mouths eased into sly little smiles. Sheep, also known as Bah-Bah, the most affable member of the Italian crew, crossed himself and snatched the phone from my hand.

"Hello? This is sports, how ya doin'?" he said. "Go ahead and gimme your husband's name."

Bah-Bah pulled up the customer's account and I leaned in closer to see the balance. The husband had placed so many bets it took us minutes to scroll through his wagering history. Ending balance: minus thirty-six thousand dollars, for the month.

"Lady, lady. Calm down! I'm lookin' at his account right now. Your husband doesn't have a gambling problem, all right? He's got a losing problem."

Bah-Bah continued to scroll. "Oh my God, is he phenomenal at picking losers! Three months without hitting one. The odds of that are astronomical!"

The rest of the Italian crew rushed over to look at the husband's account. Pointing in horror to specific wagers on the screen, they gasped and chuckled and covered their eyes. This kind of degenerate gambling was unbearable to witness.

"Lady, it's an uncanny sense to be wrong. It's the same sense as being right. You understand that? He doesn't have a problem, all right? It'll turn around for him. You watch. Odds are in his favor. Show him some support. Thank you for calling ASAP."

The men stayed gathered around Bah-Bah and me, discussing the situation's true moral dilemma: should they inform the husband— the good-natured Lakers fan who always said please and thank you when placing a bet—that his snoopy, suspicious wife was on to his gambling? They should do him a favor, they agreed, and warn him to cover his tracks.

Looking up, I found myself centered in a huddle of heavy, oily manliness. The air grew thick with body odor and hair tonic and stale breath. They belched and blew into the face of whoever was standing beside them. For the most part, I liked these guys. I enjoyed watching them work and listening to the dramatic scope of lies they invented to explain away odd credit-card purchases and abrupt changes of banking passwords. I felt for them as they suffered through the guilt triggered by family visits, arranged by their loving, adoring wives so the kids could see how hard Daddy worked.

But I missed the company of women.

So when the local brothel temporarily shut its doors, I welcomed a few of the girls into our home. My afternoon schedule spun from the plagued, paranoid interior of ASAP to sunbathing beside Vivianna, Magdalena, and Beatrice. Like the guys at the office, they spent an awful lot of time concocting lies. Parents, brothers, and husbands believed they were working at a Starbucks in Florida. It was the lie all the girls from their village used when they disappeared on a ninety-day visa to prostitute themselves through the Caribbean. At night, they lay in beds, sweaty and soft beneath the men I worked with. Beneath the beds, their stuffed duffel bags gathered dust until their visas expired. Beneath the passports, family pictures, and negative HIV documents, the gifts given to them by the Italian crew lay untouched. Clothes, jewelry, shoes, picture frames, items the girls looked forward to selling when they returned to Venezuela.

ASAP's biggest win took place over the nine-day span of the 2004 NBA finals. In one of the biggest upsets in basketball history, the Pistons beat the Lakers in five games and we made one and a half million dollars. Dusk turned the air pink as we celebrated with lobster and Heinekens from a shoreline picnic table. Bah-Bah lifted his glass and made a heartfelt toast "to Bernard! And his brilliant arbitrage system!" But despite this astonishing feat, the warm wind in his hair, and scantily clad Maritza balancing on his knee, Bernard wore the expression of a man who had just avoided a fatal car crash.

For Bernard, celebrating any win, especially one of this caliber, was rare. He disliked patting his own back. And the truth was, underneath that big, life-loving, buoyant personality of his, Bernard was a pessimist. If we lost two days in a row, he became anxious and depressed and would rearrange the sodas in the fridge while convincing himself we'd never win again. Not that winning made him feel much better. Keeping track of the money made him too nervous to sleep. As he tossed and turned, his hyperactive mind circled around one central question: how were we going to hide the money?

To receive our license from the Curaçao Gaming Commission, we had to meet many strict guidelines. For instance, an American couldn't operate a gaming business on the island without the sponsorship of a Curaçaoan and bank accounts had to be in the sponsor's name, a policy that never sat well with any of us. It took us months to adjust to the island's slow-moving banking systems and the nerve-racking apprehension we felt before sending off thousands of dollars via Internet wire services. After repeated calls to the online payment service Neteller regarding issues of anonymity, limits, and fees, they flew their corporate training manager to the island for our very own PowerPoint presentation. Moving money was no longer as simple as hopping on the D train with a Jansport backpack and meeting Lenny in the Bronx.

Soon, though, I discovered the real source of Bernard's high anxiety and it had nothing to do with pessimism and banking complications. The trauma of his 1983 Broke—the fear and disbelief of watching the stacks of millions vanish in three measly weeks—had left an indelible impression on him. So much so that any mention of money, good or bad, brought back scary memories. The simplest finance questions caused Bernard's gaze to go unfocused. He'd become jumpy and evasive, abruptly changing subjects.

"Bernard," I said. "How much money do you want in the Catalina account?"

"Is there a Quiznos on the island?" he answered. "Or did I dream that?"

"Bernard," I said. "Did we get the ten-thousand-dollar wire yet?"

"You know what I need more than anything in the world? Lobster fra diavolo."

When Bernard didn't have the energy to sidestep he'd simply say "Disaster," pop a Xanax, and then return to what he loved most, making lines, setting mathematical traps, and watching the bets roll in.

Surprisingly, Bernard suppressed his post-traumatic stress long enough to appoint two people to the finance department: Bah-Bah and me.

At thirty-eight, Bah-Bah was a friendly, though highly agitated, father of five. Before his brother-in-law introduced him to the business, Bah-Bah tended bar in Philly. Astonishingly computer illiterate, Bah-Bah was ASAP's "head figures guy," handling all of our complex financial records and transactions. At times of acute stress, he'd snag Bernard's Xanax, crack open a jug of Wild Turkey, and sputter long, senseless monologues about his desire to work for FedEx and live a clean, stress-free life. He fantasized about taking his kids to school in the FedEx truck, then working the swing shift, "droppin' off boxes."

"Figures girl," as I was called, was an unglamorous job that no one else wanted but I enjoyed. Players called me to check their balances and I like to think that the cheer in my girlish voice, even as I said, "You're down seventy-two thousand for the week," slightly softened the blow of losing money. If they claimed a balance discrepancy, I listened to the tapes. Scratchy phone lines, accents, and mispronunciations lent themselves to misunderstandings, plus a lot of people lied and tried to cheat. ASAP recorded every phone conversation for this very reason. Sitting at my desk, wearing puffy, oversized headphones that made my ears sweat, I listened to our serious action players slam receivers and cuss out our clerks. But the phones were also used for personal calls, so sometimes, following the angst and madness, there'd be a click. Steady breaths, and then:

"Dad? I got an A in art."

"I had your mother over for dinner last night, pizza with the girls."

"Good talking to you. I miss you, man. And remember, if my parole officer calls, make sure you tell him we weren't friends until 2001."

Coming upon such tender moments of human interaction within the aggressive inner atmosphere of ASAP was like stumbling upon a favorite bittersweet song while driving through a tornado. Though going offshore had given me a chance to make money and experience a new country, I hadn't realized it would be so isolating. Much of my workday was spent on the phone, or at the fax machine, or in front of a computer, tracking wires and changing odds. My co-workers and roommates (brothel guests excluded) took little interest in the outside world. They had girls, Viagra, and sports. They were happy. I was just grateful for the sweet snippets of ordinary human life. They took me out of the vacuum and recharged me. This was especially so when I came across my conversations with Jeremy. At the flash of his sweet, unexpected voice, I'd press the headphones to my ear and listen in on our conversations from days before.

"I told my dad about you," he said.

"Oh no. Did he ask what my job is?"

"No, he asked if you were Jewish."

Sometimes I'd hear Otis bark from his spot beside Jeremy's bed and I'd get sad and dreamy. My life was wide open and ready, but for what? It was sweet of Jeremy to keep Otis while I was away, but I wanted Otis in my day-to-day life. And I thought about Jeremy all the time. And I missed living in Vegas. If I really set my mind to it and pulled together all my resources, perhaps I could split my time between New York, Vegas, and Curaçao. Jeremy could quit his job and freelance and we'd shift residences depending on the seasons. To be the hustling breadwinner of a gypsy family wandering the world seemed like something I could be good at.

"Do you think of me a lot?" I asked Jeremy.

"Yes, but I have to go. I'm at work."

"No! Stay on the phone. How often do you think of me?"

"Every seven seconds. I'm on deadline, Beth. Good-bye."

A staticky click. Furious buzzing. Shouting rolled over me and I was torn from the bliss and forced back into the chaos of "Tar Heels minus four. Tar Heels minus fourRRRRR!!"

Everyone at ASAP, Americans and locals alike, worked extremely hard, putting in long hours and making themselves available for overtime on short notice. In terms of productivity, there was absolutely no difference between the clerks and the American employees. The difference lay in the salaries. American employees made five, six, seven times more than even the most experienced locals. Not to mention the beautiful homes we lived in and the big, air-conditioned company cars we drove. The clerks who worked for ASAP part-time to save for luxuries they couldn't afford from their teaching or real-estate jobs didn't concern themselves with the income inequality. But for the locals who viewed sports betting as their profession, the injustice drove them to near insanity. Some of the gamblers Bernard brought to the island were truly despicable people who referred to the clerks as "natives," deeming them too stupid or lazy to grasp the oh-so-complicated gist of sports betting. It never occurred to these hangers-on that the clerks were educated, friendly people who spoke multiple languages and often held college degrees. The only justification I ever heard for the hangers-on being there was that their mothers kicked them out of the house—and when asked for a favor, Bernard was incapable of saying no. By the time of preseason football, poor management combined with cultural insensitivity and hazardous testosterone levels turned ASAP from a corporation made up of human beings into a hotbox snaking with dozens of short fuses waiting to explode.

And then one exploded.

"I about to show my aggressivity right now you fat beetch! I will tro you over dis *focke*eng balcony. You don't know how easy it is to die, right?"

The argument boomed through from the other side of the wall. Like kids at the twitch of a lunchroom fight, we jumped from our chairs and ran to the windows and French doors, positioning ourselves for the best view.

In the pounding heat, Wladimir, our line manager, hovered over one of Bernard's hangers-on, who was standing motionless in the black of Wladi's long shadow. The middle-aged, out-of-shape chauvinist was right to be scared. Wladi was young, athletic, and six foot four. An Afro with a vengeance added three inches to his height. I once saw Wladi catch a thirty-pound double-penised iguana with his bare hands. Casually, on his lunch break.

Feeling his smallness, the hanger-on put his hands to his hips. His nostrils dilated. "Don't threaten to kill me, Wladimir. I'll have you fired."

Biting his bottom lip, Wladi reached into the bulging back pocket of his jean shorts. We didn't wonder as much as *hope* he was going for his gun. That's what a jerk the hanger-on was. When Wladi pulled out a copy of the New Testament, shoulders slumped in disappointment.

With his long, thick arm, Wladi thrust the Bible high in the air. "I don't kill no one, I am converted. I have personal contact wit *God* when I go to my knee. But I have people I will easy give dem hundred USD and dey will wait for you. And if you don't have a broken *fock*eeng face, I won't pay dem."

Through scattered claps and whistles, Bernard pulled away from the glow of his computer, bunched his shorts, and hurried to the porch. "Both of you, inside!" he scolded. "Wladi, you cannot talk like that to your manager. Houston's going into overtime."

Suddenly, Wladi looked lost. He strained his face to keep from crying. "How can you say dat, Bernard? How can you say dis mother *fock*er is my manager? He don't have papers. He not even legal! Why? Because he gringo, he my manager?"

Wladi covered his face with his large, calloused hands. He sniffled. "I am so depressed," he said. "I want to kill people."

He took the stairs two at a time. A moment later came a high squealing pitch and the rumble of an engine. In the parking lot below, Wladi sat in his purple Mitsbushi GTO. Keeping the clutch in and slamming the gas, he burned his tires against the steaming asphalt. People came out of their houses and businesses to watch the spectacle. Smoke, so much smoke, everywhere. And in the center of the scene, Wladi, spinning his car in tight circles, reversing over melted lizards, swerving off in outrageous directions, and screaming angry prayers.

*   *   *

The next morning at eight, I arrived at work to find clerks passed out cold along the breezeway's tile floor. Attempting to raise ASAP's morale, Bernard had treated everyone to an evening at Mambo Beach, an outdoor dance club where hundreds of Curaçaoans, Rastafarians, Colombian cowboys, Latina prostitutes, and Scandinavian tourists mamboed around a massive sound system. The eighty-proof rum seeping from the clerks' pores was so overpowering that I gagged as I nudged them awake. They looked up through crusted eyelashes, winced, and stumbled to their feet. When Bernard arrived at the office, I sat beside him. I hated to be the one to say it, but we needed rules.

CHAPTER TWELVE

The Power of Prayer

"Help me!"

The hushed voice rushed through the crack of my bedroom door and raised the hairs on the back of my neck. I thought I was dreaming until I heard it again. *"Help me!"* A faint knock followed.

Half asleep, I turned the doorknob and Lionel's girlfriend rushed in. She was visiting from New York and for the past week we'd all been subject to their endless, scornful arguments, which were made worse by their drinking. The girlfriend trembled, hand over mouth, as though she was trying not to vomit. My first thought was that Lionel hit her. I locked the door, immediately.

"He's out there," she said. She was a Long Islander, so even her whisper was a shout.

Her eyes and mouth twitched in either disgust or terror, I couldn't tell. My imagination went wild. "Does he have a knife?" I said.

Through hard swallows and half-sentences she managed to tell me that she and Lionel had had a fight over sex. If she didn't give him what he wanted, he'd said, he'd find someone who would. He'd left and returned with a prostitute, to whom he was giving oral sex on the living room couch.

I covered my mouth in shock and plugged my nose, something I usually did to keep myself from laughing, though I didn't find this funny at all.

"He screws hookers?" she asked herself and waited for a reply.

Days before his girlfriend had arrived, Lionel had lost the company car. He'd picked up a hooker from the side of the road and when he stopped at a quick mart for beers, the girl drove away. The story was certainly believable, but it was shot through with holes. For instance, it didn't explain why his face was beat up and his arms and legs were covered in tire marks. Or why he was wearing every piece of jewelry he owned, which was an awful lot. Showing little remorse, he shrugged the whole thing off as though he had lost not a four-door Mitsubishi Lancer, but a baseball mitt. I found Lionel's oafishness and ungraciousness detestable. I only tolerated him because I felt sorry for him, his being an outsider and coming from McDonald's and all.

I tried to think of something comforting to tell his girlfriend. Nothing came to mind. High-pitch sex groans cut through the walls.

Uh, uh, uh, uh.

The girlfriend glanced at me for a reaction. Her eyes welled with tears and she covered her face.

"Are you crying because you love him?" I whispered.

"I hardly know him! We met on the Internet." She sat on the bed. "What am I going to do?"

"You mean right now?" I said.

"Right now, tomorrow! I have three more days here."

She too worked in fast food. It must've taken her months to save enough money for a plane ticket. Most hotels on the island catered to the Dutch and were very expensive. No way could she afford a room.

Uh, uh, uh, uh.

I drew a breath. "Let's hit him over the head with something and steal all of his shit," I said. "I'm not kidding. Knock him out and take whatever money's in his pockets, in that sad-ass money clip. Credit cards. His jewelry!"

The jewelry part got me very excited.

"And then what?" she said. Her mouth hung open, drawing out her confusion.

"Anything you want! Stay at a nice hotel. Fly back first class. When you get home, pawn the jewelry."

Her face fell. "*I* am *not* a *thief*," she said.

"I didn't say you were," I said. "I'll do it. I love hitting people."

She held her stare. "Who are you people?"

I instantly hated her. Nothing enraged me more than having my bold, innovative ideas priggishly dismissed. Forget it, I thought. Let her sleep in the street.

"I'm serious," she persisted. "What are you people doing here?"

"Stop saying *you people*. The psycho on the couch is *your* boy-friend. What did he say we were doing?"

"That you made baseball uniforms, for Little Leaguers."

Now *my* face fell. I couldn't decide which was stranger, the lie itself, or the fact that this woman believed us all to be seam-stresses. For a moment, I considered telling her the truth, then thought better of it. She definitely fit the profile of a potential FBI hotline caller.

The girlfriend hugged herself for comfort and began to cry, this time harder than before. She looked so small and alone. I went from hating her to feeling sorry for her again.

"Let's just go to bed," I said. "You can sleep here."

At this slumber party gone awry, the girlfriend and I lay stiffly beside each other in my twin bed. She cried and sniffed and wiped her nose on the pillowcase and I pretended to sleep. Morning sun-light spilled through the open windows, streaking the walls and shifting shadows like a kaleidoscope. At once, the room blistered with heat so hot it buzzed. I kicked off the covers. Frogs croaked low and hollow. Lionel and the hooker started up again. Her high, fluttering moans fell in sync with the birdsong. His struggling grunts sounded like someone suffering a major heart attack. Repet-itive thuds rocked the walls. We could feel them, coming hard and fast as an animal stampede. Thick humidity sucked the air from the room, leaving the girlfriend and me to lie motionless and silent in the sticky heat with nothing at all to breathe.

At a round-table office discussion, aimlessly mediated by Bernard, I raised my hand to speak. "I want to vote Lionel off the island," I said, speaking about him as though he weren't sitting directly across the table, itching his balls through his New York Giants–themed pantaloons. "He lost the company car *and* he's a sociopath."

Our new accountant, Pamela, a Curaçaoan, agreed. Pamela was only twenty-seven, but her serious demeanor and professionalism separated her from everyone else in the office. No matter how long her workday or unbearably hot the weather, Pamela kept her movements smooth, her head cool, and managed to look good while doing so. Her style was sumptuous: shimmery, tasteful makeup, crisp white pantsuits, and silky black and red braids falling over her shoulders. I don't know how she did it. Most days I went to work in bikini top, jean shorts, no shoes, and by noon felt ill-tempered enough to steal sips of Bah-Bah's bourbon.

But even with Pamela on my side, my vote went dismissed. "Lionel is not violent," said one of Bernard's underlings. His dark, humongous post-cataract-surgery sunglasses perched upon a nose that had obviously been broken many, many times. "Wladi is violent," he continued. "He's capable of killing."

All heads turned to Wladi, slouched in his chair, scraping beach tar from his heel.

Bernard had no doubts that his friends were treating Wladi unfairly, and he had no problem saying so. Still, he felt that Wladi was out of line in threatening to pay someone to break his gringo manager's face. Final verdict: one-week suspension, with pay. "No. More. Death threats. None!" Bernard commanded, quite unconvincingly. Dying to get back to gambling, he tossed Wladi a thick roll of money and darted for his desk.

Out of nowhere, high-pitched grinding sounds amped through the office before pulverizing into Judas Priest's "Living After Midnight." Headbanging alone in the corner, Bah-Bah punched up the volume on the satellite radio.

"Nineteen eighty-five!" Bah-Bah howled. "The women, the drugs. And I only went to jail twice!" The intensity with which he strummed the air guitar turned his round, pasty face into a war zone of bulging veins, as messy and twisted as barbed wire.

Satisfied with the amount in the roll, Wladi bowed his head and pointed to heaven. "Dis is why we need to give tanks to God for all dat happen in life . . ."

In tight shorts, halter tops, and platform heels, the twenty-year-old Latina mistresses sat along the back row. In what I can only describe as a fetishized version of Take Your Daughter to Work Day, the guys now brought their girlfriends along with them to the office. They meticulously applied makeup while chatting with relatives in Caracas and Santo Domingo. Afraid of chipping their acrylics, they punched the number pad with the tips of their blush brushes.

Mamá!

Mi hijo precioso!

Estoy conociendo mucha gente en el Starbucks.

Upon receiving September's whopping $39,585 phone bill, Pamela—who had the impossible task of keeping ASAP within budget—forbade the girls from using the phones. The men acknowledged it was a shitload of money. But there was value in the girls' presence: the good luck they brought, the intoxicating smell of their skin and shower-damp hair, the reassurance that the best sex these guys had ever had in their lives was just a footstep away.

Bernard dropped a handful of chewy circus peanuts candies on top of my figure sheets and whispered, "Because you work so hard . . ."

I was in the midst of prank-calling ASAP's number one customer. Magic Epstein was known as a bridge-jumper, a gambler who bet inordinate amounts of money on heavy favorites. An upset (think no-name Buster Douglas knocking out undefeated champion Mike Tyson) can be financially devastating enough to send this type jumping off bridges. Magic held the distinction of losing the largest amount of money (one hundred seventy thousand dollars) to us in a twenty-four-hour period. It was crucial that we get his business early. Time is money, after all, so every morning at nine I gave the guy a "wake-up call."

Magic answered and I promptly hung up on him. I stretched the peanut candies as though they were Silly Putty. "Bernard," I said, wearily. "Why don't we eat something healthy today?"

Bernard considered it. "Very maybe. Very maybe."

Clerks plugged their pummeled eardrums.

"Tanks for calling sports."

"Good morneeng, dis is sports."

"Mr. Magic!" yelled a clerk. "Wants *Wee*sconsin mi*nos* six, much as he can get!"

The call worked. Awake, Magic was now ready to gamble. Bernard gave me a happy glance and projected his voice: "Give him any amount. Let him name the price."

"One hundred and eighty tousand—one-eight-oh—Magic say will make him a happy mon, Mr. Bernard."

Unable to contain his excitement, Bernard did the wave, all by himself. "Make whisky six . . . seven . . . nine. Who's ordering the *chicharrones de* chicken-o? Money line! Eight twenty. Eight forty. Eight fifty."

Phones went crazy. Monitors twinkled like Christmas lights. Wladimir continued his sermon: "Dis is why we need to give tanks to God for all dat happen in life. From every habit, we learn."

"What we *need* is more Xanax," Bah-Bah interrupted, now looking despondent. He fumbled for the pill bottles behind the emptied gallons of Wild Turkey lining his bookshelf. "I have a heart murmur. I just remembered. "

Referring to his own habits, Wladi counted on his fingers. "D*ro*g, alc*o*hol, married womans. S*o*spension from mis*con*duct."

"*Gross* misconduct, buddy," corrected Bah-Bah.

Wladi and I watched Bah-Bah kneel on the carpet. On all fours, he searched for stray Xanax. His white, meaty legs wobbled inside polyester shorts so short they looked like hot pants.

"Not even a cow looks so bad," Wladi said, in a quiet voice.

"Do you get Bah-Bah coke?" I asked him. "Tell me the truth."

"Betty, I am local people from Curaçao. I do not *fock* people up in de workplace."

"What do you mean?"

"I get him de good shit."

"Like how much?"

"I don't know. A lot. A lot." He raised his eyebrows. *"A lot."*

Bernard opened his wallet and pulled out more money. "Now! Wladi, before I forget . . ."

Though Wladi was our line manager, he spent the better part of his workweek praying, fasting, and summoning miracles for the teams we needed to win. "UCLA minus three," said Bernard. "And if it's not too much to ask, see if God can heal Scott Rolen's strained calf muscle before tonight's game."

"God bless you, Bernard," said Wladi as he snatched the money from him.

Approaching the hanger-on responsible for his suspension, Wladi adjusted the neck of his wifebeater. "Dear God," he said. He forced his smoky eyes directly through the man's skull. "Tanks so much for making me better looking dan dis *og*ly gringo defect mother *fock*er!"

"Donate your brain to primate research, you hear me?" the hanger-on shouted, once Wladi was out of earshot.

From the window I watched Wladi light his cigarette against the sun and wind and inhale the first divine breaths of a one-week paid vacation. I envied him. I was sick of staying in the office all day long, watching the guys eat fried chicken, kvetch about starting lineups, and sprinkle their feet with odor powder (which they'd then toss over their shoulder, like salt, for good luck). I wanted *out.* Not out of the business per se, just outside. In a spell of lucidity, and with no consideration for my workload, I ran down the steps. Before Wladi had the chance to floor the accelerator and spin the wheel, I hopped in the passenger seat. "I have gas money," I said, unable to roll down the windows or switch off the Jesucristo radio station fast enough. "Let's go to the beach!"

Speed was joy. We raced along the tangled, broke-down streets.

Whizzing through the downtown square, past shirtless, shoeless kids and American fast-food chains. Past hot-pink eighteenth-century mansions turned crumbled crack houses, the inhabitants drunk on cane liquor or asleep in the yard. Over the Queen Juliana Bridge, barges cruising languidly down below. Crude oil coming in. Refined oil going out. And here, the landscape broke free. Under peaceful clouds, wild pigs and blue iguanas scampered through miles of blooming cacti. Off forty-foot cliffs, we jumped into sparkling waves. A moment later we burst to the surface. Smiling, panting through the heavy, honeyed air, we collapsed onto the white powder shore.

Rainy season brought magnificent storms, as sudden and erratic as temper tantrums. Drenched, the island fogged and steamed. White light shot through the drizzle and worked its alchemy below, giving the muddy potholes a golden luster. We became rich.

So frequent were our shoreline, candlelit, surf-and-turf meals that Bernard—who didn't drink—bought the restaurant owner a new cooler, ensuring that every Heineken his dear employees ordered would be frosty. Hungry for a larger entourage, Bernard brought over scores of friends. We purchased more company cars, rented more luxury apartments, and added more people to ASAP's ever-growing profit-sharing plan. On love's impulse, he flew with Maritza to the DR to meet her family and get electricity for her village. From a pay phone in downtown Santo Domingo, he called with sad reports. *Ten people sleeping in a piece of room! Power outages every two minutes! Very. Bad. Neighbors.* He recited the routing number. We wired him money. And though eighty thousand dollars is certainly an amount worth taking into account, inside the ASAP zone it was shrugged off and referred to as a "ham sandwich." Meaning something of little substance. A snack.

With Bernard on his own escapades, I took six-hour lunch breaks. Wladi acted as my guide, showing me a whole new side of the island. Accompanying him in public was like shadowing a beloved mayor. In lively Rastafarian neighborhoods, in bars that served French fries in peanut sauce and spiced rum in Dixie cups, patrons rose from their stools to shake his hand. Bartenders offered him cigarettes and tried to get him involved in their crazy drug-smuggling schemes.

"Why is everything always free?" I said. I lifted a steaming on-the-house bowl of goat's blood soup to my lips.

"Me? I? I?" he said, tapping his own chest for emphasis, as though I were the one who didn't understand English. "Best car washer on the island!"

True, Wladi did pay close attention to detail. But surely his popularity had more to do with his street connections. Days into his first sports-book job, some four years earlier, Wladi saw an opportunity while watching his American boss and supervisors snort coke. He started to supply the drugs himself. As a middleman, Wladi made a lot of money buying drugs for them. Whatever they needed, be it more weed, more blow, or more crack, the bosses would send Wladi out with a wad of cash that included a generous tip for taking the risk. Efficient and resourceful, he always knew where to go, and whom to call, even in the toughest of jams. In his boss's condo, surrounded by an ocean view and central A/C, the supervisors showed their gratitude by inviting him in to freebase.

How do you say in English? Adrenalina! Wladi felt like he was shifting into third, gas pedal to floor, heading toward a cliff with no brakes. Which is how he lived his life for the next two years. Racing, overheating, crashing, living like he wanted to die, up until the moment he almost did. High on crack while buying crack in a cracked-out neighborhood, Wladi got into a fight. The man reached for his gun. Wladi backed toward his car. The man cocked his gun. Wladi apologized. The man pulled the trigger. The gun misfired.

The next morning, Wladi opened the *Vigilante* and saw his would-be killer's picture. Overnight, the guy had shot and killed someone else. Staring into the Rasta man's bloodshot eyes, Wladi heard the voice of God. *Wladimir,* God said, *I love you.* Everyone was always telling Wladi how much God loved him. But now he *knew*. On the north side of the island where the water is rough, Wladi stood waist high in the ocean. The minister absolved Wladi of his sins and Wladi fell backward in his arms.

Meanwhile, the Feds busted Wladi's boss, whose wife had visited the island, discovered his prostitute girlfriend, filed for divorce, and turned him in. In his house they found guns. And a million dollars cash stuffed inside the walls. No wonder Wladi had always assumed *The Sopranos* was a reality show.

A lot of sports books come down to the island and most of them disappear pretty quickly. For whatever reasons—bankruptcy, fear of getting busted, rampant VD contagion—they hold a fire sale and flee in the middle of the night. And in their wake they leave inflated prices at the snack shacks and whorehouses, a drug-addicted clerk or two, and scores of unemployed islanders feeling used and angry, frantically looking for another job. This betrayal reinforces their belief that Americans, however generous they are when times are good, are nonetheless faithless, wasteful children. Children who think they're more powerful than God.

Born again, Wladi felt his burdens lift. The shame and guilt were gone. There was nothing for him to hide, and no one to hide from, anymore. God knew how much Wladi had lied and cheated— He knew about all the bad shit—and He still loved him. It was such a relief. At church, Wladi learned that gambling was a sin. He also learned that a new sports book was hiring. Finding it easier to abstain from sex than the business, Wladi attended the ASAP interviews at the island's Denny's. Right away Wladi saw that Bernard wasn't like his other gambling bosses. He didn't do drugs or brag. He wasn't Italian. He didn't wax his eyebrows. From what Wladi could tell, he just liked to eat. Wladi felt safe with him.

Even so, "the zone," as locals refer to sports books, is no place for a recovering drug addict. There's too much yelling, blaming, and negativity, and not enough encouragement. Nothing to achieve, really. Each time Wladi's ideas went dismissed, his feelings of inferiority grew and he internalized the judgment of others. Within two months at ASAP, he relapsed.

"*Dee*stroyed," Wladi said, rocking on the Quinta Cindy hammock. "My Savior told me to take off Saturday morneeng shift but I did not leesten." Looking tired and acting restless, he chain-smoked and rambled, "I hate how unfair sports book is. Fat Italian gringos make it hard for me. Dey tink I'm lazy, dey tell Bernard I'm sucks."

Our live-in servant brought us strips of green mango dipped in crushed chilies. Around us, landscapers worked to the rhythm of the slow waltz playing on their radio.

Wladi placed a bump of coke at the end of his cigarette and smoked it in one go. I jumped rope. We were on our lunch break.

"Wladi. What if, right now, Jesus is on his way down to earth? He's going to get here and you're going to be high."

I had used this tactic on my sister once and it worked.

"Betty, believe me. Jesus is my friend. If He is coming to Curaçao, He will tell me." He scowled at the black spiral of smoke hanging over him. "I pray for God to give Bernard wisdom, to guide ASAP in de right way. But de question is always at my mind: Why are Americans *soch* big dickheads?"

"Not all Americans are. The guys in the office, it's their M.O. Bernard doesn't have very good taste in friends."

"I dream of Bernard taking my NBA advices. I dream he stand up and shout 'our *nom*ber one handicapper, Wladimir, say Peestons mi*nos* two for two hundred tousand USD. Go! Go! Go!' *Fock*ers ignore my NBA *o*pinion."

He turned pensive. "I do not know when de devil may grab me and tell me to *com*mit murder."

I stopped jumping rope. "Wladimir! You cannot murder people just because they don't respect your NBA picks. I'm sure the Bible says something to that effect."

Wladi's on-again-off-again born-again extremes, relapses, and crying spells made him seem, at times, an out-and-out psycho. Still, he was turning out to be the closest thing I had to a friend on the island. Whether fired up on drugs or the Holy Spirit, he stopped by the house at crazy hours, eager to share his latest spiritual epiphany and include me in his life. Every day, he took me somewhere new. He showed me the island's boxing gym, where I started training twice a week, and secret coves teeming with seahorses, where I did my morning workout routine. At Plastic Baai, the part of the ocean where the garbage company dumps all the dead animals, we helped his friends hunt octopus the size of bathtubs. Adventures slipped effortlessly from one to the next and, fairly quickly, I created a life for myself. On her day off, Pamela picked me up and took me shopping along the promenade. Sometimes after lunch we visited her witch doctor. The Italian crew picked up on my diminishing work ethic and tried to hypnotize me. *You are not working in the Caribbean,* they said, in a dreamy tone. *You are working from a basement in South Philly. It's snowing. You have to work the phones.* I nodded. It didn't work. The mounting afternoon heat made it impossible to wear clothes or change betting lines. The only realistic thing for me to do was drive to a beach and find a shaded spot to slip in and out of consciousness. When it was dark enough, I skinny-dipped. Floating on my back, I looked up at the moon, already bright at dusk. Soft warm waves lapped against my skin and I felt the lightness and pleasure of being surrounded by water, completely cut off from the rest of the world.

We thought we were imagining it, but no. The calypso band really was playing "Purple Haze."

Hand in hand, Jeremy and I walked along the promenade. The sun's glare off the white coral walls made his eyes squint that one-eyed pirate stare of his. He peered across the harbor, at the oil refineries' rusty networks of pipes and silos, as though he couldn't quite believe he'd just spent seven hours on a plane to look at an industrial landscape complete with gas flares licking the sky.

"Isn't it pretty here?" I said, trying to direct his attention to the lovely pontoon bridge.

He held my curls from my face and spread SPF 55 across my cheeks. "How is it you see beauty where none exists?" he said. "Did you have a traumatic childhood?"

Smiling in the unfaltering sunshine, he waited for me to do the same. He was a smart aleck, albeit a lovable one, and at that moment I found him irresistible.

For five months, I'd been sending Jeremy eleven-page love letters, inviting him down, but he was unable to get time off work. Finally, he pitched a story about hedge funds moving to Curaçao to avoid certain tax laws and his editor sent him on a one-week assignment. Wanting everything to be perfect, I set him up with a neat desk and phone line inside ASAP.

Our day-to-day island life was free and easy, brisk and pure. After a sunrise skinny-dip, we'd throw on our shorts and sandals, grab a papaya milkshake, and head to the office for a few hours of work. Late afternoon Amstels at the Golden Seahorse beer stall and we'd make it back to the beach in time for sunset. On the ocean's edge, at an improvised restaurant with no outdoor lighting, not even candles, we enjoyed our surf and turf in pitch darkness, talking, laughing, and sharing a joint between courses.

No rain, no fights, lots of kissing at traffic lights. Then why, I wondered, did I feel so anxious? At first I assumed it was due to the amount of time I was spending with Jeremy. Six consecutive days was a long time for me. My longest relationship—which lasted nine months—was thirteen years earlier when I was a sophomore in high school. So even though I was twenty-eight, I was an amateur in the art of sharing space. Yet the emotional shift I underwent each morning as Jeremy and I pulled into ASAP had nothing to do with feeling that Jeremy's mere presence was an assault on my independence (that would come later). It was more as if I were a self-conscious child with yet another long day of show-and-tell in front of her. And no matter how hard I tried to make my line of work look interesting, it was just a matter of time until he saw through the façade and realized just how unchallenging and soulless my job really was and that I was, basically, a highly paid customer-service rep. Compared to Jeremy and the burgeoning career that infused every part of his life, I felt like a loser.

At first, Jeremy was in awe of the office, as I knew he would be.

Its setup was cool and the high-level way we made money was interesting. When Bernard was gone and the TVs were allowed on, Jeremy loved watching the games with the guys. Their knowledge of sports and strategy and the confidence with which they answered all of his questions impressed him. But days later the novelty wore off, as I also knew it would, and Jeremy eagerly threw himself into his article. Hearing his fast, fluent typing—which made him sound busy and passionate—agitated my already plummeting mood. I fought the wild impulse to pick a fight and, instead, opened up about how I was tired of drifting and ready to pursue something else. It surprised me how difficult it was for me to admit this aloud.

Jeremy was happy to hear that I desired a change. He'd heard enough of my gambling stories to know that even the most successful gamblers are incapable of having healthy relationships or interests outside gambling. I was different, he said. Once I decided what it was I wanted to do, he assured me the transition into an on-the-up job wouldn't be as difficult as I thought.

But gambling wasn't just a job. It was a lifestyle and a family. Yes, it was small and highly dysfunctional. But it was unlike any other family any other person generally experiences—and that's what made it so special to me. I was afraid to let go of what I had, no matter how stifling it was. If I turned my back on it, what else did I really have?

"You have me," he said. "Give me an idea of what you want to achieve. Let's at least try to live in the same city."

"Uhm . . ." I said, feeling embarrassed. Like I was talking to a guidance counselor on whom I had an awfully big crush. "Can I be your reporting assistant? You do the reporting and I'll transcribe your interviews. I'll write sentences too. Descriptive ones."

"Hell yeah!" Jeremy said. "But don't you have to do two dimes on Atlanta under thirty or whatever?"

I did, but it didn't matter. I put on the puffy, oversized headphones I wore to listen to ASAP's tapes, sat at my desk, and transcribed. Jeremy thought I'd find his interviews boring, but he was wrong. Hedge fund managers were interesting. It was a whole other world to learn about with new stories to listen to. Around me, the office charged into raging insanity with the four o'clock kick-offs. Turning up the recorder's volume, I drowned out the chaos and imagined how cool it would be to do my own reporting and have my own desk in a newsroom. Maybe I'd try for a part-time internship at the *Vigilante*.

Finally, a plan.

The sound of gunfire came from the wooded area just beyond our shoreline dinner table. At high speed, three cars broke free of the bush: the bad guy, the *Vigilante* reporter, and the sheriff, in that order. Headlights reflected off the iron-black sea, making the choppy waves glimmer like switchblades. The bad guy drove directly into the ocean. In an instant, his station wagon was afloat. The reporter—not the sheriff—rushed from his car, plunged into the sea, and returned to shore with the bad guy in a headlock. Reporters are so brave. The thought made me miss Jeremy.

Citronella torches splashed shadows like war paint across our faces. Drunk and hungry, we returned to our surf-and-turf platters. Except for Bah-Bah, who held his heart in pure, utter terror. Days before, he'd announced his impending departure, blaming his need to leave on "a nasty case of island fever." I didn't know what that meant. Was Bah-Bah homesick? Had he done someone wrong? Did he have AIDS? No one dared inquire, for, around the same time that Bah-Bah asked the ASAP cleaning woman to turn out her pockets and accused me of talking in code over the phones, his strange, paranoid fears lost their charm. Now he was just plain mean. Recently, he'd moved out of his spacious, sunny bedroom in Quinta Cindy and into the dark, dank, detached guest quarters. His own private hideout, which he nicknamed the Barnyard. Each morning, he emerged wrapped in a spongy comforter and railed bitterly against our looks of concern.

With Bah-Bah leaving, I was the Figures Department. It was a big job for one person and Bah-Bah's sloppiness about entering information into the computer was making the transition increasingly difficult. I found that he hadn't logged past transfers into the software. He wrote them on pieces of scrap paper and stuffed them into swollen manila folders. Initially he said he'd make himself available for any questions or problems I had. Then he flim-flammed. It would be too dangerous, he said, to talk shop or send faxes from Philly. The Feds might be watching.

Leading an entourage of Latina party girls, Bernard arrived with Maritza. Over the past month, her considerable weight gain had spawned pregnancy rumors. But Dr. Chocolaté, the state-certified brothel's ob-gyn, confirmed that Maritza was not with child. She was just getting fat. Inevitable, considering how much time she spent with Bernard. Her belly pressed between the button and the hole of her jeans, so she fastened them with a large safety pin.

"She's capable of getting very, very heavy," Bernard said, watching her eat an entire fried-calamari platter. "I have an eye for these things."

Moonlit, Bah-Bah looked even more consumptive. "Is island fever contagious?" I asked. He turned his head to me. He managed to find demeaning most everything everyone said to him, and my question was no different. "Fuck you," he said, and I stared back, sucking drawn butter from my lobster tail.

Days after Bah-Bah left the island, I arrived at the office at five a.m. to balance the books. It was the only time of day the office was calm enough to concentrate. No fights, ringing phones, shouting of orders, or blaring heavy-metal music. Just Pamela and me entering sports scores into software, tracing transfers, making lists of people late on paying, filing wiring receipts, and organizing our dozens of on-line accounts. In the eight months since the opening, our customer base had grown exponentially, with two hundred–plus players betting between twenty dollars and two hundred thousand dollars on games. More often than not, there were discrepancies—

transfers still in progress, botched bets, customer claims—but I wasn't prepared for what I found this morning.

"How come we have no money?" I said. I checked the amount on the computer and ripped through Bah-Bah's figure sheets. Useless, considering every third number was unreadable. Sevens could also be ones, or nines. Confused, I glanced at Pamela. Laboring over three different calculators, she did not look her normal, determined self.

We spread the printouts across the floor and studied the calculations as though they were cryptic maps that could lead us to buried treasure. How was it that we were making money on paper but had no money in our accounts? In the long hours of heavy silence to follow, we tried to make sense of the available balance: $461.39.

In walked Bernard, briefcase swinging at his side. He situated himself in front of three monitors and checked the morning odds. "How'd we do yesterday?" he said.

I approached him, reluctantly. My throat tightened. "Bernard?" I said. "I don't think we have any money."

He reached for the papers I handed him. With each whip of a page, he slouched deeper into his chair.

"Oh no," he said.

"What?"

"Low funds."

I grew agitated. "This is what I'm saying, Bernard: WE DON'T HAVE ANY MONEY!"

Astonishment. Emergency meetings were called. Wild claims were made. Perhaps there was a bank account we were forgetting, and that's where all the money was. Maybe it was a hack job. Maybe the Feds had frozen our accounts. Maybe Omar, the quiet, polite guy who worked in marketing, had stolen it. Finally, I couldn't take it anymore.

"Come on, you guys. *Island fever*?!" I said. Bah-Bah had five kids he could barely support. Not to mention his coke addiction. Of course he'd been stealing. The numbers had always added up.

Now, suddenly, he was gone, and this number wasn't real and that number wasn't real and this guy didn't get paid and that transfer never took place.

Bernard dismissed my rant. He felt bad accusing anybody without being absolutely sure. "It could be an honest mistake, Beth. There could be a rational explanation."

"Like what?"

"Could the Internet have stolen it?"

"The Internet doesn't steal, Bernard. People do."

After the day's last game, we listened to taped phone calls. The office was packed with cleaning ladies, clerks, the marketing team, and Bernard's friends. At first, we went through the calls slowly, rewinding and pausing each time we heard something that sounded fishy. But it soon became clear we were wasting our time. There were hundreds of tapes. Our investigation could've continued for weeks. And even if we did finger the culprit, what then? We wouldn't have him beat up or tortured until he coughed up the money, and since whoever it was would know that, all threats were idle. That's assuming he still *had* the money. Thieves tend to snort or gamble their booty away in mere hours. And it's not like we could take legal action. This is what so profoundly sucks about being in Bernard's position. When roughed up and kicked around, gambling bosses don't have many options. All they have is each other. When they're in trouble, gamblers go straight to their friends, not the cops, for help. But those same friends are the ones who often cause the trouble, by lying and embezzling.

During one of Bernard's longer Xanax stupors, I went behind his back and called Bah-Bah. On his elm-lined suburban street, hiding in the safety and warmth of his family, he acted shocked about the stuff I was certain he screwed us on days before. When I pressed harder, he asked that I never call his house again. Red hot with anger, I wanted to rip him apart. I wanted to tell him that we had listened to the tapes and overheard him conniving. That we had hired someone to shoot him in his fat, bald head and that someone was on the way to his house at that very moment. But before I could say a word, the line went dead and stayed busy until it was later disconnected.

To this day, we don't know if Bah-Bah took the money. Afterward, we heard that he lost one million dollars in an all-night coked-up on-line blackjack spree. We heard he went to rehab for drugs and gambling. Then again. And again. One morning back in New York, I passed a newsstand and saw Bah-Bah's face smiling at me from the front page of the *Daily News*. He'd been arrested on charges of conspiracy to defraud the NBA. Federal authorities alleged he paid an NBA referee to throw games. Soon there'd be a trial. Staring at his picture, I found myself wondering if he had a collaborator or, at least, a confidant—his wife, a friend, a dog. If there was anyone left in his life who liked him, anyone whose faith he hadn't shattered. As much as I disliked Bah-Bah, I didn't like the thought of anyone suffering through depositions, court dates, and lingering prison sentences all alone.

Back at ASAP, however, we knew everything that needed to be known. We were spectacularly broke and owed people money. We tried to save as many jobs as we could, but we had no money to pay anyone. Clerks stopped coming to work. The tech team downstairs sold desks and computers and pocketed the money. Cutting our overhead, we got rid of cars and houses. The hangers-on and the Italian crew fled. Stopping by the whorehouses to give their girlfriends a good-bye kiss, they held the women's faces in their hands and promised to send for them—which was funny, because it was the same thing I said to Otis before I left. I moved in with Bernard. We drove to and from work together, ate together, and worried together. Barely able to stay a step ahead of calamity, we tried to prepare for what came next: the struggle, the hustle. The phone calls.

"Sports, Beth. Name and password?"

"Six two four five mortgage. You fuckers owe me! Sixty fucking grand!"

"Sir," I said. "I'm sorry. We have a lack of available funds."

"Sports, Bernard, who's this? . . . I've been desperately trying to get a hold of you. I'm in desperate need of cash flow and I'm absolutely buried. Listen to me. I can't pay people! It's embarrassing. I need help."

"Sports, Beth. Name and password?"

"Three nine four oh plane crash. How can a book go broke during the middle of fucking football season? Tell me that, bitch."

"Oh, like you're really going to get paid now, talking to me like that."

Click.

"Sports, Bernard, who's this? . . . Listen, I need some cash. I really need cash. I'm absolutely, totally disappointed. I'm being so conservative it's sickening. Will you please find me some cash? Please?"

"Sports, Beth. Name and password?"

"Two four four four Dinky."

Dink, on speakerphone.

"Beth. I know you'll feel like a deserter if you leave, but it's time. ASAP's done. You need to leave the business and get on with your life."

The great care with which these words were said twisted my heart. "I wouldn't leave you if you were in this position," I said.

"I'd never be in that position. And I'd certainly never put my employees in that position," Dink said. "Come home. Just for football then you're fired for good. Six hundred a week and you can live in the condo. Do the math. You don't save money anyway."

"Come home, Bethy!" Grant shouted in the background. "We miss you."

"Sports, Bernard, who's this? . . . I'm in surrendering mode. Could I meet you at the Miami airport? I need a buck. I know I already owe you a buck but the thing is, my credibility is shot. I'm beat up. I need a buck total. If it doesn't work out with you, there are no other options. It's not like I have nothing to sell. On paper I have a hell of a business, but in real life . . ."

In real life, Bernard's wife asked for a divorce. Did she find out about his affair? Did she see the American Express bill? Was she tired of being alone? Bernard couldn't bring himself to ask her.

THE POWER OF PRAYER / 203

Whatever the reason, he knew it was his fault. He wondered how he'd be able to pay alimony and child support. He lost his libido. Feeling unworthy, he sent Maritza back to the DR and cut her weekly allowance 10,000 percent. None of Bernard's friends called to see how he was doing. They were all too afraid he'd ask them for a loan.

In real life, it was me, Wladi, Bernard, and a bunch of empty workstations. I doodled and wished we had something to blow up for insurance. Bernard clipped his nose hair, pressed the opposite nostril, and blew out the trimmings before he inhaled them. Wladi spoke of heaven and redemption. He prayed for God to help us prepare for the hard times ahead.

In the end, God offered us something so much better than guidance. He got us a bailout. A sports book in Costa Rica agreed to pay our customers. In return, the customers would be theirs and Bernard would work for the outfit, helping them tweak their mathematics. Though I was relieved for Bernard, I didn't want to go to Costa Rica. I was burned out and I missed Jeremy and wanted to go home, wherever home was. But seeing Bernard in such an altered state and overhearing his phone calls with his psychologist, I couldn't bring myself to leave him.

San José was just as much a dump as it was when I visited with Dink, three years earlier. Like fugitives, Bernard and I moved into an anonymous two-bedroom efficiency and Wladi moved in next door. The neighborhood was loud and the wet air-conditioning made everything damp and moldy. We woke up and counted the mosquito bites. For dinner, the three of us sat on the outside curb and ate soggy empanadas.

Men with machine guns guarded the building we worked in. The new boss questioned everything Bernard did. He didn't appreciate Bernard's genius. He didn't let Bernard bet millions. It made me feel embarrassed; it was like watching your father work a job that's beneath him.

The sun set at four p.m. It rained for days on end. At night, I cleared bugs from the tub so I could take a bath. Centipedes and roaches I smashed with my flip-flop. But the beetles were too colorful to kill. They lay on their backs, kicking, and I admired the designs on their bellies. Picking them up, one by one, I wondered how something with wings—something that knew how to fly—could find itself, night after night, upside down, flailing, fluttering, and stuck. And I didn't know for whom the image spoke better, Bernard or me.

CHAPTER THIRTEEN

Sucker

I arrived in New York to find a newly groomed Otis napping at the foot of Jeremy's bed, right where I'd left him ten months before. Delighted by my early retirement, Jeremy prepared healthy dinners and gave me access to his laptop, complete with my own log-in. He'd fixed the tub's drain and grouted the tile for my evening baths. I found fresh-cut flowers on the bedside table. I loved the pampering. But despite how brightly the days started out, before bed, as we lay close together, I could not keep remorse at bay.

"I totally abandoned Bernard," I said, sobbing into Jeremy's chest hair. "He's unhappy so he's eating and getting fat again. He's going to die."

Jeremy smoothed my ponytail. "Bernard'll be fine. He'll get his shit together."

"But I haven't even told you the worst part. Remember how we left the island in such a rush? We accidentally forgot someone."

"Who?"

"Lionel."

"You hate Lionel!"

"So! Just because you hate somebody doesn't mean you abandon them. Wladi heard he's addicted to crack and lives in the McDonald's parking lot. He has no one! We left him behind!"

"Babe, relax. It wasn't Vietnam. You didn't leave anyone behind."

Jeremy's reassurances helped loosen the tiny knots in my heart. Eventually, having him and Otis back in my life convinced me that I'd made the right choice by leaving Costa Rica. In his tenth-floor apartment, Jeremy and I got to know each other by simply spending time together. It felt strange after months of expressing ourselves through high-emotion love letters. The routine of daily life together marked a drastic shift in our relationship. I looked forward to packing Jeremy's lunches, doing his laundry, and helping him think of story ideas. I loved soaking in the bathtub and watching him shave at the sink. The only problem with this new, exquisite little world was that I needed a job. I was getting restless, and, of course, I needed the money.

"No dealerships are hiring," I said, searching the classifieds. "Do you think cleaning people's teeth would be gross?"

As usual, Jeremy approached the morning paper fretfully, as though it were an outstanding bill he hadn't the money to pay. Living in constant fear of getting scooped, he winced with each turn of the page. Only when he realized he was in the clear did he allow himself coffee and small talk.

"I thought you were going to apply to journalism school," he said.

"Applying to school doesn't pay the bills," I said, considering the colorful adult entertainment ads. But it was the tiny "Miscellaneous" job that caught my attention: boxing trainer needed to help start a program for overweight kids. Fun and physical, I thought, but kind of square. Still, the boxing enticed me, and I thought it would make for a nice transition over to the clean-nosed side of the law.

At a sports bar in midtown, I interviewed with the program director. Dave Greenberg was tall and goofy in his oversized leather jacket, Jets ball cap, and Jets wristwatch. He asked for a copy of my résumé and I hesitated. Earlier, I'd decided I would be honest about my jobs. I had plenty to offer any boss and if gambling put a bad taste in their mouth, screw 'em. But face-to-face, my confidence wilted. Professional gambling, bookmaking, and offshore betting businesses might give pause to anyone, especially job interviewers in the straight world. More often than not, it's easier to make something up on the spot. In hindsight, I probably should have.

"Actually," I said, pulling my hair across my upper lip like a moustache, "I don't really have a résumé."

He asked if I had any experience.

Did I ever.

I highlighted my qualifications: a 7-and-3 boxing record, a quick jab, and a soft spot for chubsters. Looking bored, Dave got lazy and no longer tried to hide the glances at my breasts. I knew that I was losing him so I took a chance and mentioned sports betting. The words jerked his gaze back to eye level. He looked starstruck, as if it weren't me sitting across from him, but Vinnie Testaverde.

"Oh my God. I love sports betting!" he said. Adding, rather sweetly, "It's my passion."

And I realized all those MASH fortune-telling games I'd played as a little girl were wrong. I wasn't going to marry a banker, drive a Rolls-Royce, and live in a shack. I was going to spend the rest of my days with a middle-aged Jewish gambling addict from Long Island.

Dave was so excited I could feel his knees bouncing beneath the table. I asked what he bet on.

"Anything that moves," he said.

After more gambling talk, Dave asked if I would put him into an office. By doing so, I'd become his agent, which meant I'd give him ASAP's phone number in Costa Rica, a password and credit line, and he'd be able to bet. This is common practice in the Internet age, since most bettors are wary of sending thousands of dollars to faceless bookies in third world countries.

If I became his agent, I'd be responsible for making sure ASAP paid him when he won and he paid ASAP when he lost. In the event that Greenberg couldn't pay, it was still my responsibility to make sure Bernard got paid. This was the risky part. There was always a chance I'd get stiffed and have to foot the bill. And I couldn't complain to the cops about it since the whole thing was illegal. In return for taking the risk, though, I'd receive a twenty-five-percent kickback on his losses—not a bad way to supplement one's income. Looking across the table at Greenberg's big, stupid smile and his big, wiggling ears, I felt the allure of easy money.

"I can get you an account," I said and wrote the office number on the back of an ASAP business card. Bernard had passed them out the day we opened and I was happy to finally use one. It made me feel professional.

"But what about the boxing program?" I said. "Did I get the job?"

He took my card. "Eh, that thing'll never get off the ground. I'll never get enough money for advertising. I'd rather do this." He kissed two of his fingers—the ones you use to touch a mezuzah—and turned them to me. His way of waving good-bye.

That evening, after I'd set up Dave's account and he'd made his first bet, Bernard called to congratulate me. "Where'd you find this guy?" he said. "He's trying to win fifty bucks on the Jets and he's willing to risk nine hundred to do it! He has the makings of a Very. Good. Customer."

Something was different, I noticed. The undertone of wrist-slitting depression in Bernard's voice had vanished and that alone made me happy. It occurred to me that to hit rock bottom, adapt to it, and then crawl out of it was probably the most familiar situation Bernard knew. Setting him up with a sucker would be profitable for both of us and made me feel better about leaving him. Days later Greenberg called and referred three more customers. I happily took them on.

Wind and sleet rattled the bedroom windows. Steam hissed and curled from the radiator. The sound of Jeremy's electric toothbrush buzzed through the walls. I didn't realize that when I vowed to leave the gambling world forever, forever meant two weeks.

I was seeing life like a gambler again and domestic life had no thrill to it, no stakes. The *bzzzzzzz* of the toothbrush sounded like the drone of daily drudgery, of monogamy, madness, and death. By the time Jeremy settled into bed with his guitar and book of Jewish camp songs, I'd made up my mind.

"I'm moving to Vegas," I said. "Tomorrow." I drew up the covers.

I glanced at him for a reaction. Instead of showing anger or disapproval, he strummed. I'd always been grateful that Jeremy gave me the independence I required. But at that moment, a little domination would've gone a long way with me. I took his passivity for rejection.

"If I go," I said, "I won't lose interest in you as quickly."

He looked at me as he though he saw only imperfection. "*Jesus, Beth!* You're not a girlfriend, you're a fucking flight risk! You come on so strong . . ."

"Use I statements! And stop looking at me like I'm ugly."

". . . All you did in Curaçao and Costa Rica was tell me how much you missed me. And no sooner do we get into some kind of relationship than you run away. You've been here two weeks! I feel like a single father raising a little kid who has never been loved!"

"Jeremy. I am not a little kid. I have a strong sense of self. I know when I'm bored."

But I wasn't bored. Or maybe I was. I wasn't sure. But I did know I was getting cold feet. Even if I knew how to make a living in New York—which I certainly didn't, not without gambling—I wasn't ready to live with Jeremy. I needed my own space, preferably in a hot climate with a swimming pool. I needed Vegas.

Truth be told, Jeremy wasn't ready to live with me, either. What we both wanted was simply to date, but my bouncing around made things chaotic. "Quit your job and come with me," I said. "We can rent rooms a few blocks from each other."

"Do you not understand I'm trying to be a reporter here? I'm done hopping from experience to experience. I'll visit, but I'm not moving to Las Vegas."

"Then will you be my pay and collector?" I asked. It was the part of my job Jeremy thought the most interesting. When we first met, he sometimes accompanied me on my drop-offs. I needed someone I could trust.

"Will it hurt my chances, if I go into politics?" he said.

"No. It'll help. I like when politicians have diverse backgrounds."

He gave it more thought and then smiled.

"I'm your boss now!" I straddled him.

"You are not my boss."

"Yes I am. You're my employee. You get a hundred bucks for every appointment. Save it for something special."

"Yeah," he said. "Like my own bail."

"We're home!" I shouted as Otis and I ran up the steps of Dink's house and into his den. Dink now conducted his gambling business from home, claiming he could no longer afford Dink Inc.'s overhead, though I think his decision to work from home had to do with the fact that he had grown frightened of going out into the world. Huddled in the cramped darkness of his corner desk, he held his jaw as though it were displaced and tugged at his wild, overgrown hair. "I had a good, long run," he said regretfully. "But it's over. My life is over." He fidgeted his way through his symptoms: memory loss, bouts of vertigo, burps that tasted like rotten eggs, sticky urine, slimy teeth, an inability to digest anything but double cheeseburgers. Allergic to air and paper (though not money, he made that clear), he handed me a brochure of a bubble community for people who could no longer tolerate society. It showed porcelain trailers at the end of an isolated cul-de-sac. Dink was on the waiting list. It felt great to be back.

Tulip, sun-kissed and svelte in a fitted "Got Gelt?" T-shirt, held both my hands and admired me as though I were a daughter she'd grown to be proud of. "He's all yours," she said.

I sat beside Grant, the last employee standing. "I have customers," I said, and explained how I met Dave Greenberg.

"That's unbelievable!" Dink said. "How do you meet someone

for a job interview and end up being their agent? God must have a crush on you."

"Do you even know how to be an agent?" Grant sniped, obviously jealous.

"*Yes*, I know how to be an agent."

"How much have they lost?" Dink asked.

"They haven't. They've been winning."

"They always win," he said. "I've never had a square that didn't beat me the first month."

Just as Dink predicted, my customers continued to win and the New York pay and collect circle worked without a glitch. From Ronkonkoma, Mikey the miserable limo driver drove bagfuls of money to Franky the Fireman, ASAP's New Jersey/Manhattan chief associate. On Mondays, I reported to Franky how much my customers won and he gathered the money owed and hopped in his pickup to go meet Jeremy. On the corner of 140th and Convent Avenue, he'd hand over twenty, thirty grand, which Jeremy would then break down into individual packages. At random Starbucks around the city, Jeremy—the only face my customers would connect to the whole operation—pulled stuffed envelopes from his Manhattan Portage bag and paid out the winnings.

Days before New Year's, my customers finally went on a losing streak. They owed $25,000. My cut: $6,250. I had visions of gleefully blowing the cash like on that old game show where people tossed all kinds of crazy shit into their cart as they flew down the aisles of a fantasyland supermarket. I called Jeremy and begged him to come out for the spree.

At the airport, I was so nervous and excited to see him that I hadn't paid attention to the missed calls and messages on my cell phone. When I found a spot with good reception, I listened to them. Then I closed my eyes and wished I hadn't.

Hey Beth, it's Dave; I wish you were pickin' up. Listen, I got a very disturbing phone call. I was in trouble in the stock market years ago, I don't know if I told you that, but I'm on probation. And, uh, my parole officer wants to talk to me about who I've been speaking to on

my cell phone. He has all the numbers—you, the office, Jeremy. I
have to go downtown at three o'clock. I'm scared as hell. Don't call
me on my cell. I'll call you from a different phone. Good-bye.

He's lying, I thought, and called his cell immediately. There was
no answer.

Oil paintings of the King and Queen of Thailand hung over our
heads and Jeremy sat beside me, merrily sipping a Thai iced tea.
We were at Komol, the restaurant I worked at when I first moved
to Vegas, sitting in the same front booth where Amy the masseuse
had offered to put me in touch with Dink. That was four years ago.
Jowtee, the invisible spirit who controlled the restaurant's destiny,
was still sitting at his table, set with noodle dishes and fresh-cut
flowers. My ex-boyfriend was still waiting tables. He took our
order.

But what if Greenberg wasn't lying? Staring at the untouched
food on my plate, I felt the sting of dread work its way through my
guts. I didn't care what happened to me. But if Jeremy got arrested,
he could be booked on charges of conspiracy to conduct illegal
gambling business. People in his position certainly had. And God
knows what would happen to Bernard. It was 2005 and the Department of Homeland Security was now cracking down on gamblers. Feeling shaky, I needed to rest my head on something. I
leaned on Jeremy's shoulder and repeatedly told him that I loved
him.

"I love you, too. This pad thai is amazing."

"Remember how I told you my customers lost?" I started.

"Yeah."

"Well, I want you to listen to something."

I held my phone to his ear and played Dave's message.

"Jesus Christ, Beth!" He laid his fork in the bed of noodles.

"Before you worry," I said, "I'm pretty sure he's lying."

"He's not lying."

"I'm ninety-eight-percent sure he's lying. He just doesn't want to
pay. Or he can't pay. I mean, even if Dave *has* a parole officer, I
doubt he's asking him who his bookie in Costa Rica is."

Jeremy closed his eyes and spoke slowly. "Beth. If Dave Green-berg has a parole officer it seems entirely possible that he would want to know who his bookie in Costa Rica is and for Dave to cough up his contacts."

"I think you're just feeling scared because you might go to jail."

"Look, if we need a lawyer, I'll call my parents . . ."

The thought of Jeremy explaining the situation to his mom and dad, board members of their synagogue and graduates of Wellesley and Oxford, respectively, sent me over the edge.

"Jeremy, I swear to God, if you tell your parents about this I will never, ever talk to you again."

The hamsters ran inside their exercise balls, rolling around the car-pet and bumping into walls. Grant picked one up and spun it on his pointer finger as though it were a basketball. "They probably bet more than they had and now they're tryin' to get their money together," he said, passing my phone to Dink.

"Grant!" Dink yelled. "Put Murray down or you're fired." Dink listened to the message. "I think he's trying to stiff you," he said. "He must think you're stupid."

I fell back onto the couch. "Well, he's right! I am stupid! I never got their home phone numbers and they're unlisted. The only numbers I have are their cell phones and they've turned them off."

Grant laughed himself into a fit. Dink held a pocket mirror to his tongue and examined the fungus growing from it.

"Grant, help me get a gun," I said. "The only way I'm going to get this money is to go to New York and wait for Dave at his work. If I end up shooting him, I'll say it was self-defense. I'll say he was stalking me and I was scared. I'll say he raped me."

"You don't need a gun," Grant said. "I'll beat his ass. I've never been to New York. Let's go next week. The Knicks are playing at home."

Dink raised his voice. "*Nobody's* buying a gun and *nobody's* going to New York."

"You don't understand!" I yelled, my voice cracking with panic. "Bernard just had his fucking life ruined because someone stole from him. And in return for everything he's done for me, I give him the biggest stiff package in history. If I don't get him that money I can't live with myself."

That evening I called Bernard and asked him to shut down my players' accounts. It was something I'd been avoiding because it would let on that I was having problems. Bernard asked if everything was okay.

"Everything's okay . . ." I said. "But I'm going to need a little time."

"How much little time?"

"No longer than three weeks."

"I have ya down for a little time, no longer than three weeks. Check?"

"Check."

Grant, Jeremy, and Otis stretched out on the floor watching football, Dink played party poker, and I sat at the computer and started my investigation. From my interview with Dave and the e-mails and conversations that followed, I had a few clues to go on. I knew his wife's name was Marcia and that they had a four-year-old son, Jacob, but I couldn't remember where on Long Island they lived.

There were hundreds of listings for Dave Greenberg, zero for a Marcia, and nothing about them on the Internet. I called all of the boxing gyms on Long Island and no one had ever worked with a Dave Greenberg. Seeing my growing frustration, Jeremy came to my rescue. As a reporter, he had access to a Web site used by law enforcement to track people down when only fragments of data were available.

"I could get in a lot of trouble for doing this," he said, typing in the ID and password needed. "It's super-unethical."

"I won't tell anybody. I promise."

Dave Greenberg+New York produced hundreds of addresses. Marcia Greenberg, New York, produced only five.

"Massa-fucking-pequa!" I shouted. "That's it!"

Not only did it give me the Greenbergs' address, but also it gave me the names of their neighbors, parents, and siblings. It told me what year Marcia (maiden name Edelstein) and Dave got married, the schools they'd attended, and how much they'd paid for their condo. It didn't give me their phone number, but it did give me Marcia's parents' number. I stepped into the hallway.

"Hello, Mrs. Edelstein?" I said. Putting on the most mature voice I could muster: "This is Becky Frompkin, Marcia's friend from high school."

"Well, hellloooo, Becky dear."

In her shaky voice, Mrs. Edelstein recited her daughter's phone number, double-checking to see I got every numeral right.

As relieved as I was to finally have Dave's number, it was hard for me to decide who had the upper hand. The information I had certainly helped, but I was still the one doing something illegal. If he really wanted to, Dave could blow the whistle. The cops would come for Jeremy and me, not him. If I came off too strong, Dave might blow, but if I came off as too soft, he wouldn't take me seriously.

Back in the den, I turned down the televisions.

"Okay, I got his number."

"Gooood," Dink said, as though talking to a child. "Now, call him and tell him you didn't appreciate the parole officer don't-call-me-I'll-call-you bullshit. You don't like people making a fool of you and if he pays by Friday no one else needs to know about any of this."

"What do I say when he asks how I got his phone number?"

"Tell him the guy you owe the money to gave it to you."

"What if he says he doesn't have the money?"

"Tell him you'll ruin his marriage."

This is the beauty of having a mentor.

I wandered toward the safe and peaceful master bedroom where Tulip, in silk panties and bra, sat in a fan-back vanity chair. In the white glow of a light-therapy box, she plucked her eyebrows. I sat on the edge of the bed and asked that she made sure I stayed assertive.

"Go for it, girlfriend," she said.

At the sound of Dave's hello, I felt like a gun that'd spent its whole life between mattresses and now had the opportunity to fire.

"Dave, it's Beth."

Dead. Silence.

"Bethy! Happy New Year! Listen, listen. Can I call you back in five minutes?"

"I have the phone numbers of your in-laws, your boss, and your sister," I said. "If you don't call me back in five minutes I'm going to call every one of them and tell them about your gambling debt."

"I'm at home with my family," he whispered. "Let me call you back from another phone, will you?"

"Five minutes," I said.

"If I were you," Tulip said, "I'd tack on a heavy aggravation fee for the way he's fucking with you."

My phone rang.

"Beth, listen, I'm calling from a pay phone . . ."

"Dave, you owe me twenty-five thousand dollars."

"Way, way, wait. I owe how much? Whatever the other guys lost, whatever they're not paying you, I'm not responsible."

"*You* turned me on to them, *you* guaranteed them, *you* probably told them that if worse came to worst they could take a shot at me. I'm holding *you* responsible."

"I'm not paying anyone's debt. If you want I'll give you their numbers."

"I have all the numbers I need, Dave. I have your number, your wife's parents' number, your address, your credit-card numbers." The last one was a lie.

Tulip set down her tweezers and gave me an enthusiastic two thumbs up.

"Christ, Beth, you gotta believe me here. I am in no position to be talking to you about this and where the hell do you get off telling me you have my address and credit-card numbers?"

"What do you think? I just run around the streets handing out thousands of dollars in credit limits? You don't think I work for someone? You and your buddies win five weeks in a row and get paid the exact amount, on time, and the first time you lose you turn your phones off? It's the most scumbag thing you can do in this business."

"I told you, my parole officer . . ."

"Even if you *do* have a parole officer, Dave, he is not my problem."

The receiver went silent and I listened to the sound of blood in my ears. Then came a delicate, high-pitched squeak, the kind of sound a lobster makes when dropped into a pot of boiling water. Dave Greenberg was crying.

"I can't pay you," he said, and for a second I felt for him. After all, this was the same guy who wanted to start up an exercise program for fat kids in his hometown.

I pushed my forehead to my knees and listened to his story. Of how the Feds busted him for selling fake stocks on Wall Street and the judge made him choose between ninety days on Riker's or a fifty-thousand-dollar fine and a felony. "I couldn't have my mom see me go to prison," he sobbed. "I wish I'd gone to Riker's. I wouldn't have to work at that real-estate place and get paid shit."

"You paid six hundred and twenty-five thousand for your condo," I said. "I don't consider that shit."

"How the fuck do you know that?" He blew his nose. "My in-laws put the money down for that house. I don't have the money to pay you."

By the expression on my face, Tulip could tell something was wrong. "Tell him you're gonna tell his wife that the two of you've been fucking," she said.

"Get Grant," I said.

Grant strutted into the room eating a peanut butter and jelly sandwich. I held the phone to my chest. "Will you pretend you're my boss?" I whispered. "And scare him a little?"

He took the phone from my hand.

"Listen here, you dirty-ass kike, you're talkin' to the boss man, you hear?"

I cringed. Tulip covered her mouth and widened her eyes in disbelief.

"I've dealt with lots of bitches in my life, but at least the bitches I'm used to dealin' with have some common motherfuckin' sense." He paused to lick peanut butter from his fingers. "You don't know who the fuck you're dealin' with. I ain't some pussy-ass faggot on Wall Street. I want two grand a week for the next twelve weeks. The first time you miss a payment, I'll knock every single one of your fuckin' teeth out."

If there is a moral to this story it's this: never trust anyone from Long Island. Greenberg submitted to Grant's threat, but his promise to pay was nothing I could actually bank on. My instincts told me I'd never see that money and I couldn't remember a time they'd ever been wrong. Though I took great pleasure in getting in touch with my inner thug—with the help of my partners in crime, of course—I couldn't get the metallic taste of dread out of my mouth. It bothered me how carelessly I'd put Jeremy in danger and I wondered what he must think of me. If Jeremy got picked up, he could be convicted as a felon and fucked for life. I hadn't considered any of this until I heard Greenberg say Jeremy's name. Only then did I feel foolish and ashamed.

Jeremy waved off my apologies. He wasn't nearly as bothered as I was. From a reporter's standpoint, he found the process interesting and thought it was a cool way to get to know the city. On the days he brought packages with him to work, he took the money out of his pocket when he went to the bathroom, just to look at it. He said he'd miss that. If anything, the whole episode seemed to strengthen his attraction to me. Without warning, he'd launch into declarations of love and praise so earnest they took me by surprise.

"You were a master at managing that crisis," he said, cutting my steak for me. "Very strategic. Extremely confident. Not once did it get beyond your control."

"Jeremy, you're missing the point. I haven't solved anything. It remains a crisis until the money's in my hands."

He refilled my wineglass. "Forget journalism school. Apply to Wharton business school. I can help you get references."

It took Dave one month to come up with the money and he agreed to pay me on two conditions: I meet him in person and alone. "Just you and me, Beth. Don't even *think* of bringing the ape," he said, referring to Grant. But I doubted his motives. If Dave was, in fact, paying what he owed, why was he so concerned who I brought along? But I was already late in paying Bernard and so eager to get this over with that, despite my concerns, I agreed to meet him alone and flew to New York.

From a booth in the sports bar, I watched Dave walk in from the street. He brushed the snow from his leather jacket as though he had just crawled out of a sewer. His eyes watered from the cold.

"Have you been crying again?" I said.

"No, I'm not *crying*," he said, as oversensitive as a ten-year-old boy.

He fished a thin pile of money from his front pocket and set it on the table. I made a point not to look at it.

"That's all I have," he said. He wiped his mouth.

"How much is it?"

"Count it."

"I'm not gonna count it. Just tell me how much it is."

"It's a thousand dollars. You can call my in-laws, wife, whatever you want. I told all of them what happened. There's nothing you can do. If you call, they're just going to hang up on you. I canceled my credit cards . . ."

"I know," I said. "You told your wife you lost your wallet."

A deep crease appeared between his thick black brows. "Tell me how you know that," he said.

"I don't. It was a guess. But now I can tell her you left it in the hotel room we shared."

"Are you that"—he searched for the word—"*cold?*"

It took all I had not to spit in his face. "Dave, you're the one who chose to do business this way, not me. You're the asshole. Look in the mirror and try to convince yourself you're not. See how stupid you look."

"You can do whatever you want but here's the deal. I'll have Jeremy locked up in about five seconds. You want to get paid? Reopen my account. That's the solution. If I win, you can deduct my winnings from what I owe. The only reason I'm giving you that"— he tapped the cash—"is because I have the heart of a lion."

And that's when I realized that Dave Greenberg had psychiatric problems. Up to this point, I had considered Dave a degenerate, the gambling equivalent of a functioning alcoholic. Degenerates' friends and family wonder when they'll bottom out; ashen circles appear beneath their eyes and their skin takes on an enervated yellowish tint. But degenerates have one saving grace: they pay their bookies. Dave was what we referred to as a sicko. Sickos don't care if they win or lose, how much they owe or who they owe it to. The only thing that matters is that they get down. Come the opening pitch, the tip-off, the coin flip, as long as they have action on the game, the sun will continue to rise.

My mind raced through plans of action. One grand was a far cry from what he owed and I hardly considered reopening his account a *solution*. Successful gamblers say that if you really want to excel in their line of work, you must be able to "ride the wave," the "wave" being losing streaks, the fear of getting busted, and the sickening feeling that strikes with smiting force when you realize you trusted someone you shouldn't have—that you were taken for a sucker.

I wasn't sure if I had the stomach for the business, but one thing was certain: I no longer had the appetite. With Bernard waiting for his money, what choice did I have? To put Dave Greenberg back into action was a straight-up stupid gamble. Defeated, I took it. Knowing that I might lose credibility with everyone in the business or get myself into even deeper debt with Bernard, I kept my nausea to myself and, without stirring much notice, called and asked Wladi to reopen Dave's account.

*   *   *

The six o'clock alarm sounded. I sat up and faced the window. Beneath the streetlamp's pool of light, snowflakes shot across the still-black sky. I whined about the weather and fell back into bed. Jeremy rose to admire it.

"Babe, what could be more beautiful than a fresh snowfall?"

"Six Flags Atlantis," I said, solemnly.

The room was dark and its every surface was cold to the touch. Each time I started to pack, I stopped, and crawled back beneath the covers and into the heat of Jeremy's body. We interrupted our kisses to talk about the things we'd do to each other when we saw each other again, when we had more time. Unhurried in his movements, Jeremy rolled out of bed and tucked away his morning hard-on. He pulled a book from his workbag and set it in front of me.

"Will you marry me?" he said.

The book was thick with hundreds of pictures of engagement rings. I touched its cover, hesitantly, as though it might bite. I looked up at him.

"You don't have to do this," I said. Thinking: I'm not pregnant.

"I didn't want to ask without a ring," he said. "But I've never seen you wear jewelry and I don't want to get you something you don't like. We'll pick one out together."

Astounded by his sweetness, I felt dizzied and charmed. But I was also confused. "Jeremy, are you being serious?"

He nodded, but his expression stiffened and I noticed an illness of ease. As though the slipstream that propelled him this far had veered, forcing him to swim against the rapidly strengthening current of his better judgment. He acknowledged that things were moving fast, and he wasn't entirely prepared, then kicked me out of the room so he could call my dad and ask for his blessing. I was happy Jeremy was being so respectful, but I worried what my dad might say. He never paid much attention to the guys I dated. As long as they were white and drove an American-made car, he was fine with them. Jeremy drove a sixteen-year-old Volvo and I wasn't convinced Dad considered Jews white. Concerned, I eavesdropped from the living room couch. *Yes, Mr. Raymer. It is early, I'm sorry.*

A moment later, Jeremy walked toward me. Smiling hugely, he

got down on one knee and held my hand. Despite the fact that we were sitting in the living room and looking bed-rumpled in nothing but our underwear, the occasion took on a sense of formality so strong I straightened my posture and stopped giggling long enough to concentrate on Jeremy's proposal. "I love you. I don't want to go through life without you. Will you marry me?"

Forgetting everything in the world, I said yes. And without meaning to, I cried.

Our engagement intoxicated us like a heady wine. Between romantic dinners and heavy snowfalls, we wandered the city in a daze and dreamed of our future. We invented a game where we imagined winning one hundred million dollars. If we agreed on how to spend the money, we won, and winning meant we were destined to be together.

"We buy my mom a house wherever she wants, we get my dad a Rolex and a new 'Vette, and we find a really nice rehab for my sister," I said. "We have to take care of Tulip and Dink too. They don't have kids."

"We buy my mom and dad a summer home and offer to pay the hotel and airfare for our wedding guests," Jeremy said. "And we go somewhere exotic for our honeymoon." He wrapped his arm around me. "It's important to me we have a Jewish wedding."

"That's fine."

"And that the kids be raised Jewish."

"Okay! It's important to me I travel alone up to three months a year."

"Will you be faithful forever?" Jeremy asked.

"I don't think infidelity is the worst thing," I said. "From my experience, it's the absolute norm. And easier to get over than people think."

"What's the worst thing, then?"

"I don't know. Disappearing? Like, if you dropped me off somewhere and never picked me up."

"Well, Jesus. I'd never do that."

"Good. Me either."

"But Beth, I do not want an open marriage."

"I don't know how *open* it has to be. We could do things and keep them to ourselves."

He stopped walking and crossed his arms over his chest.

"Jeremy," I said, steps ahead of him. "Please don't be so rigid."

In the days to come, when I was left alone with my thoughts, I tried to make sense of my shifting moods. Marriage struck me as romantic and courageous one moment, and unimaginably wretched the next. What bothered me most was the sense that I was betraying my own nature. Becoming someone's wife didn't seem like an honest expression of who I was. When I told people I was engaged, they'd exclaimed, "Beth, you're blushing!" It wasn't a blush; it was a pink, blotchy rash that ran down my neck and across my chest. I had always taken pride in my independence, but I had underestimated just how extreme it was if even the *idea* of forfeiting a bit of it could produce a physical reaction. I was afraid of becoming a hypocrite. I had condemned conventional marriage as an impractical way to live. Yet all these sentiments didn't explain away my admiration for Jeremy or my need to be loved by him. Worried that in my absence he'd change his mind, I'd call him at the newsroom.

"Beth, I'm on deadline."

"Okay, but I just want to make sure we're still getting married."

"Babe, of course we're still getting married."

Everything in my life was new. Every plan, thought, daydream—the fact that I now needed Greenberg to *win*. My mouth went dry and my breath shortened each afternoon as I checked his account. Late at night, he logged onto ASAP's online casino and played blackjack. Knowing the site's managerial password, I watched him play his hands from Jeremy's laptop. Greenberg felt a little too safe with seventeens for my taste. I sent him telepathic messages and screamed for him to hit. He wouldn't. He'd lose. And I'd go to bed in despair, too agitated to sleep, wondering if it was only a matter of time before my tongue turned green.

Dave had always taken pleasure in betting long shots, and the day he called me with the big news was no different.

"Bet you didn't know I was a whiz at baseball!" Dave said. He chuckled. "Check my tab and call me back."

Dumbfounded, Jeremy and I stared at the computer. Dave had bet the most unlikely seven-team parlay, including a bet I'll never forget: San Fran at Colorado total to go over 17. It was an extremely high total for a baseball game even in the thin, dry, home-run-happy air of Coors Field.

Final score: Giants 13, Rockies 6. Dave Greenberg had won forty thousand dollars.

"Do you know the odds of winning a seven-team parlay?" I said.

Jeremy leaned back, pensively. "Don't pay him. He doesn't deserve it."

Jeremy was right: Dave had put me through the wringer. But I couldn't contemplate keeping his winnings for myself without imagining him and his buddies lying in wait for Jeremy outside the newsroom. Or simply turning Jeremy in to the cops. The right thing to do was to pay Dave, turn off his account, and be grateful that Bernard got his money and nobody went to jail.

But the thought of giving Dave one penny made me feel like I was betraying even stronger principles. I paced the room and twirled my hair. "But what if you get kidnapped?"

"I doubt anything like that will happen."

"But what if it does?" I said. "What would you do?"

"Call 911."

"From the trunk? What if you're handcuffed?"

"Beth, I'm not going to let anybody put me in a trunk."

I couldn't help but smile. As absurd as this conversation was, I found something very comforting about our exchange. Jeremy was being brave and savvy, steadying me in a time of vacillation. I liked the way he was taking control.

Days later, when Dave called wanting to schedule our pay and collect, I couldn't think straight. My mind had become preoccupied with silly, superstitious games. If I made it to the 2 train without seeing a cop car, I'd keep the money and Jeremy wouldn't get kidnapped. If the first thing I saw when I walked into the bodega was a primary color, I'd keep the money but something bad would definitely happen to Jeremy.

"Enough being shitty to each other," Dave said. "We'll meet near my office. I know a place that has killer chicken Caesars. My treat."

HIS TREAT? Now that was insulting. I seethed. Sleet underfoot, bare black branches overhead, I couldn't stop my teeth from chattering in the cold. Enough! I'd rather slit my wrists, I thought, than fight this weather to go into midtown and sit across from Greenberg and eat a chicken Caesar.

"Lunch would be great," I said, politely. "Let me see when I can get the money and I'll call you back."

I called ASAP and spoke to the new figures girl. We deducted the money I owed Bernard. My commission, plus the amount I owed Greenberg, came to $21,500.

"How would you like your player to receive his package?" she asked me.

"Actually, why don't you just send it to me," I said. "Is there any way you could Western Union it, to Rio de Janeiro?"

I made a mistake, I learned from it, and now I needed a vacation to forget about everything else. Jeremy was right about my habit of running away from things. But wasn't this time different? I wasn't shirking my duties; I was standing up for myself. And, anyway, I was taking him with me. We arranged for Otis to go to sleep-away camp in the Catskills, Jeremy finagled time off work, and two weeks after my arrival, he'd be meeting me at the condo I rented overlooking Ipanema Beach. In the meantime, Carolina and I would finally realize our South American adventure. She borrowed a diesel truck and we mapped out our entire trip. But really our goal was to stay lost, which, in the end, takes a lot more effort. Leaving the Brazilian consulate, expedited visas in hand, I swayed to the samba rhythm in my head. Squeezing into a Brazilian-cut bikini in the Bloomingdale's dressing room, I could virtually taste the *caipirinha*.

Not until I was packing did I consider the life I was leaving or the one to which I'd return. Part of me looked forward to quitting the business, once and for all, getting a new job and trying my hand at being a wife. But did I honestly think I could do that? Another part of me thought—perhaps hoped—that I couldn't. But I truly loved Jeremy and it would shame me not to try. Listening to him play the guitar, I kept my thoughts to myself. I zipped my backpack, threw it over my shoulder, and kissed him good-bye.

Welcome to flight 2540, bound for Rio de Janeiro.

I settled into my window seat, pulled up my table tray, and took immediate advantage of the first-class amenities. I was a little queasy at the thought of leaving Jeremy to deal with Dave's phone calls, but on the other hand, I trusted that Jeremy would competently handle whatever situation arose with his usual terseness and innate sense of justice. A warm washcloth on my forehead eased my worried mind, and for the fun of it I changed the greeting on my cell phone. "You have reached Beth," I said. "I'll be gone for a long time. Please leave a message."

The plane lifted into the air and I felt the spinning sensation of being swept off my feet, a feeling that always works its magic on me. In an instant, all of New York City lay below me. Somewhere down there beneath the big clock at Grand Central, Dave Greenberg waited for me to show up with his money, just like I said I would. At the thought of him *plotzing,* I ordered champagne.

Rising above the cloud bank, I tilted my face to the sun. I didn't even need the plane. I could fly to Rio all on my own, hot with the rush of getting the best of it.

Acknowledgments

The earliest iteration of this book was a letter I wrote to Jeremy from Curaçao. Before I ever thought of myself as a writer, he believed in me. Thank you.

To agree to be a character in a work of nonfiction takes an enormous amount of generosity and courage. Dink, Tulip, Grant, Bernard, Jeremy, Wladimir: thank you for trusting me.

To all the gamblers—and their moms—who shared their memories, I couldn't have written this book without you.

I would like to acknowledge all my professors at Columbia University, especially Stephen O'Connor, for his unending encouragement, and Samuel Freedman, who helped me see my own character—in the book, as a writer—more clearly and guided me as I took my first steps from book proposal to publication.

I am grateful to the Fulbright Program for its generous grant, which allowed me to focus on writing and gave me the opportunity to live in Central America.

Thank you, Las Vegas: the Capital of Second Chances!

Thank you, Peter Gethers, for being so cool. And D. V. DeVincentis, for snapping my author photo and for becoming a friend.

While I was writing this book, several people dogsat Otis and offered me sunny and quiet writing nooks and moral support: Jamie Fox, Alexi Villedrouin, Peter, Susie and Dougal, the Shusters, Carolina Freitas da Cunha, Dr. G., Michael Herzig, Clifton Leaf, and Ed and Lorrie Scanlan and their lovely Villa Vista Mar (villavistamar.com).

Mom, Dad, Sis: thank you.

Thanks also to Katharine Smyth for her wise and thoughful advice (on *all* subjects) and Brendan Beirne for being an awesome President of Manufacturing.

Gratitude to my editor and publisher, Julie Grau, whose incisiveness and attraction to risk make her a savvy gambler in her own right.

An immense thanks is due to my loyal agent and friend, Andrew Blauner, for making it all happen.

And lastly, Ryan Carrasco, your unerring eye, off-the-wall humor, and reading—and rereading—of drafts saved me from all kinds of embarrassment. There's no one else like you in the entire universe.